GFOA BUDGETING SERIES
Volume 8

Capital Project Planning and Evaluation
Expanding the Role of the Finance Officer

Joseph P. Casey and Michael J. Mucha, editors

Government Finance Officers Association

Copyright 2007 by the
Government Finance Officers Association
 of the United States and Canada
203 N. LaSalle Street, Suite 2700
Chicago, IL 60601-1210

Library of Congress Control Number 2007930424
ISBN 0-89125-291-6

Printed in the United States of America.
First printing, October 2007
Second printing, November 2013

Contents

Foreword

As local governments transition to focus more on performance and accountability, government leaders must direct more attention on careful planning and evaluation of both operating and capital expenses to position the organization to provide required services. A well prepared capital budget is necessary to ensure proper planning, funding, and implementation of essential projects that provide important government services. Finance officers have an opportunity to contribute valuable insight to all stages of capital plans and help insure capital project investments align with long-term service goals, objectives, and strategies.

With this book, the Government Finance Officers Association (GFOA) takes a practical approach to capital planning. Focusing on common essential projects, this book provides finance officers enough information to become "educated consumers" of capital projects and allow greater participation in all aspects of the capital planning and evaluation process, including needs assessment, project planning, project evaluation, and project implementation.

This book is the eighth volume in a series related to the National Advisory Council on State and Local Budgeting (NACSLB) recommended budget practices. The NACSLB framework consists of 59 practices, covering all aspects of budgeting, to guide state and local governments.

The GFOA would like to thank the many authors and reviewers that contributed to this publication. The authors and reviewers drew from years of experience with capital project planning and evaluation within local governments of all sizes. The GFOA would also like to thank Joe Casey and Mike Mucha for editing and contributing to the book along with Amy Stewart and Nicholas Greifer for their involvement and effort with this project.

Finally, the GFOA and the editors would like to express their appreciation to Rebecca Russum for editing and producing the final manuscript.

Jeffrey L. Esser
Executive Director/CEO
Government Finance Officers Association

About the Authors

Editors

Joseph P. Casey has been the Deputy County Administrator for Hanover County, Virginia, since 2004, previously serving as the Director of Finance and Management Services since 1990. He formerly worked with KPMG, where he became a CPA. Since 1998, he also has also served as an adjunct professor for Virginia Commonwealth University's (VCU) graduate public administration and non-profit program and as a national trainer for the Government Finance Officers Association (GFOA). He received his undergraduate degree from the University of Richmond in 1986 and a graduate degree in public administration from VCU in 1995. He currently sits on the GFOA Executive Board and is a Past-President of the Virginia GFOA. In addition, he has served the GFOA as a reviewer for the Awards for Excellence and Distinguished Budget Presentation Awards programs; he has reviewed books for and written articles that appeared in *Government Finance Review*; and he was selected as the 1991 MBIA Scholarship recipient to GFOA's Advanced Government Finance Institute. He also received *Inside Business'* "Top 40 Under 40" award and the Virginia Association of Government Accountants' Local Government Leadership Award. He expresses his appreciation to his family and co-workers in their support of this endeavor.

Michael J. Mucha is a Consultant/Analyst with the GFOA Research and Consulting Center and focuses on management and technology research and consulting. He is involved with several GFOA publications on performance measurement and financial management. Before to coming to the GFOA, Mr. Mucha worked with the Sports & Exhibition Authority of Pittsburgh and Allegheny County. He received a master of science in public policy and management with a concentration in both economic development and financial management from the H. John Heinz III School of Public Policy and Management at Carnegie Mellon University and a bachelor of business administration in economics from the University of Iowa.

Contributors

C. Brooke Beal is the Executive Director of the Solid Waste Agency of Northern Cook County, Illinois, a regional government charged with managing solid waste for over 900,000 people in suburban Chicago, and has served in that capacity since September 1993. Mr. Beal joined the agency's staff in January 1989 and served as its Assistant Executive Director prior to his current appointment. Previously, he was a Program Analyst for the State of Illinois' Capital Development Board. He holds a master's degree in political science from Illinois State University and a bachelor's degree in political science/economics from Illinois State University. Mr. Beal has been involved in the site selection and permitting of two transfer stations and a landfill. In addition, Mr. Beal has made presentations on topics ranging from solid waste management operations to capital financing options at the National Solid Waste Management Association's Waste Expo, Solid Waste Association of North America's WASTECON, the Government Finance Officers Association's annual conference, and at Deutsche Bank's Institutional Investor's Conference.

Bradley G. Black is a licensed architect and a Facilities and Development Manager with the City of Eugene, Oregon. He has acted as the project architect for the renovation of a major university research library and as the owner's representative and project manager for construction of the City of Eugene's new public library. Prior to his employment at the city, he served as a project manager for two Oregon school districts, worked as a practicing architect in a private firm for more than twenty years, and was a professor of architecture at the University of Oklahoma. His publications include the contribution of a chapter in the *Architect's Studio Handbook,* by Terry L. Patterson.

Greg Canally is currently the Budget Officer for the City of Austin, Texas. He has been with the city for eight years and is a member of the GFOA's Committee on Economic Development and Capital Planning. Prior to his work in municipal government, he served as a project manager/economist for HDR Engineering, working with all levels of government to implement water planning solutions. He spent his early career working as Equity Research Analyst for ABN/AMRO Bank. Mr. Canally holds a bachelor of science in economics from Villanova University and a master of science in economics from the University of Texas at Austin.

Allan M. Carmody is the Director of Budget & Management for Chesterfield County, Virginia. He has enjoyed twenty-plus years of employment in public sector budgeting and the engineering and construction management industry. As budget director, he has responsibilities for capital improvements, debt management, operations, and growth management initiatives. As a member of the county's executive leadership team, he participates in setting overall county policy and strategic guidance. Mr. Carmody earned a bachelor of science in engineering technology from Old Dominion University and has completed the core course work for a master's in engineering from Virginia Tech. Professional memberships include the GFOA, where he has served on the Committee on Economic Development and Capital Planning. Special honors include two gubernatorial appointments to the Commonwealth of Virginia's Design-Build Construction Management Review Board.

Julia H. Cooper is the Deputy Director of Finance for the City of San Jose, California. She has two decades of local government finance experience, including management of the city's debt management program involving the issuance of over 100 debt financings totaling over $3.0 billion. The city's debt portfolio includes general obligation, special assessment, community facilities districts, airport revenue, sewer revenue, certificates of participation, lease revenue bonds, multi-family housing revenue, and tax allocation bonds. The city's portfolio includes tax-exempt and taxable debt in fixed, variable rate, auction rate, and commercial paper securities. In addition, Ms. Cooper has daily oversight of the city's investment and cash management functions, which includes approximately $2 billion of investments. Ms. Cooper received a bachelor of science in political science from Santa Clara University and a master of public administration from San Jose State University. She is also a member of the GFOA, California Municipal Treasurers Association, California Society of Municipal Finance Officers, and Association of Public Treasurers, and serves on the GFOA's Committee on Governmental Debt Management.

Sue Cutsogeorge has worked at the City of Eugene, Oregon, since 1995 and serves as the city's Financial Analysis Manager. She was responsible for creating and managing the financing plan for construction of the $36 million library that opened in Eugene in 2002. Prior to her work at the city, Ms. Cutsogeorge served as an independent financial advisor to state and local governments for twelve years with the firms Public Resources Advisory Group and Government Finance Associates.

Michael J. Daun is Deputy Comptroller for the City of Milwaukee, Wisconsin. As the city's Chief Financial Officer, the Comptroller is responsible for all city accounting, financial reporting systems and related policies, payroll, debt management, audit, financial administration of all grants, and revenue budgeting. Mr. Daun also directs the performance of capital investment analysis for proposed city economic development projects. He is a part-time instructor for the University of Wisconsin as well as a past GFOA instructor and has worked with US AID and the City of Vladivostok, Russia, on economic development initiatives. Prior to joining the City of Milwaukee, Mr. Daun was a consulting services manager at Arthur Andersen & Co. and a senior budget officer in the Governor's Office-Illinois Bureau of the Budget. Mr. Daun has written articles for the GFOA on auditing, debt issuance and other topics. He has a bachelor of science degree in civil engineering from Marquette University and a master of public administration degree from Cornell University.

Eric Johansen is the Debt Manager for the City of Portland, Oregon. He is responsible for the city's $2.6 billion debt program, including new debt issuance, refunding analysis, arbitrage rebate compliance, continuing disclosure, and debt systems management. Before joining the City of Portland, he worked as a financial advisor for five years with Public Financial Management (1988-1993) where he specialized in utility revenue finance, advance refundings, arbitrage rebate compliance, and quantitative analysis. Prior to that, he worked as an investment banker with Shearson Lehman Brothers (1983-1988). Mr. Johansen is a member of the GFOA Committee on Governmental Debt Management.

Shayne C. Kavanagh is the Senior Manager for research in the GFOA Research and Consulting Center. He is the author of the GFOA's 2007 publication *Financing the Future: Long-Term Financial Planning for Local Government;* co-editor of the award-winning GFOA publication *Technologies for Government Transformation: ERP Systems and Beyond;* co-author of the GFOA publications *Technology Needs Assessments: Evaluating the Business Case for ERP and Financial Management Systems* and *Financial Policies: Design and Implementation;* and has written several articles on technology for *Government Finance Review* and *Public CIO* magazines. Kavanagh also provides direct consulting services, including IT governance and planning for clients like Collin County, Texas, and Sacramento County, California, as well as financial planning services for clients such as the City of Gresham, Oregon, and the City of Montclair, California. Mr. Kavanagh received his master of public administration degree from Northern Illinois University, where he was the ASPA Student of the Year for his graduating class.

Soliman Khudeira is currently a Project Director with the Chicago Department of Transportation – Division of Engineering where he manages all phases of major projects. He has over twenty years of experience in the various disciplines of civil engineering including civil design, structural design, surveying, and construction management. He has a PhD in civil engineering from Illinois Institute of Technology. He is a licensed professional engineer and structural engineer in Illinois.

Nancy Leavitt is a Financial Analyst with the City of Virginia Beach, Virginia. Ms. Leavitt was a member of the team that developed the city's policy on public-private partnerships explained in Chapter 9. She also developed the program to monitor and report on the performance of the city's TIF districts. She previously served as Financial Planner for the City of Norfolk, Virginia, where she worked on the financings for many economic development projects. She held several positions at the Denver Water Department, including Financial Analyst, Rates

Analyst and Manager of Water Rates. She has over twenty-five years of local government experience. Ms. Leavitt received her bachelor of arts degree from the University of Texas and her master of business administration from the University of Denver. She is also a Certified Employee Benefits Specialist.

Marcia Maurer currently serves as the Chief Financial Officer for the Sacramento Regional County Sanitation District. She has worked for Sacramento County, California, for more than twenty years. She has been a member of the GFOA since 1999 and is currently the Vice-Chair of the Committee on Economic Development and Capital Planning. While at the sanitation district she has been involved in financing the construction of more than $1.2 billion of capital improvements including pipelines, pump stations, and process improvements at the treatment plant.

Huy Nguyen is a Consultant/Policy Analyst in the GFOA Research and Consulting Center. Mr. Nguyen specializes in market research and enterprise software selection. He has contributed to several GFOA technology procurement consulting projects, including those for the City of Springfield, Illinois; Clark County, Nevada; Inland Empire Utilities Agency, California; Newport News Public Schools, Virginia; Montgomery County Public Schools, Maryland; and Humble Independent School District, Texas. Mr. Nguyen also participates significantly in GFOA technology research. He also wrote the *Government Finance Review* article "Beyond ROI: A New Framework for Measuring the Value of Technology Investments." Mr. Nguyen received his bachelor of arts in economics from the University of Illinois at Urbana-Champaign and his master of public administration degree from the University of Illinois at Chicago.

Donald W. Penfield, Jr. is the Facilities Management Director for the City of Scottsdale, Arizona. He has been employed with the city for twenty-five years and has served in a variety of positions involving capital projects design and construction management, improvement district project management, purchasing management, capital improvement program planning and administration, and facilities maintenance management. He received his bachelor of science in engineering from Arizona State University in 1972. He is a registered professional engineer with proficiency in civil engineering in the State of Arizona.

Patricia A. Phillips is the Director of Finance for the City of Virginia Beach, Virginia, and has held this position since 1992. The finance department is responsible for financial systems, financial reporting, procurement, payroll, risk management and debt management. Previously, Ms. Phillips served the City of Virginia Beach as the Director for the Office of Research & Strategic Analysis. She also worked for Coopers and Lybrand as a public accountant. Ms. Phillips received a bachelor of science in business administration, graduating *magna cum laude*, and received her graduating class accounting award. She also holds a master in business administration from Old Dominion University. She is a CPA in the Commonwealth of Virginia and a member of the American Institute of Certified Public Accountants as well as the GFOA.

John H. Tuohy is currently the Chief Financial Officer for the City of Falls Church, Virginia. He has previously served as the Director of Finance for Schools and General Government for Fauquier County, Virginia. He has been a member of the GFOA since 1986 and has served on the GFOA Committee on Cash Management and as President of the Virginia GFOA. During his career, he has been involved in the construction of two middle schools and one elementary school, and the renovation of four other schools.

Nicole Westerman currently serves as the Chief of Staff to the Secretary of Budget of the Commonwealth of Pennsylvania, and is also on the GFOA's Committee on Economic Development and Capital Planning. Previously, she worked as a consultant for Public Financial Management, specializing in capital program planning and municipal budget analysis and development. She also served the City of Philadelphia as an Assistant Deputy Mayor in the Capital Program Office with responsibilities alternately including capital project and capital budget management. She has a master of government administration from the University of Pennsylvania, and a bachelor of architecture and bachelor of fine arts from the Rhode Island School of Design.

James C. Willett is the current Superintendent of the Pamunkey Regional Jail in Hanover, Virginia. He is a current Certified Jail Manager through the American Jail Association, and has over ten years experience in the correctional field, with the past nine years as a supervisor. In addition, he holds an eligibility status as a Certified Correctional Manager through the American Correctional Association. Mr. Willett is a member of the American Jail Association (AJA), the American Correctional Association (ACA), and sits on the board of the Virginia Association of Regional Jails, and is a previous member of the Offender Aid & Restoration (OAR) Board.

Fred Winterkamp currently serves as the Manager of the Fiscal and Business Services Division for Orange County, Florida. Prior to this position, Mr. Winterkamp was the Senior Treasury Administrator and Cash Manager for Orange County Public Schools. In those capacities, Mr. Winterkamp has overseen the issuance of more than $3 billion of municipal debt in the form of notes, bonds, and lease obligations to finance schools, capital equipment, correctional facilities, courthouses, utilities infrastructure, and convention centers.

Reviewers

The editors and authors thank the following individuals who served as reviewers or advisors on this book:

Brad L. Ashley, Director of Parks and Recreation, Hanover County, Virginia

John F. Berry, Jr. President and CEO, Richmond Metropolitan Convention & Visitors Bureau, Virginia

Eddie Buchanan, Fire/EMS Division Chief, Hanover County, Virginia

Michael Carter, Director for Operations, Department of Public Works, District of Columbia Government

Steve Chidsey, Chief of Public Works Operations, Hanover County, Virginia

Chris Chronis, Chief Financial Officer, County of Sedgwick, Kansas

Cathy O'Connor, Assistant City Manager/Finance Director, City of Oklahoma City, Oklahoma

Fran Freimarck, Director, Pamunkey Regional Library, Virginia

Adam A. Frisch, Chief of Computer Support Services, York County, Virginia

Phil Heins, Emergency Communications Director, Hanover County, Virginia

Shirley Hughes, Chief Financial Officer, City of Beaufort, South Carolina

Thomas F. Kuehne, Finance Director/Treasurer, Village of Arlington Heights, Illinois

Kent Pfiel, Director of Finance, City of Richardson, Texas

Patricia A. Phillips, Director of Finance, City of Virginia Beach, Virginia

Jim Shrum, Budget Coordinator, Douglas County, Colorado

William Stafford, Chief Financial Officer, Evanston Township High School District 202, Illinois

Doug Straley, Development Manager, Sports & Exhibition Authority of Pittsburgh and Allegheny County, Pennsylvania

Michael Thornton, Assistant Superintendent of Business and Operations, Hanover County Public Schools, Virginia

Jeff Tyne, Budget Officer, City of Peoria, Arizona

Marc S. Weiss, Director of Economic Development, Hanover County, Virginia

Nicole Westerman, Chief of Staff to the Secretary of Budget, Commonwealth of Pennsylvania

Joseph E. Vidunas, Roads Engineer, Hanover County, Virginia

1

Introduction:
The Finance Officer's
Role in Capital Projects

By Joseph P. Casey

Finance officers' responsibilities for capital projects in most mid-size jurisdictions have traditionally focused on their base of strength: budgeting, fiscal management, debt management, and accounting. These skills are critical to ensure that budgets are formulated, funding sources secured, and that the project is properly monitored through the financial and budgetary reports. However, these basic tasks by themselves do not provide the opportunity for the finance officer to contribute in determining the appropriateness, scope, and priority of capital projects. The chief administrative officer or city manager and department managers generating the capital project request primarily assume these roles.

The finance officer's role in capital project planning has great potential to expand into a leadership role. In assuming a greater responsibility for project leadership, the finance officer can help position the local government to consistently make decisions aligned with overall goals and objectives. Centralized oversight can decrease the competition for funds between departments, and help ensure long-term plans are followed to achieve the best outcomes for the jurisdiction and its citizens. The finance officer can also expand the capital improvement program formulation to be not just a project-funding exercise, but rather a strategic plan that aligns projects to overall jurisdictional goals and strategies and works to complete projects that encompass the right scope at the right time.

How Finance Officers Contribute to Capital Projects

Typically, department managers develop a brief description of the project, along with preliminary cost figures. This limited information is given to the finance officer, where it forms the basis for budgeting, funding, prioritization, and incorporation into the capital improvement program. Within this restricted role, the finance officer is relegated to serving as merely a bookkeeper for capital projects, simply compiling the requests of the many department managers and performing an affordability and political exercise to determine which projects get funded, depending on funding constraints or applicable debt capacity limits.

In some government jurisdictions, project requests are limited by available funds and have the scope reduced to fit a budget constraint, often without proper analysis into whether or not the reduced project can still effectively provide the desired service-level outcome. Occasionally, it may be possible to defer projects to later years when they might better serve citizens and staff. If finance officers are to be involved with these decisions, they need a much greater understanding of proposed capital projects than they typically have.

Exhibit 1.1 illustrates the typical level of involvement for department managers, chief administrative officer, and finance officer for a mid-size jurisdiction during common phases of capital projects. Relative to the department manager and chief administrative officer, the finance officer has little involvement early in the process when criteria is developed for evaluating projects, needs assessments are conducted, alternatives are generated and considered, and cost estimates are prepared. While the finance officer may be aware that the capital project process has begun, his or her limited participation at this stage can result in later challenges. When the finance officer finally gets involved, a knowledge gap exists that presents problems with project prioritization, funding source allocation, budget formulation, and project oversight or cost control. In some situations, governments may not have a process that encourages careful analysis early in the project to define service levels, develop criteria for potential projects, properly conduct a needs assessment, and evaluate all viable alternatives, and information that would normally be supplied to the finance officer does not exist.

What Finance Officers Need to Know About the Projects They Evaluate

While preparing the operating budget, the finance officer will often accumulate a tremendous amount of supporting documentation to back up departmental requests, but often capital project requests do not include the same due diligence. Finance officers will only get enough information to classify the project under an oversight department, produce a brief description and schedule for the project,

Exhibit 1.1 Traditional Roles for Capital Projects

Step	Description of Steps	Dept.	Chief Adminis- trator	Finance Officer
1	Define service levels	High	High	Medium
2	Develop capital improvement criteria correlated to service level	Medium	Low	Low
3	Conduct a needs assessment to determine short- and long-term requirements	Medium	Medium	Low
4	Develop viable alternatives	Medium	Low	Low
5	Estimate costs to support each alternative	Medium	Low	Low
6	Select an alternative and prepare the capital budget	High	Medium	Low
7	Prioritize department capital budget requests	Medium	Medium	Medium
8	Determine availability of funding sources and debt capacity in meeting requests	Low	Medium	High
9	Match potential capital projects with funding sources	Low	High	High
10	Prepare budget document illustrating capital projects proposed	Medium	Medium	High
11	Hold meetings for the public and elected officials to review the proposed budget	Low	High	High
12	Make adjustments to the proposed budget	Low	High	High
13	Initiate the project	High	Medium	Medium
14	Monitor project for completion within the project timeline and budget	High	Medium	High

estimate an approximate cost, and begin to identify funding sources. The following are questions used to supply the finance officer with necessary information:

◆ When will the project begin and end?

◆ How much does the project cost?

◆ What is the projected cash flow during the project life?

◆ Is it possible to delay the project?

◆ Do opportunities exist to cut costs?

To provide answers to these questions, the finance officer must rely on individuals deeply involvement with the project. Those individuals, however, may lack an organization-wide perspective. Department managers and others responsible for a narrow segment of the jurisdiction's total services compete with other department managers for funding and will attempt to provide answers that will convince the finance officer and other decision makers the project is worth funding. Often specific projects can be highly technical, based on complicated assumptions, or require advanced knowledge to completely understand. These requests may justify the project in language outside the realm of knowledge for finance officer, which can be intimidating for the finance officer who is trying to balance the needs of each department with the needs of the jurisdiction as a whole. For example, it could be difficult to balance requests from the following department representatives, all of whom may present information that the finance officer may be unfamiliar with.

- ◆ **Engineers.** Engineers, often representing public works or utility departments, work on technical projects. Highly technical project requests could be difficult for the finance officer to understand and almost impossible for her to provide substantive input into how scope changes could better achieve overall goals.

- ◆ **Public Safety Leaders.** Police, fire, or EMS chiefs often argue the importance of security and the potential for loss of lives or damage to property. The importance of public safety facilities and the public attention these projects generate make adjusting the capital requests of public safety leaders a delicate and often time-consuming exercise.

- ◆ **School Boards and Superintendents.** Education leaders often appeal to parents and advocate for projects that appear to best represent student interests. School projects also tend to generate considerable public attention.

- ◆ **Information Technology Directors.** Technology staff provides the support services that are essential to many high profile government services, but often deal with complex terminology and costs that can be difficult to comprehend. Information technology projects should not only involve technology considerations. Often technology enables changes to business processes and must be understood by all. Even though these projects may be complicated, finance officers should make sure that technical issues are properly communicated.

- ◆ **Other Department Managers.** Individuals within each department are the experts on specific services and often have developed skills to best leverage support to acquire funding to meet their needs.

Evolving from Traditional Roles in Capital Projects to Strategic Roles

As government management practices evolve to focus more on measuring outcomes and aligning resources to meet strategic goals, the finance officer's approach to capital project planning, evaluation, and budgeting must also change. To better position the jurisdiction to accomplish goals and objectives, the finance officer should take a more strategic role throughout the entire capital planning process, beginning with the development of service-level goals helping to determine current deficiencies as part of a needs assessment. Defining realistic service outcomes and setting up a system to accurately measure impact is where the finance officer can excel. With an expanded strategic role, the finance officer can be involved with helping to answer the following questions:

◆ What service-level objective is correlated to the capital project, and if none exist, how can one be best developed?

◆ What is the impact on service-level objectives of deferring a capital project?

◆ How will changes to the project scope impact changes to service levels?

◆ Have alternatives been considered that would mitigate the need for the capital project by achieving desired service levels using less costly strategies?

◆ Is there an opportunity to combine capital project requests to take advantage of economies of scale or other efficiency gains?

◆ Were the factors used to determine and support the costs of the project reasonable and justified?

◆ Is this project in alignment with the strategic priorities of the entire jurisdiction?

Correlating Service-Level Goals to Capital Needs

Service-level goals or objectives are the fundamental means by which a local government can illustrate to its citizens what level of service can be provided with available resources. This requires that goals be clear enough to show a direct relationship to the need for capital infrastructure. Having objectives that support operating activities can focus the attention on the importance of capital needs and projects to service delivery. After defining objectives, the jurisdiction should develop a set of performance measures to track the progress and communicate results to citizens, elected officials, employees, and other stakeholders.

Needs Assessments

A needs assessment should address any gaps in service delivery and form the basis for a capital project request. The needs assessment for any potential project should also identify the development of the project as the best method for achieving these stated goals. The process for a needs assessment will generally involve on-staff expertise, such as department managers and other staff experts, and professional consultants with advanced knowledge of the specific service area. Needs assessments should consider time and begin to account for available resources to determine if the project is even feasible. All levels of involvement in the needs assessment require a familiarity with basic operating practices for service delivery and understanding of desired outcomes. Including the finance officer throughout the needs assessment process will only help to develop more accurate budgets and more appropriate capital financing strategies. In addition, in the event that the jurisdiction ultimately needs to limit the project scope, the finance officer will be in a much better position by understanding project components and the resulting service delivery implications of potential cuts. Specific elements to consider for needs assessments under each type of capital project are discussed in section II of the book.

Involvement of Other Key Players

Finance officer involvement in strategic decisions regarding a jurisdiction's capital improvement plan is not meant to replace or diminish contributions by other key staff. Generally, department staff or subject matter experts usually have more specialized skills related to the functions of their department, and the finance officer's role is not to try and compete with such expertise, but rather to complement it. An approach that combines budgeting and finance strengths of the finance officer with specific operational expertise of other staff will provide the best opportunity to position the potential capital project to achieve its stated objectives. The following list identifies other key staff or professional consultants that play an important role in most capital projects:

- ◆ **Engineers.** Engineering skills can best help in determining construction challenges that may exist with potential sites.
- ◆ **Attorneys.** Attorneys will often be needed for land acquisition and complex procurement and contractual agreements.
- ◆ **Planners.** Capital projects may be subject to zoning regulations or other land use restrictions. Planners will help the jurisdiction comply with or change applicable regulations.
- ◆ **Building Inspectors.** Building inspectors' knowledge of the local construction industry makes them a valuable resource to check any cost estimates. Additionally, final construction plans will need to be approved for compliance with all local codes.

◆ **Information Technology Staff.** Many capital projects require information technology assistance as most facilities are equipped to provide the appropriate network connections.

◆ **Facilities Managers.** The facilities management department can provide advice to ensure that buildings are designed to operate more efficiently and reduce operating costs over the facility's life.

◆ **Public Information Officers (PIO).** The PIO should release information to the public and press to provide updates on the project's progress. The PIO can be especially helpful when trying to gather community support for a project.

◆ **Subcommittees of Elected Officials.** Subcommittees on either the budget committee or facility committee are often used to solicit feedback from elected officials without the formality of an elected officials meeting.

◆ **Procurement Officials.** Understanding procurement processes is important to determining project timing and estimating costs. Keeping the purchasing manager informed of the project helps make resources available that are critical to maintaining the project schedule.

Evaluation and Disclosure Goals – Project Checklist

The proper disclosure and communication with elected officials, department managers, employees, and most importantly, citizens will allow a better understanding of the proposed capital project. Additionally, providing information will generate more focused feedback during public input sessions, and if necessary, will prevent any modifications after project initiation. The following is a sample of twelve important questions that should be answered as part of the presentation of any capital improvement project:

1. Has a needs assessment determined that the capital project would help achieve any applicable service-level standards?
2. Does the project fit with the jurisdiction's long-term plans?
3. Has a timeline been developed for the relevant steps in the capital project, such as opportunities for public input, action from elected officials, proper evaluation, procurement processes, permitting, design, and construction?
4. Has the funding source(s) for the capital improvement been identified and are there financial plans that link the timing of funds with part of a balanced plan (e.g., the general fund's ability to fund improvement in three years, grant award potential, debt service for debt, etc.)? If debt funding is used, is it within policy parameters?
5. What is the project's impact on the operating budget?
6. Is the estimated capital improvement cost supported by appropriate cost variables and inflated to reflect estimated costs at the time the contract will be awarded?

7. Has a location been determined for the capital improvement, and does the location allow for service delivery in the best manner?
8. Do current land use plans illustrate that the capital project is in compliance with land use laws?
9. Are efforts underway to acquire land far in advance of the project start date to minimize costs and mitigate the chance of condemnation being necessary?
10. Are there appropriate summary models of all the capital improvements illustrating all projects, funding sources, timing, fund, and other summary information to use as a guide for reviewing compliance with debt policies, and balanced operating plans to support such funding over the stated time period?
11. If the project is part of an ongoing improvement or multi-phase project, are there appropriate disclosures identifying future funding sources and amounts?
12. If multiple jurisdictions or levels of government are participating in the project, do appropriate disclosures illustrate the level of involvement at each level?

Getting Involved in the Process

If the finance officer currently has had little involvement in the early stages of the capital project planning and evaluation process, development of a more strategic role may take time. It is important that the finance officer earn his seat at the table by providing useful feedback and demonstrating the value of his participation. To participate, the finance officer will need knowledge on the entire scope of the most common capital projects. Having that knowledge will assist the finance officer not only in traditional roles, but should also have an impact on the planning, evaluation, and management of the entire project. Some examples of common benefits resulting from the expanded role of the finance officer include:

- ◆ Better documentation for elected officials, citizens, and other stakeholders to support the project in the budget document;
- ◆ Better development of performance measures and initiatives that can be correlated to capital project needs;
- ◆ Better utilization of the pre-budget process to address capital needs and coordination of in-house resources to ensure projects have been properly evaluated;
- ◆ Better development of long-term strategic capital plans;
- ◆ Better debt management programs that prevent over committing debt capacity in the short term on projects that may not be as high of a priority as other long-term projects; and
- ◆ Better connection between the capital and operating budgets to account for capital projects' impact on the operating budget.

This book was written to provide some of the basic knowledge that will enable finance officers to serve an expanded role during the capital project process. It is divided into two sections: the first section discusses considerations associated with most capital project types and the second section reviews twelve of the most common or important local government capital project types.

Section I: Essential Components of All Capital Projects

While specific capital projects such as schools and solid waste facilities differ significantly, many aspects of the capital project planning and evaluation process are similar. Section I will discuss general themes including: public participation, cost estimation and budgeting, project oversight, common funding sources, and the potential for public/private cooperation on projects. Each chapter is intended to provide basic information, not act as a complete detailed resource. The following topics are covered in section I:

Chapter 2: Public Participation. Citizen involvement is extremely important to development of publicly accepted service-level goals and to the success of capital projects. This chapter discusses the use of surveys, community meetings, and citizen committees to gauge public perspectives and provide services and service facilities to more closely meet the community's needs and expectations.

Chapter 3: Cost Estimation and Budgeting. Expanding the finance officer's role requires involvement with not only cost estimation, but also in discussions on the project scope in addition to traditional budgeting responsibilities. This chapter discusses issues related to defining the appropriate scope to meet service-level goals, estimating costs for proposed projects, and making recommendations for preparing capital project budgets.

Chapter 4: Project Schedule and Oversight. Once project work has begun, the finance officer is ideally positioned to participate in project oversight responsibilities. This chapter provides information on project schedules and key project phases, including land acquisition, design, other pre-construction activities, and construction.

Chapter 5: Common Funding Options. While capital projects may have many different funding sources, several sources are especially common. This chapter highlights both pay-as-you-go and pay-as-you-use financing, and contains information on necessary steps in establishing a debt program.

Chapter 6: Public/Private Partnership Agreements. Governments have many opportunities to partner with private sector organizations to meet service-level goals. Often these projects achieve goals that would be impossible without a combined public/private approach. This chapter presents a method to evaluate potential agreements and discusses common strategies for financing partnership agreements.

Section II:
Project-Specific Considerations

To participate productively in strategic discussions and assist in setting service-level objectives and developing performance measures for each capital project type, the finance office will need project-specific knowledge. Section II of this book provides a short description of twelve important capital project types and basic information to assist with the needs assessment. The chapters also provide information on development standards or industry best practices, project management tips, potential alternative funding sources, and likely impacts on the operating budget. Section II covers the following project types:

Projects for Public Health and Safety

Chapter 7: Emergency Communications Systems. These facilities are an essential and vital public safety function that require proper security and must operate 24/7 without interruption. The communications system is the primary means by which public safety agencies communicate with each other and are deployed. Because of rapid advancements in technology, greater awareness of security issues and interoperability objectives requires an organization-wide focus for these projects.

Chapter 8: Fire/EMS Stations. Fire/EMS stations are needed to house firefighters/EMS personnel and accommodate a variety of ambulances, fire trucks, and other types of rescue equipment. Fire/EMS facilities must be continually evaluated to ensure proper coverage of growth areas and so that stations are positioned to reliably allow adequate emergency response times.

Chapter 9: Correctional Facilities and Jails. As jail populations increase, plans should be developed to ensure that overcrowding does not negatively impact service delivery. Because of unique design and construction requirements, jail facilities should be carefully planned.

Projects to Enhance Local Government Efficiency

Chapter 10: Roads. Having defined service levels that guide road construction will assist in the development of long-term plans to reduce congestion, promote economic development and efficiency, and help control costs over extended time periods. As communities develop, road project planning and evaluation becomes increasingly important to ensure adequate capacity.

Chapter 11: Water and Wastewater Systems. Perhaps nothing helps guide a jurisdiction's development plans more than determining the capacity and location of water and sewer lines. In addition, water and sewer treatment facilities are expensive and highly regulated facilities that require significant planning efforts.

Chapter 12: Administrative Facilities. Unlike many other government facilities, administrative facilities are similar to private sector offices. Most administrative space is designed to permit staff to perform necessary functions, interact with other employees within and between departments, and allow convenient access for citizens wishing to acquire permits or conduct other business, obtain information, or attend public meetings.

Chapter 13: Planning and Evaluating Technology Investments. While not the most visible kind of capital project, both from a citizen and a staff perspective, information technology infrastructure is often the backbone for essential local government services. Investments in information technology can include business applications such as financial management systems, geographic information systems, or other infrastructure supporting department operations.

Chapter 14: Solid Waste Facilities. Changes to many environmental regulations, along with development of the private sector waste management industry, have altered the way governments deal with solid waste. At the same time, solid waste removal remains one of local government's most important services.

Projects to Enhance Quality of Life

Chapter 15: Schools. Perhaps one local government's most visible and common facilities, schools require advanced planning to accommodate future student populations and comply with any mandated student: teacher ratios and other requirements. School projects are also routinely subjected to intense public involvement.

Chapter 16: Public Libraries. Libraries provide children and adults with resources for continuing education and learning. Facilities should be designed to accommodate any expected growth and located in strategic areas that are accessible to the maximum number of users.

Chapter 17: Parks and Recreation Facilities. Similar to libraries, parks add to citizens' quality of life. Communities should have strategic goals to guide the type and location of parks to best meet citizen needs. Capital projects can provide active sites such as water parks or athletic fields, or passive use areas such as nature preserves or hiking trails.

Chapter 18: Convention Centers and Meeting Facilities. The construction of convention centers and other exhibition or meeting facilities can be a tool for increasing economic activity within the area. Convention centers have specialized requirements and are intended to be economically self-supporting to the greatest extent possible, so market conditions must be carefully analyzed and an effective finance plan is especially important.

2

Public Participation

By Greg Canally and Joseph P. Casey

Public participation during the planning, design, and construction of capital projects is extremely important. Both large and small projects will require and benefit from public involvement or knowledge. For example, public involvement for small projects, such as replacing a storm drain, might include mailing notices to citizens informing them of the timing and scope of the work. Larger projects, such as the construction of a recreation center, will benefit from greater public involvement, such as surveys to establish citizen preferences, committees to help suggest design elements, and regular informational meetings to update the public on the project's progress. Developing a process to involve the public during project planning is a key step in determining if the project will meet service-level goals and community expectations. Active participation will also help avoid public outcry after completion and can work to create citizen advocates for the project. Jurisdictions need to carefully balance the level of public involvement, however, with the need to plan, develop, and construct the project in a timely manner. Processes involving too much citizen involvement are often inefficient and can lead to problems that cause significant delays and increase costs. This chapter will discuss different methods of public participation, including the use of surveys, community meetings, different communication methods, and citizen committees.

A New Era of Public Participation

In December 1962, the New York City Board of Estimate unanimously rejected the city's proposal to build a Lower Manhattan Expressway. The blocking of this expressway was due in part to efforts of community activists and concerned citizens and helped usher in a new era of public participation for government capital projects. While the project may have failed without public involvement, this event introduced the role of citizens into project planning.

Forms of Public Participation

Citizens can become involved in capital project planning process in several ways. In a larger sense, public involvement in jurisdiction-wide planning processes such as the development of strategic or comprehensive plans allows citizens input into the type of projects and the overall community preferences and priorities. These plans usually define service-level goals and anticipate the required public services and facilities to achieve or maintain those standards. For individual projects, citizens are often asked to provide feedback on specific plans through surveys, community meetings and/or citizen committees. Even when the jurisdiction is not soliciting feedback, it is important to communicate plans and results and keep the public informed. This can be accomplished by any of the previously mentioned methods, or by other means of communication including citizen newsletters, press releases, or through the jurisdiction's Web site.

Surveys

Surveys help gauge overall citizen viewpoints and perspective on controversial issues. When conducting surveys, the statistical accuracy of the survey should be assured. Participant selection and careful crafting of questions will result in an unbiased survey that does not suggest a favored response. For example, it would not be appropriate to distribute surveys on a potential library expansion plan at the library, as it would include only library users and thus not represent the community at large. Similarly, presenting a question that implies only the positive benefits of expansion without mentioning required tax increases would bias the results. The following are a few sample survey questions that could be used to gauge community preferences on broad planning objectives or specific projects:

Schools:

- ◆ What would you like the student: teacher ratio to be?
- ◆ Would you be willing to have your taxes increased to lower the student: teacher ratio?

Parks:

- ◆ What recreational activities do you participate in most often?
- ◆ What recreational activities/opportunities do you wish were offered?
- ◆ Would you be willing to pay recreational fees to fund such activities?
- ◆ Have you used the nature trails located in City Park?
- ◆ Do you think taxes should be increased to provide more nature trails?

Libraries:

- ◆ How many books do you generally check out from the library each year?

◆ Would you support additional library fees to purchase more computers for the library?

◆ Is the nearest library too far from your home?

Fire/EMS:

◆ The current average response time is seven minutes; do you favor increasing taxes for more fire/EMS facilities and staff to reduce response times?

Roads:

◆ The current average grade of roads on a commonly used scale is C with no roads graded below D. Do you favor increasing taxes to improve the average grade to B with no roads graded below a C?

When developing survey questions, it is extremely important that questions are relevant and easy to understand. Surveys should be piloted to ensure that questions are not worded in a way that allows for multiple interpretations. There are some national firms that use standard questions for many local governments and can provide benchmarks in gauging how citizens' perspectives compare to national averages. Consideration should be given to having the surveys conducted every few years with similar questions each time to gauge changing opinions. Questions therefore should be developed with the anticipation that they will be used for many years, making proper planning and testing the survey essential. The capability for trend analysis can be a strong tool in helping a jurisdiction determine community preferences.

Community Meetings

There are many community business and civic organizations that can be a resource for obtaining citizen-based feedback or providing an audience to present information. Groups such as the Ruritans, Lions Club, Rotary Club, VFW Clubs, homeowners associations, civic organizations, and others meet regularly and will generally allow for a presentation by local officials. There are also many groups in the business community such as the local chamber of commerce, business leagues, trade associations, and employee unions that will offer feedback on planned capital projects or other important issues. In addition, many faith-based organizations have become more active in the community and can provide yet another venue to reach citizens.

It may be a beneficial for the jurisdiction to coordinate among these groups and align presentation updates on local government and capital project plans as necessary. Speaking with community groups will show the public that the jurisdiction is transparent and responsive and will encourage citizens become more involved with government.

Communication Methods

Public engagement also involves communicating progress and results of capital improvement plans and projects. Some jurisdictions have a public information office (PIO) that serves as a conduit between local government, local media, and citizens. The PIO is often responsible for writing newsletters and press releases, maintaining the jurisdiction's Web site, and answering inquiries from citizens. The PIO is a great resource to include in capital project planning and evaluation since this office usually has a better understanding of the "citizen perspective." Jurisdictions without a dedicated PIO still provide all of the same information, but the central administration or decentralized departments hold responsibility for contact with the public.

Dealing with Opposition

As with most issues, capital projects will most likely face opposition from strong critics who do not want to see tax changes or who argue the government should adopt a completely different course of action. When dealing with negative participation, policies should be developed to provide a forum for disagreement without allowing the spirited arguments of a few individuals to dominate the prevailing preferences of the community at large. It is important that the jurisdiction consider opposing viewpoints, but also remain focused on established service-level goals and broader planning documents that were already subjected to prior public participation processes.

Newsletters

Newsletters published by the jurisdiction are one example of how the public can remain informed on topics, projects, or issues that may not be covered by newspapers and other media. Newsletters with brief articles on upcoming projects or important events are designed to inform the public and direct the reader to further information.

Press Releases

The jurisdiction can keep the public informed on specific capital projects by issuing a press release. Press releases provide information to local media that can form the basis for larger articles. Some jurisdictions also provide "letters to the editor" in local newspapers explaining the need for a certain capital project and the impact on service delivery and costs or taxes. Jurisdictions should be careful when using this method and understand that providing such a letter may encourage others to write letters critical of the project.

Web Sites

Web sites can be one of the most useful forms of keeping citizens informed with the plans and progress for capital projects. Web pages dedicated to capital projects on the jurisdiction's Web site can provide information on upcoming projects and progress on current projects. The Web site can also be an effective way to advertise or inform citizens about any of the other forms of citizen participation already discussed and list meeting notices, provide committee information, contain links to complete surveys, and forms to send e-mail to staff.

Committees

Jurisdictions often form committees to develop recommendations or provide feedback on proposed capital projects. Citizen committees are a great vehicle for public participation. As part of the committee meeting agenda, a committee should allow for citizen input at its regularly scheduled meetings. Preferably this should occur near the beginning of the meeting, and there should be a time limit per speaker as well as overall time allotment. This is a very simple, efficient way to establish credibility with the community and media, as well as a way to gather project-specific input. While the range of what committees can do varies greatly based upon their scope, the overall structure, appointment, administration, and goals are generally similar. Many departments within local government may also form official committees to solicit feedback. Specifically, citizen committees are often formed for fire/EMS projects, parks, schools, libraries, and other highly visible projects that garner the most citizen interest and knowledge.

- ◆ **Fire/EMS.** Many fire/EMS departments have their roots in a volunteer force, or continue to utilize volunteers. The input of this group, especially its leaders, can greatly assist the jurisdiction's definition of service levels and future fire/EMS facility needs. In addition, a general citizen-appointed public safety committee can be a resource for 911 centers/communications systems and jails.

- ◆ **Parks.** Parks and recreation programs often include athletic leagues whose leaders can be great information sources. Clubs that utilize parks for their activities might have members willing to provide feedback and input into future facility needs.

- ◆ **Schools.** Each school traditionally has a parent-teacher association (PTA) and schools may have citizen-appointed committees for different curriculum areas.

- ◆ **Libraries.** In many areas, each library division may have a citizen-appointed group that serves as the "friends of the library." These advocates can offer insight into the needs of library facilities, including the many programs that libraries offer (e.g., book clubs, children's story time, etc.).

Bond Committees

The remainder of this chapter focuses on establishing a bond committee. Bond committees are formed for capital projects to provide feedback on bond referendums. Information can also be applicable to the formation and organization of other citizen committees, such as those discussed earlier.

Jurisdictions establish bond committees to provide recommendations and support for an upcoming bond referendum. In many communities, capital projects are first proposed as part of a larger bond referendum that includes multiple projects. A bond referendum may be required under state law, be used to help ensure the lowest cost financing, and/or confirm the public's commitment to proposed projects, especially if such projects require a tax increase. Bond committees are formed to provide public input and recommendations on how to proceed with a bond referendum or to gather support and advocate for the referendum. They are also an important part of the public participation process. Some bond committees are established by elected officials who appoint citizens to serve as members. For other bond committees, the establishment and the selection of members may be the result of a "grass roots" citizen-based effort. These committees are more common in states where restrictions limit the ability of governments to advocate for a bond referendum. In these instances, staff may assist the committee with information and be available for community meeting presentations, but would defer any advocacy role to committee members.

Why Have a Citizen Committee?

Local officials generally know what projects are needed, how much they cost, how much the jurisdiction can afford, and any constraints on the jurisdiction's ability to issue debt. The citizen committee, however, serves several purposes that should not be overlooked. Committees generally provide the following advantages:

- ◆ Allow officials to reach out into the community and involve citizens in the policy-making process;
- ◆ Allow the jurisdiction to hear directly from a group of citizens about specific projects and plans; and
- ◆ Allow for representation by many different groups that have a direct interest in the project.

Who Should Be on the Committee?

The purpose behind a citizen committee is to create an open, public process that reaches out into the community. This is best accomplished by appointing key stakeholders and community members who are civically active, able to commit time to the project, and respected in their subject area. Most importantly, the make-up of the group should mirror the diversity of the community. Possible committee members could include:

- ◆ Former elected officials;
- ◆ Representatives of other governmental bodies;
- ◆ Business leaders;
- ◆ Environmental leaders;
- ◆ Community activists; and
- ◆ Customers and/or clients of the service provided through capital project.

The size of the committee is often dependent on several factors, such as the size of the community, the number of elected officials, and the size or impact of the bond issue being considered.

Committee Roles and Responsibilities

When initially establishing the committee, the elected officials should give clear it direction on the rationale for its establishment and specific instructions on its roles and responsibilities. Usually, this information is included in a resolution approved by the elected officials before the committee is formed. Examples of committee responsibilities can include:

- ◆ Determining the size of the bond program;
- ◆ Identifying potential projects;
- ◆ Prioritizing projects;
- ◆ Holding public meetings; and
- ◆ Producing a report to elected officials.

Committee Organization

The success or failure of a bond committee process hinges on the members themselves, the staff assigned to work on behalf of the committee, and most importantly, the way the committee organizes itself. An early task for the committee should be to establish its rules: quorum rule, voting rules, attendance rules, public input, and citizen communication rules concerning time. Upon convening the first meeting of the committee, staff should have the group elect officers, such as a chairman and vice-chairman. Depending on the techniques used to arrive at committee decisions, rules, especially those for voting, may need to be amended as the committee gets closer to finalizing the recommendation. The committee should also determine its schedule including, when full committee meetings will be held, and, if applicable, when subcommittee meetings will occur. It is important to be cognizant of meeting times and duration. While committee members have willingly volunteered to serve, the meetings should be scheduled to ensure attendance from as many members as possible. One of the main roles of most committees is to gather public input, so meeting times may also need to be convenient for the public. Some committees may be required to establish themselves as non-profit organizations under IRS guidelines. This is especially true for those committees that will be involved with fundraising.

Establishing Guiding Principles

Before identifying and prioritizing projects, the group as a whole needs to define the broad guiding principles for the process. Examples could include: equity, diversity, input, sustainability, quality of life, accountability, or affordability. It is likely that the committee will establish these principles early in its work, but after going through the process and listening to the public, it may decide to refine some of the principles.

Forming Subcommittees

Depending on the size of the committee and the recommendation in front of them, the committee may choose to break up into subcommittees. Generally, subcommittees will either be charged with functional areas for committee administration (such as marketing, Web site content, fundraising, or community presentations) or project-related areas (such as parks, public works, or schools). Another option would be to group similar projects included in the recommendation; for example, the grouping of "drainage and transportation" would include street projects, sidewalks, traffic signals, storm sewers, and other projects in the "right of way." If a committee does choose to use subcommittees, the decisions about how to split up the whole committee are important. These categories will form the basis of early communication about the bonds, how the public refers to them, and how it views the process.

A subcommittee process allows members to focus on their areas of expertise or interest, while moving simultaneously through a range of issues in a timely manner. The one major downside of the subcommittee concept is the time it takes to get the rest of the committee "up to speed" on the subcommittee's issues/projects when the final recommendation needs to be determined.

Staffing Committees

Ideally, staff assigned to the committee should be members of the jurisdiction's finance or budget staff who can not only coordinate the information flow on projects and programs, but also be able to communicate the necessary financial information about tax impacts and costs. The staff should ensure that the process moves forward, but should not influence specific committee decisions or recommendations. Other potential staff duties include keeping meeting minutes, providing information to committee members, and handling certain housekeeping duties, such as organizing meals.

Soliciting Public Input

As previously stated, one of the committee's main tasks is to seek public input. Methods of public input are generally the same as those discussed earlier in the chapter, such as committee meetings, community meetings, and direct input from surveys. This can be accomplished during regular committee meetings, at public hearings, and through surveys. Committees also can hold public hearings to solicit feedback on their work. For example, the bond committee could put forward a draft recommendation and ask for public comment. If there are going to be a series of public hearings, it is recommended that they are held out in the community. Scattering the public hearings in different parts of the community, in various schools or park buildings, makes it more convenient for citizens and gives residents of each area the opportunity to speak out.

Committee Recommendation

Often, the committee's ultimate goal is to provide elected officials with a recommendation. Getting to that recommendation however is not always easy. A clear process should be established to determine how the committee will arrive at a final recommendation. Methods for making proposals for the committee to vote on and voting rules must be set early on. For example, one method has a committee member put forth a proposal that is then voted on and amended until a voting standard is met (unanimous, majority, super majority) and a decision reached.

Final Report

Once the committee decides on a recommendation, a final report is usually created. This is an important document, as it will be viewed by elected officials, staff, and the community. Most reports include an executive summary, an explanation of the final recommendation, a description of the committee's guiding principles, a summary of the public input process, and an overview of the process used to decide the recommendation. After the report is issued, the jurisdiction must determine if it will modify elements of the recommendation or pass along the recommendation directly to voters as the basis for a referendum.

If the referendum failed, local officials will need to determine the best path to proceed, especially for essential projects. In some states, a failed referendum may require that the project be delayed for a few years before alterative debt financing methods are permitted. With this in mind, it is imperative to hold a bond referendum far in advance of the need to arrange for alternative financing. If the referendum passes, it is crucial to keep the public informed. An oversight committee can provide public monitoring of the project and keep citizens involved.

| Conclusion |

There are many ways in which to engage the public constructively in capital projects. Traditional methods of public participation such as citizen committees and community meetings can be further enhanced with the use of Web sites, surveys, newsletters, and other forums that help gauge the public's preferences and priorities and keep them informed of the status of previously approved projects. Individual jurisdictions and communities may each have preferred ways of public participation, but common throughout all is the need for facilities and government services to meet the needs and expectations of citizens, which can only be accomplished with citizen involvement in the capital project planning process.

City of Austin Bond Election 2006 – Bond Election Advisory Committee

This case study was based on the City of Austin, Texas, bond election advisory committee report and recommendation, presented to the city council on February 2, 2006. Unless otherwise noted, all figures and examples were taken from the final report.

The City of Austin, Texas, formed a bond election advisory committee to recommend an investment program that meets critical current infrastructure needs while positioning the city for future growth.[a] The committee consisted of twenty-one members that took suggestions and requests from staff and citizens representing projects estimated at $1.1 billion and recommended $614.8 worth of improvements for the city to include in a bond referendum.

The Process

The city council passed a resolution in February 2005 creating the committee and appointed members in April. To divide up responsibilities, the committee formed into subcommittees. Members of each subcommittee met twice per month for seven months to hear testimony and presentations from staff, community advocates, and outside experts. In November, each subcommittee prepared recommendations for the entire committee. The initial recommendation from each subcommittee totaled $851 million, far exceeding the target of $600 million established at the beginning of the process. The committee was then able to amend the recommendation and arrive at the total recommended amount that was presented to the community during two public hearings and later submitted to the city council. Overall, the entire process included six public hearings, twelve full committee meetings, forty subcommittee meetings, the review of 500 proposed projects, a survey with 900 responses, 900 e-mail messages from the public to the committee, and the participation of eighty-five community groups and over 1,000 citizens at public hearings. Exhibit 2.1 shows the entire process and timeline for the committee.

Subcommittees

The committee organized itself into six subcommittees: affordable housing, drainage and transportation, facilities, open space, public communication and outreach, and inter-jurisdictional cooperation. The first four subcommittees collected and evaluated proposed projects. The public communication and outreach subcommittee oversaw the planning and implementation of the committee's interaction with the community, including content on the city Web site, citizen surveys, public hearings, and presentations to community groups. The subcommittee on inter-jurisdictional cooperation addressed issues related to other governments and regional stakeholders.

Exhibit 2.1 Bond Election Advisory Committee Process

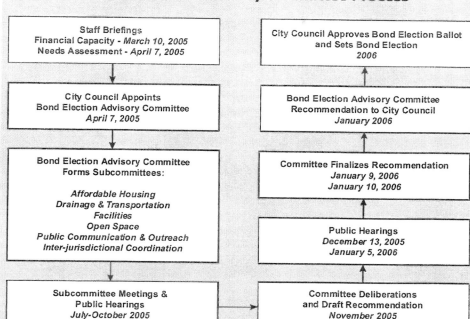

Guiding Principles

In May 2005, the committee adopted the following principles that would guide the process and final recommendation:

- **Equity and Diversity.** The committee will create a proposed bond program that responds to community needs in all parts of the city and among all demographic and lifestyle groups. In addition, the bond program will include a diverse array of projects that will create choices and opportunities for a diverse community and provide innovative solutions for specific community needs.

- **Expertise and Input.** The committee will seek and use the best information available from stakeholders. The proposed bond program will also reflect public input and the committee will make every effort possible to ensure that communication channels remain open and accessible to all citizens.

- **Leverage and Relationships.** The committee will identify and give priority to opportunities that leverage city capital investments with additional resources from other city sources, other jurisdictions, and agencies, and the private and non-profit community. Additionally, the committee will evaluate relationships among proposed projects and make recommendations designed to enhance the effectiveness of the city's investments.

Final Recommendation

In its final report, the committee recommended $497.0 million of the $769.1 million in projects that staff had presented in needs assessment at the beginning of the process. In addition, $117.8 million in projects not included in the staff needs assessment, but suggested by citizens and community groups during the process, were included to bring the total to $614.8 million. Exhibit 2.2 shows the recommended total cost of projects in each category the committee used. As part of its final recommendation, the committee voted to recommend the city set a bond election for the entire $614.8 package at once and that the city set up a citizen oversight committee and evaluation strategy for implementing the bond program.

Exhibit 2.2 Final Recommendation

($ Millions)	Recom-mended by Committee	Staff Needs Assess-ment	Amount from Staff Needs Assessment	Amount from Citizen Requests
Affordable Housing	67.5	25.0	25.0	42.5
Drainage	122.1	198.6	122.1	
Facilities	144.0	203.6	114.8	29.2
Central Library	90.0	106.7	90.0	
Open Space	92.3	50.0	50.0	42.3
Transportation	98.9	185.0	95.1	3.8
Total	**614.8**	**768.9**	**497.0**	**117.8**

Bond Election

On November 7, 2006, the citizens of the City of Austin voted on seven different propositions totaling $567.4 based on recommendation by the committee. Final recommendations of the committee were adjusted slightly by the City of Austin to develop the following propositions,[b] all of which were overwhelming approved by voters.

- **Proposition 1.** "The issuance of $103,100,000 in tax-supported general obligation bonds and notes for reconstructing roads and streets, constructing, reconstructing, and improving drainage facilities related to the roads and streets; constructing, reconstructing, and improving bicycle and pedestrian mobility infrastructure; improving traffic signal synchronization and controls systems, acquiring and installing traffic signals; and acquiring land and interests in land and property necessary to do so; and the levy of a tax sufficient to pay for the bonds and notes."

- **Proposition 2.** "The issuance of $145,000,000 in tax-supported general obligation bonds and notes for designing, constructing, and installing improvements and facilities for flood control, erosion control, water quality, and storm water drainage, and acquiring land, open spaces, and interests in land and property necessary to do so, including, without limitation, acquisition of land including fee title and easements in the Barton Springs contributing and recharge zones to provide for the conservation of the region's water quality; and the levy of a tax sufficient to pay for the bonds and notes."

- **Proposition 3.** "The issuance of $84,700,000 in tax-supported general obligation bonds and notes for constructing, renovating, improving and equipping public parks, recreation centers, natural areas, and other related facilities, including, without limitation, playgrounds, hike and bike trails, sports courts, and swimming pools; and acquiring land and interests in land and property necessary to do so; and the levy of a tax sufficient to pay for the bonds and notes."

- **Proposition 4.** "The issuance of $31,500,000 in tax-supported general obligation bonds and notes for constructing, renovating, improving, and equipping community and cultural facilities including, without limitation, the Zachary Scott Theater, an African American Cultural and Heritage Facility, an Asian American Resource Center, the Austin Film Studios, the Mexican American Cultural Center, a Mexic-Arte Art Museum, and acquiring land and interests in land and property necessary to do so; and the levy of a tax sufficient to pay for the bonds and notes."

- **Proposition 5.** "The issuance of $55,000,000 in tax-supported general obligation bonds and notes for constructing, renovating, improving, and equipping affordable housing facilities for low income persons and families, and acquiring land and interests in land and property necessary to do so, and funding affordable housing programs as may be permitted by law; and the levy of a tax sufficient to pay for the bonds and notes."

- **Proposition 6.** "The issuance of $90,000,000 in tax-supported general obligation bonds and notes for constructing and equipping a new Central Library facility and acquiring land and interests in land and property necessary to do so; and the levy of a tax sufficient to pay for the bonds and notes."

- **Proposition 7.** "The issuance of $58,100,000 in tax-supported general obligation bonds and notes for constructing, renovating, improving, and equipping public safety facilities, including, without limitation, a public safety training facility, police stations, emergency medical services buildings and facilities, a municipal courthouse, an animal shelter, and other related facilities and acquiring land and interests in land and property necessary to do so; and the levy of a tax sufficient to pay for the bonds and notes."

---

a. The city council passed Resolution No. 050217-50 on February 17, 2005, to create the bond election advisory committee. A copy of the resolution is available on the City of Austin, Texas, Web site, http://www.ci.austin.tx.us.
b. The ballot language for each proposition was taken from the City of Austin, Texas, Web site, http://www.ci.austin.tx.us/bonds.

|3|

Cost Estimation and Budgeting

By Nicole Westerman and Joseph P. Casey

Key to the new strategic role of the finance officer for capital projects is the ability to scope projects to best meet the service-level goals of the government. After appropriate projects are identified, costing and budgeting projects correctly is vital for successful project completion. This chapter reviews common issues in estimating costs and budgeting for capital projects.

| Scope Definition |

Capital needs arise for different reasons: growing or declining service demand, the introduction of new services, changes in technology, mandates from state or federal government, or the deterioration of assets. These needs can often be anticipated with good planning and sound management. Monitoring growth or decline in service use relative to defined service-level goals will help plan some kinds of projects; for example, if emergency response times are not meeting current targets, perhaps another fire/ EMS station is needed.

Once a need is identified, the scope of a potential project must be defined more clearly. Establishing project scope means:

◆ Defining the need or needs the project is meant to address, and whether they are meant to be addressed in a temporary or permanent way;

◆ Deciding how the needs are to be addressed;

◆ Identifying any other needs or goals that will be created by the project;

◆ Defining what the finished project should be like;

◆ Deciding – and articulating – what should and should not be included in the project; and

◆ Defining what role the private sector has in provision and/or funding of service.

The process of scope definition should involve the input of people with different viewpoints and areas of expertise. Exhibit 3.1 shows how multiple participants contributed to scope definition during the City of Philadelphia's project to convert an old school building into a police forensic science building..

Exhibit 3.1 Participants Involved with Scope Definition: Example from a City of Philadelphia Project

Participant	Role
Agency heads	• The Police Commissioner and Deputy Commissioner for Science and Technology advocated for the proposed project to ensure that it received the attention it deserved.
"Clients" or end users	• The people who will use the building are usually more than willing to tell you what they need (or think they need). • In this case, the clients were DNA and chemistry lab technicians, and police officers who do crime scene work and firearms identification.
Engineers	• Mechanical, electrical, and structural engineers helped evaluate the existing building envelope, structure, mechanical/plumbing systems, and electrical system and define the extent of work required for the new use.
Architects	• By developing a building "program," the architects helped define all the activities that will take place in the building and the associated space/ area requirements.
Industry experts	• A laboratory consulting company worked with the architect to develop the program and plans and specifications, applying best practices in lab design. • Members of the American Society of Crime Lab Directors can perform reviews to help ensure that the new labs will be accredited.
Risk management	• An industrial hygienist in the law department's risk management section helped to make sure the ventilation systems would exceed safety standards and reduce potential liabilities to the city.
Operations and maintenance managers	• Those with the responsibility for running the facility when it is completed had input in the selection of systems, materials, and fixtures to ensure ease and affordability of operation.

The involvement of people with technical or operational experience to identify factors that could later increase project costs, such as structural design issues, is critically important. Once the project scope is defined, it is important to use it as a limit beyond which the project shall not grow. Scope creep is a potential problem at every stage of the project's life. As the term implies, scope creep can increase the duration, complexity, and most important, the cost of the project with little and/or noticeable warning.

It is important to note that the project's scope may be memorialized in and restricted by bond referenda or other financial or contractual instruments. Keep in mind, however, that it may be possible to deal with the identified need in a way that limits the jurisdiction's involvement. For example, a jurisdiction may be able to rent a facility rather than purchasing or constructing one. It might also be able to enter into an agreement with a private partner under which capital costs of purchase or renovation are shared. In such cases, the capital costs of both acquisition and construction must be carefully weighed against rent, maintenance costs, and other operating costs. A cross-disciplinary working group including a planner, real estate manager, facility manager, capital program manager, and, of course, the finance officer can help to identify and weigh such alternatives.

Guarding Against Scope Creep

Project scope must be controlled by careful project documentation and good project management. Before project approval, scope should be defined by a detailed narrative explanation with supporting back-up. Before project design work begins, the scope should be described in a request for proposals (RFP) that tells the architect or engineer what work or service is expected and what the final product should be. During the design process, scope will be further defined in more detail. The end design will transform the original narrative form of the scope into a set of drawings and specifications. If the project requires multiple prime contractors, the work of each contractor must be defined clearly, without any gaps or redundancies.

Those with project management responsibilities need to constantly educate the finance officers about the risks associated with scope definition and the project budget. If a significant change in budget is necessary, the finance officer should have been sufficiently familiar with the project's progress so it is not a surprise and there is some lead time in understanding and dealing with budgetary consequences. Conversely, finance officers should stress the importance of meeting the budget and the consequences of failing to do so.

After the design is finalized, and throughout the construction process, the project manager or construction manager must be relentless in preventing unnecessary change orders or contract amendments. The danger of scope creep is omnipresent. There are legitimate reasons for change orders and contract amendments, such as unforeseen conditions or real changes in project requirements, but keep in mind it is the end user's job to try to get the very best, nicest, or most out of this project, and keeping costs down is simply not the contractor's priority. Normally, it is the project manager and the finance officer's responsibility to keep a tight rein on the scope, and in effect, on the cost of the project.

Unforeseen Conditions and Project Scope

As noted previously, project scope can grow for legitimate reasons, including changing functional needs, new regulatory requirements, or unforeseen conditions (e.g., asbestos insulation found hidden inside of walls or the discovery of an underground tank that requires remediation).

Even if proposed changes are legitimate, it is important to make sure any changes to the scope are reviewed and approved at the appropriate level before they are implemented. Preferably, the same decision makers who approved the project originally will approve any major changes. Any changes in cost that may result from changes in scope must be part of the information used by the decision makers and, if approved, must flow through to changes in the overall capital budget. Scope changes must also be reviewed for compliance with any applicable legal requirements, such as bond covenants. The scope of the project, as defined in the bond referendum and to a lesser degree supporting bond referendum literature, should not change. In some cases, the project scope is not allowed to change at all. Depending on the way projects are monitored or on the nature of the project, public disclosure of changes may be appropriate or necessary as well.

| Cost Estimation |

Project scope definition and cost estimation go together. As the project scope is refined, estimates of the total cost should be developed to ensure the project remains feasible. On an even more basic level, cost estimation is an important factor in the decision whether or not to include the project in the overall capital plan. That means resources should be dedicated to cost estimation outside the scope of approved projects. There are books, software, and construction cost indices available for in-house cost estimation. The bigger the project, the more carefully the cost should be estimated. Cost estimation might be done in-house, by architects or engineers, or by a consultant. If you have a big capital program, or if you do not have in-house design or project management staff, it is useful to have a cost estimator on a retainer. Under typical capital eligibility rules, the services would not be chargeable to a particular project, but they would be chargeable to the capital budget.

> **Construction Budget vs. Project Budget**
>
> One of the most important things to recognize is that there is a difference between a construction budget and a project budget. A project budget will incorporate all of the costs associated with the project, such as design, consultant fees, land acquisition, site preparation, and project management expenses. The construction budget will incorporate just the portion of the project costs that are paid to the contractor(s).

During project development, the owner's representative or project manager should secure independent assessments of the cost of constructing the project. The names of this analysis may vary; common names include a statement of probable construction cost or a construction estimate. The intent is to have an estimate that includes the estimated cost of all bids that are expected to be received to complete the project. Often construction cost estimating services are included as part of the architect's or engineer's services, but for all projects, the jurisdiction should secure independent assessments in addition to these. Architects, engineers, and other professionals with a financial interest in the project moving forward may underestimate costs to make the project look more favorable. It is important that consultants specialize in construction cost estimating, preferably with experience in your community. Estimates of probable construction costs should begin as early as possible. Estimates should be conducted during schematic design, design development, construction documentation, and finally just prior to advertising for bids.

Cost estimating is an iterative process because as the project design is developed and finalized with each successive design phase, more detail is displayed and the cost can be more accurately predicted. Each estimate builds upon any previous estimates. Generally the more expensive or complex the project is, the more frequently a cost estimate should be developed. With large projects, there is more at stake; even a small percentage deviation from budget can be big in terms of dollars. Despite all of this effort to estimate the cost of a project, an effective finance officer must plan for an all too common situation where actual bids differ, sometimes significantly, from the final estimate of construction cost.

Value Engineering

Scope definition and cost estimation have a push-and-pull relationship in the process of "value engineering." Value engineering is a process that, when successful, can lower project costs. The project manager, along with designers, cost estimators, and those with an operational perspective need to work together to identify ways to trade quality or program elements for savings, or identify ways of getting the same quality and program elements for less money. They should provide a menu of options from which the project decision makers can choose. Of course, the decision makers might decide that none of the options are acceptable and that more money simply must be found.

Are Estimates Accurate?

One way to determine the reasonableness of the cost estimates is to survey other recently constructed projects. The projects could include other public buildings constructed by the same jurisdiction or other similar projects constructed by other governments. In making these kinds of project cost comparisons, it can be difficult to get a true "apples-to-apples" comparison because other project scopes

Value Engineering

The Society of American Value Engineers defines value engineering as "the systematic application of recognized techniques which identify the function of a product or service, establish a value for that function, and provide the necessary function at the least overall cost. In all instances, the required function should be achieved at the lowest possible life-cycle cost consistent with requirements and/or performance, maintainability, and aesthetics." Value engineering is also called value methodology, value analysis, or value management.

The typical characteristics of candidates for value engineering are:
- Projects that substantially exceeded the initial cost estimate;
- Complex or multiple phase projects;
- Items using high-cost materials;
- Items requiring difficult construction or fabrication procedures;
- Items performing questionable functions;
- Items appearing too costly to build, operate, or maintain;
- Projects that have grown complex, possibly by development over a long period of time; and
- Large projects.

Benefit of a Value Engineering Program

Value engineering has proven to be an effective management tool for achieving improved design, construction, and cost effectiveness. Value engineering techniques can be used to improve productivity or the benefit-to-cost ratio in nearly every aspect of capital planning, including preliminary engineering, maintenance, standard plans and specifications, design criteria, and guidelines. Value engineering provides a means to analyze and control total project cost. This total cost control is accomplished by a systematic analysis and development of alternative means of achieving the function and cost.

Source: Information provided by Soliman Khudeira, City of Chicago Department of Transportation – Division of Engineering. More information on the Society of American Value Engineers can be found at www.value-eng.org.

may differ. It is important to look at the cost components for other projects to determine if they are truly comparable to the proposed project. Inflation should also be considered when comparing past construction projects.

Nationally published cost figures can provide some indication of the appropriate cost ranges for a capital project. While valuable as an initial place to begin looking at costs, national cost figures should be used with some caution. There is little ability to ensure that the costs being considered are actually applicable to your specific circumstances.

Other Cost Components

Other cost components common to most capital projects that should be included in a project cost estimate, but are often not found in the construction cost estimate, include land acquisition; project management or soft costs; costs for technology and communications; financing costs; furniture, fixtures, and equipment; moving costs; inflation or cost changes over time; and a contingency amount.

◆ **Land Acquisition.** For a capital project that needs a new site, the land acquisition process needs to be planned for and performed as part of the capital project. For many jurisdictions, land acquisition is accomplished far in advance of the capital project as such anticipation can better position the jurisdiction to negotiate and review multiple sites. In addition, having the site already defined can provide for better project cost estimates as site development factors such as utility availability, transportation, water/sewer and stormwater infrastructure, and site development factors can be better quantified. Land acquisition costs may also include relocation and demolition costs for any businesses, homes, or existing structures on the land.

◆ **Project Management/Soft Costs.** Soft costs include professional services during the project and typically include the work of an on-staff or outside architect or engineer. Larger, more complex projects require a wider range of expertise and a much larger team of professionals. Jurisdictions will also commonly hire an owner's representative for large projects where necessary project management expertise is not available on staff.

◆ **Technology and Communications.** Data connectivity is an increasingly important requirement for government facilities. The design of the project should define and plan for any necessary technology and communication components.

◆ **Financing Costs.** The cost estimate for the project should include costs associated with raising money to fund the project. If the project will be funded with debt, costs would include costs of bond counsel, underwriters, financial advisors, or any consultants. These issuance costs may be charged to the project and included in the debt financing or may be separately funded through the operating budget. If debt financing includes capitalized interest and/or debt service reserve funds, these costs may need to be captured in the project cost as they would be recognized in the debt proceeds.

◆ **Furniture, Fixtures, and Equipment.** Furniture, fixtures, and equipment (FF&E) costs are less likely to be overlooked than other costs because the future users of the building tend to be vocal about their FF&E needs. Nonetheless, it is important to determine costs early in the project and include them in the project budget, the operating budget, or some other financing plan.

◆ **Moving Costs.** If the building is accommodating a function already in operation, you will eventually have to move it from the old location to the new. The cost of the move needs to be estimated, whether it is to be charged to the operating or the capital budget. Also, there may be costs in renovating the old location to accommodate a different use. If the facility cannot be used during any renovations, there will also be costs associated with a temporary facility during construction.

◆ **Price Changes Over Time.** Estimating what costs are going to be is difficult but necessary. Projects occurring in the future will most likely cost more than they would have today due to increases in the prices of labor and materials. A project that is expected to take multiple years to build may need inflation factors applied during the construction period. It is important to develop project cost models that can easily be updated as projects may be deferred or accelerated during capital budget formulation. If a project is deferred, there is risk of understating a project cost if inflation is not applied. Many different indices exist for calculating expected inflation rates, and the jurisdiction should be careful to use the most appropriate inflation estimate. Regional inflation indices are generally more accurate than national estimates and will reflect regional labor and material prices.

  Market conditions also can play a huge role in determining local prices. Some years may be more active for contractors, and as a result, fewer will be available to bid on the project, driving up prices. During slower times, hungry contractors drive down prices. Also, prices for commodities such as steel or concrete also fluctuate and can have a significant impact on project cost.

◆ **Contingency.** Because many factors can make a cost estimate inaccurate, setting aside an amount, usually a percentage of the total estimate, for contingency is critically important for financial planning. The goal of a contingency is to plan for unexpected financial obligations or costs that will be disruptive to the budget or divert resources from other projects or needs. The earlier the stage of project development, the bigger the contingency should be.

Exhibit 3.2 shows a sample project budget template used by the City of Eugene, Oregon, on its public building construction projects. This template is also used to track the project costs during design and construction against the original budget and to make adjustments as needed.

Exhibit 3.2 Sample Construction Project Cost Template

SITE ACQUISITION/PRE-DESIGN		
1	Site acquisition cost	
2	Site survey	

3	Geotechnical testing and recommendations	
4	Environmental clean-up	
5	Tree mitigation	
6	Archaeological consultant and legal fees	
7	Utility relocation fees	
8	Bond issuance costs	
9	Subtotal	
10	Site acquisition/re-design contingency @ ___%	
TOTAL SITE ACQUISITION AND PRE-DESIGN		
DESIGN AND ADMINISTRATION		
11	Project management – owner's representative costs	
12	Architectural fees – base contract	
12A	Amendment #1 – list purpose	
12B	Amendment #2 – list purpose	
13	Construction insurance	
14	Promotional materials	
15	Subtotal	
16	Design and administration contingency @ ___%	
TOTAL DESIGN AND ADMINISTRATION		
CONSTRUCTION CONTRACTS		
17	Site improvements	
18	Underground parking	
19	Construction contract	
19A	Alternate – list purpose	
19B	Alternate – list purpose	
20	Excavation	
21	Staging requirements and building lock/key	
22	Hazardous material clean-up	
23	Subtotal	
24	Construction contingency @ ___%	
TOTAL CONSTRUCTION CONTRACTS		
FURNISHINGS, FIXTURES, AND EQUIPMENT		
25	Furnishings, fixtures, and equipment	

TOTAL FURNISHINGS, FIXTURES, AND EQUIPMENT		
RELATED PROJECT COSTS		
26	Telephone and computer cabling and equipment	
27	Moving and storage expense	
28	Signage allowance	
29	Artwork	
30	Geotechnical testing	
31	Structural testing	
32	Plan check, building permits, and impact fees	
33	Printing, reproduction, and legal advertising	
34	Commissioning and systems balancing	
35	Utility fees (water and electrical)	
36	Temporary costs for relocation to alternate site during construction	
37	Financial management staff costs	
38	Interest on interfund loan	
39	Subtotal	
40	Miscellaneous contingency @ __%	
TOTAL RELATED COSTS		
ESTIMATED PROJECT COST		
41	Site acquisition and pre-design	
42	Design and administration	
43	Construction contracts	
44	Furnishings, fixtures, and equipment	
45	Related project costs	
ESTIMATED PROJECT COST		

RESOURCES AVAILABLE FOR PROJECT	
A. General obligation bonds	
B. Other bonds	
C. State construction grants	
D. Urban renewal funds	
E. Private donations	

F. Development impact fees	
G. Local improvement district revenues	
H. Temporary property tax levies	
I. Increased sales, income, or other taxes	
J. Miscellaneous one-time funds	
K. Energy conservation grants	
L. Savings from moving out of private leased space	
M. Parking fees	
N. In-kind donations	
TOTAL AVAILABLE PROJECT FUNDING	
PROJECT FUNDING LESS ESTIMATED PROJECT COST	
TOTAL CONTINGENCY BUDGET	

Source: Sample project cost template is used and provided by the City of Eugene, Oregon.

Sustainability Issues and Green Building Options

One issue for the community to consider during the needs assessment process is whether it is important to include sustainability and "green building" practices into the project design. In order to avoid scope changes, the decision whether to incorporate such practices must be made before design begins. These practices will most likely add cost to the project budget, but may save significantly on operations costs over the years.

One way to incorporate sustainability ideas into the construction project is to seek a rating under the LEED (Leadership in Energy and Environmental Design) Green Building Rating System.® LEED is a voluntary national standard for sustainable buildings that is designed to promote integrated, whole-building design and operation practices and to promote environmental leadership in building projects, among other goals. The impact on the project budget from incorporating LEED certification into the process varies. Estimates for incorporating LEED certification into the project budget range from a slight cost decrease to an increase of as much as 10 percent of the construction cost versus the normal standard of construction (not versus building code). On the other hand, projects that qualify for LEED certification are expected to cost less to operate over time, so the trade-off is the possibility of an increased up-front cost of up to 10 percent, against lowered operating costs over the building's life.

More information on the U.S. Green Building Council can be found at http://www.usgbc.com.

Changes to Operating Costs

Any changes to operating costs, such as utility, maintenance, and security costs, should also be identified so the jurisdiction can prepare the operating budget. For example, the use of environmentally friendly, energy efficient building designs and materials has the potential to save a jurisdiction money over time with reduced heating, cooling, and lighting expenses. However, current technology and advancements for electrical systems, HVAC systems, and other features may be more energy efficient, but may also require more specialized maintenance. Changes may include revenues as well as expenditures.

Cost Estimation Pitfalls

While many resources exist to help with cost estimation, there are many potential challenges. One common pitfall is the omission of cost components. Not listing all costs associated with the project will result in a negative budgetary impact when the omission is discovered. Costs that are occasionally overlooked include moving costs and inflation. Any disruption to the project schedule such as unforeseen conditions or misalignment between costs and funds has the potential to delay a project and raise project costs. Similarly, any approval requirements, such as compliance with federal and state regulations, can have negative impacts on project timing and costs that are difficult to predict.

Cost Estimating Tools

There are many types of tools available to the finance officer or project manager to quickly determine the estimated project cost such as the Marshall-Swift index or R.S. Means. The Marshall-Swift index uses certain project attributes to arrive at an estimated cost per square foot. The estimated cost per square foot can then be applied to the total area of the project to calculate an estimated project cost. The Marshall-Swift index is also used by many governments in assessing real property, valuing building permits, and estimating property loss from natural disasters or fire.

Many project types discussed in section II of this book can be found in a Marshall-Swift table that is based upon a hierarchy of project quality attributes of exterior walls, interior finish, plumbing, mechanical and electrical, and HVAC. This hierarchy can range from a wood-framed structure with linoleum floors and heat pump to a highly ornamental brick structure with carpet and zoned HVAC of hot/chilled water. Generally, each project falls into one of five classes (A-E) and within each class are three quality attributes of excellent, good, and average for a total of fifteen different choices to match the project scope.

To account for regional variation in prices, a local multiplier is then applied to the square foot cost to equate the square foot price to an area in close proximity to the locality. The following example can be used to estimate costs for a high school with the following characteristics.

◆ Total square feet: 250,000

◆ Exterior walls: Face brick, stone, concrete or metal panels, solar glass

◆ Interior walls: Plaster or drywall, acoustic tile, carpet and vinyl

◆ Lighting, plumbing, and mechanical: high-level lighting, audio visual wiring, good plumbing

◆ HVAC: Hot and chilled water (zoned)

Based on the description, the project would be classified as a class "A", type "good" project resulting in an initial cost estimate of $196.57 per square foot. To illustrate the use of local multipliers, costs associated with five cities are shown in Exhibit 3.3. The local multiplier adjusts for overall price differences between regional markets. The cost multiplier adjusts for inflationary trends over large areas of the country.[1] It is important to note that cost estimating tools must be properly scrutinized and not used as the only way to budget capital projects. The use of these tools helps supports the reasonableness of the estimated project cost, but generic models will not be appropriate for every project and do not take in account any unique cost factors that could have a considerable impact on overall project costs.

Exhibit 3.3 Marshall-Swift Index Example

	Austin, Texas	Newport, Rhode Island	Richmond, Virginia	Olympia, Washington	Milwaukee, Wisconsin
Construction/ Equipment costs:					
Square feet	250,000	250,000	250,000	250,000	250,000
SF cost: Class A - Good	196.57	196.57	196.57	196.57	196.57
Local multiplier	0.87	1.07	0.95	1.11	1.09
Cost multiplier	1.00	1.04	1.04	1.00	1.00
Adjusted square foot cost	$ 171.02	$ 218.74	$ 194.21	$ 218.19	$ 214.26
Total construction costs	$42,753,975	$54,685,774	$48,552,790	$54,548,175	$53,565,325

Inflation

Inflation estimates are an important part of cost estimates for multi-year projects or projects experiencing a delay between cost estimation and bid. Exhibit 3.4 shows the impact of inflation assumptions on project costs over five years. Estimating inflation can have an impact on cost estimates. For construction projects, the industry has experienced inflation approximately double the general economy-wide rate of inflation estimated by the consumer price index (CPI). In the future, construction cost inflation estimates are expected to remain approximately 6 to 8 percent, but significantly higher inflation rates could be possible.[2]

Exhibit 3.4 The Impact of Inflation

Project Cost ($Millions)	Assuming 4% Inflation per Year				Assuming 8% Inflation per Year			
	Year 1	Year 2	Year 3	Year 4	Year 1	Year 2	Year 3	Year 4
$ 10.0	$ 10.4	$ 10.8	$ 11.2	$ 11.7	$ 10.8	$ 11.2	$ 11.7	$ 12.1
$ 25.0	$ 26.0	$ 27.0	$ 28.1	$ 29.2	$ 27.0	$ 28.1	$ 29.2	$ 30.4
$ 50.0	$ 52.0	$ 54.1	$ 56.2	$ 58.5	$ 54.0	$ 56.2	$ 58.4	$ 60.7
$100.0	$104.0	$108.2	$112.5	$117.0	$108.0	$112.3	$116.8	$121.5

Budgeting for Capital Projects

Once cost estimates are developed, the finance officer can also assist in ensuring that the capital improvements program is structured to best illustrate the required resources for each year. Some projects may take many years complete, and their budgets may be allocated over the years, or many governments require sufficient appropriations to exist before awarding contracts. Capital projects that span multiple years may have land acquisition funding budgeted in one year, followed by engineering and design funding in another year, with the construction and remaining costs in the final year. A properly prepared and adopted capital budget is essential to ensure proper planning, funding, and completion of capital projects.[3] The Government Finance Officers Association's (GFOA) recommended practice on capital project budgeting lists elements to include in the capital budget, which are:[4]

◆ A definition of capital expenditure for that entity;
◆ Summary information of capital projects by fund, category, etc.;
◆ A schedule for completion of the project, including specific phases of a project, estimated funding requirements for the upcoming year(s), and planned timing for acquisition, design, and construction activities;

◆ Descriptions of the general scope of the project, including expected service and financial benefits to the jurisdiction;

◆ A description of any impact the project will have on the current or future operating budget;

◆ Estimated costs of the project, based on recent and accurate sources of information;

◆ Identified funding sources for all aspects of the project, specifically referencing any financing requirements for the upcoming fiscal year;

◆ Funding authority based either on total estimated project cost, or estimated project costs for the upcoming fiscal year. Consideration should be given to carry-forward funding for projects previously authorized; and

◆ Any analytical information deemed helpful for setting capital priorities (this can include any cost/benefit comparisons, and related capital projects).

NACLSB Criteria Relevant to Capital Project Analysis

The GFOA has also developed best practices in public budgeting as part of its ongoing efforts to encourage implementation of recommended budget practices established by the National Advisory Council on State and Local Budgeting (NACSLB). As they pertain to capital budgeting and in particular to some of the concepts of this book, five specific practices are summarized below:

Practice 2.2 - Assess Capital Assets, Identify Issues, Opportunities, and Challenges

◆ **Practice:** A government should identify and conduct an assessment of its capital assets, including the condition of the assets and factors that could affect the need for or ability to maintain the assets in the future.

◆ **Rationale:** The capital assets of a government and their condition are critical to the quality of services provided, and hence are important in determining whether the needs and priorities of stakeholders can be met.

◆ **Outputs:** A government should have a process for inventorying its capital assets and assessing the need for and the condition of these assets. The assessment should include an evaluation of issues, challenges, and opportunities affecting the provision of capital assets in the future, such as community needs and priorities; the impact of deferred maintenance; funding issues; changes in technology; economic, demographic, or other factors that may affect demand; and legal or regulatory changes. This review may be undertaken in conjunction with an evaluation of the program or service utilizing the particular assets. The assessment of capital asset condition should consider the impact of any deferred maintenance and needed improvements. Identification or development of measurement standards for the condition of capital assets (including what is regarded as acceptable) is a valuable output of this practice.

Practice 5.2 - Prepare Policies and Plans for Capital Asset Acquisition, Maintenance, Replacement, and Retirement

◆ **Practice:** A government should adopt policies and plans for capital asset acquisition, maintenance, replacement, and retirement.

◆ **Rationale:** Policies and plans for acquisition, maintenance, replacement, and retirement of capital assets help ensure that needed capital assets or improvements receive appropriate consideration in the budget process and that older capital assets are considered for retirement or replacement. These policies and plans are necessary to plan for large expenditures and to minimize deferred maintenance.

◆ **Outputs:** Policies may address inventorying capital assets and evaluating their condition, standards for acceptable condition, criteria for continued maintenance versus replacement or retirement of an existing asset, and identification of funding for adequate maintenance and scheduled replacement of capital assets. Plans should be developed to establish ongoing, multi-year replacement and renewal schedules, and should recognize the linkage of capital expenditures with the annual operating budget. Plans for addressing deferred maintenance may also be an output of this practice. Stakeholders should have an opportunity to provide input as capital asset policies and plans are formulated. Once adopted, the policies and plans should be made publicly available, particularly as set forth in budget, management, and planning documents. Policies and plans should be incorporated into decision making in the budget process.

Practice 6.2 - Develop Options for Meeting Capital Needs and Evaluate Acquisition Alternatives

◆ **Practice:** A government should develop specific capital project options for addressing capital needs that are consistent with financial, programmatic, and capital policies and should evaluate alternatives for acquiring capital assets.

◆ **Rationale:** Capital project planning is necessary to give adequate consideration to longer-range needs and goals, evaluate funding requirements and options, and achieve consensus on the physical development of the community. An evaluation of alternative mechanisms helps ensure that the best approach for providing use of a capital asset or facility is chosen based on the policies and goals of the government.

◆ **Outputs:** A government should have a process that identifies capital projects that are needed to achieve goals and a general time frame in which these assets will be needed. This assessment should consider need, life cycle costs (including operating costs), impact on services, beneficiaries of the project, financing issues, and other impacts. Plans for acquiring capital assets should be part of or consistent with land use, transportation, or other long-range plans of the community or area. Options for acquiring the use of capital assets and facilities should be examined. In some cases, the process for evaluating capital acquisition alternatives is linked with a corresponding process for evaluating service delivery alternatives.

Practice 9.6 - Develop a Capital Improvement Plan

◆ **Practice:** A government should develop a capital improvement plan that identifies its priorities and time frame for undertaking capital projects and provides a financing plan for those projects.

◆ **Rationale:** The total cost of desired capital projects will usually substantially exceed immediately available funds in most governments. Development of a capital improvement plan provides a framework for prioritizing projects and identifying funding needs and sources.

◆ **Outputs:** A process should exist for evaluating proposed capital projects and financing options, and developing a long-range capital improvement plan that integrates projects, time frames, and financing mechanisms. The plan, including both capital and operating costs, should project at least five years into the future and should be fully integrated into the government's overall financial plan. The process for developing the plan should allow ample opportunity for stakeholder involvement in prioritizing projects and review. The capital improvement plan should be included in a budget document, either in a single document describing both the operating and capital budgets or in a separate document describing the capital improvement plan and capital budget. The plan should be approved by the governing body.

Practice 11.5 - Monitor, Measure, and Evaluate Capital Program Implementation

◆ **Practice:** Governments should monitor, measure, and evaluate capital program implementation.

◆ **Rationale:** Monitoring the status of capital projects helps to ensure that projects progress as planned, problems (such as delays in key milestones and cost overruns) are identified early enough to take corrective action, funds are available when needed, and legal requirements are met.

◆ **Outputs:** Reports on capital project implementation should be prepared for decision makers and other stakeholders. Summary information should be considered for projects that are progressing as planned. More detailed information will probably be needed for projects where there are issues. Project milestones, such as dates for completion of such tasks as planning, land acquisition, engineering and design, and construction, should be identified and progress in meeting these milestones should be reported. Governments should also monitor quality compliance and financial performance.

Conclusion

Cost estimation and budgeting is a vital exercise to ensure that the defined scope is funded and successfully completed. Estimates need to have reasonably supported assumptions that also are inflated to the year in which projects costs will committed and/or expended. Underestimating the cost is a risk that can result in scope reductions, project deferral, project cancellation, and/or reduced funding for other projects or increased debt financing. Overestimating the cost is also a risk that may have overly committed funding to one project that could have otherwise been more timely utilized in other government programs, projects, or returned back to the taxpayers via tax rate reduction. Therefore, it is imperative that those people responsible for cost estimating fully understand the scope and schedule of the project and any project challenges that may arise in order to provide a supported cost estimate model. If in-house expertise in cost estimating is unavailable, appropriate professionals should be contracted to assist in providing such services.

Notes

1. Local multipliers are generally specific to the city, whereas cost multipliers are applied based on the location being in the Eastern, Central, or Western U.S.

2. Taken from Ken Simonson, "ACG's Construction Inflation Report," the Associated General Contractors of America, September 2006. The whitepaper can be found at http://www.acg.org.

3. Taken from the Government Finance Officers Association's Recommended Practice, "Capital Project Budget," 2007.

4. Ibid.

4

Project Schedule and Oversight

By Sue Cutsogeorge and Bradley G. Black

Often the finance officer's role during construction is limited to monitoring the project's sources and uses of funding for budgeting and/or financial reporting, but the finance officer can also contribute to critical decisions in many areas of project oversight. The finance officer, working together with the project manager, is ideally positioned to monitor progress towards milestones, financial incentives, or penalties in the construction contracts. By reviewing the project schedule, the finance officer can provide advice about ways to best position resources in the correct year of a capital improvements program and align cash outflows with inflows to determine the most effective timing for any debt issuance. The finance officer can also better assist with essential stages of the project, such as land acquisition, selection of professional consultants, preparation of the bidding documents, execution of the construction contract, and reporting on the project. The following are a few examples of project oversight issues that could benefit from greater involvement by the finance officer:

- ◆ Selection of design professionals and contractors;
- ◆ Preparation and execution of the bidding process;
- ◆ Construction contract oversight; and
- ◆ Review of proposed contract changes.

Project Oversight

One key to effective project management is centralizing responsibility for overall project oversight.[1] In addition to the finance officer, the project oversight team should include engineers, architects, and managers that have expertise in construction projects. If such expertise does not exist on staff, it is important to contract with outside professionals to carry out these oversight responsibilities on behalf of the jurisdiction. It is essential that the primary oversight person be able to assemble the right people at the right time to ensure that the project is properly planned, will meet service-level goals and needs assessment thresholds, and can be positioned in long-term capital plans with identified funding sources. It is also crucial that the project manager be empowered by the organization to make project decisions.

Selection of Professional Consultants and Contractors

At the beginning of the project, decision makers should determine the method that will be used for selecting and contracting with professional consultants, architects, and contractors. The role of the finance officer and management staff will be determined in part based on the method of selecting and contracting for services. Government often has stringent requirements that regulate procurement processes. It is important to review, document, and comply with all applicable purchasing and reporting laws and regulations from project inception and understand their impact on the project's schedule and cost.

The professional consultant team needed for the project can be selected in many different ways, depending on the procurement requirements of the jurisdiction and the nature and scope of the project. Whenever possible, a qualifications- or quality-based process is recommended. A qualifications-based process focuses on the knowledge, skills, and experience of the professional consultants or consulting team and capabilities of the team to meet the project's needs. It is a labor intensive approach requiring a request for qualifications (RFQ) and interviews with a few short-listed respondents. An RFQ is similar to a request for proposals (RFP), except that with an RFQ fee proposals are not involved in the selection process. After consultant selection is made, the jurisdiction and design team negotiate contracts and fees for services.

Generally, the make-up of the professional consultant team is based on the complexity of the project. A simple project may only require an architect and a few engineering consultants, whereas a complex project will demand a much larger team of professionals that includes architects, interior architects, mechanical, electrical and structural engineers, environmental engineers, vertical transportation consultants, waterproofing consultants, traffic engineers, landscape architects, technology consultants, and commissioning agents.

Use of an Owner's Representative

Managing a construction project to successful completion is a team effort in which the jurisdiction or owner needs to remain fully involved. For complex projects requiring advanced construction management knowledge, the use of an owner's representative is a necessity. The owner's representative is an outside consultant with construction expertise that will provide oversight, manage the

---

Risk Mitigation

Before the start of any construction project, jurisdictions need to ensure that proper steps have been taken to safeguard against risk. Every jurisdiction should consult with members of its risk management department or outside experts to determine the proper levels and types of coverage for each project. At a minimum, jurisdictions should ensure the following conditions are met:

1) The project is covered with builder's risk insurance.
2) All contractors and design professionals used in the project carry adequate insurance policies covering general liability and workers' compensation policies and provide the jurisdiction with a certificate of insurance listing the jurisdiction as an additional insured.
3) Proper indemnification clauses are included in the contract with each contractor.

---

project, and coordinate activities between all members of the project team, including the design professionals and the contractors in the jurisdiction's best interests. Often these professionals are involved with the project from the beginning. Use of a qualified owner's representative is an effective way to manage costs and provide necessary project and construction management expertise that is not in the jurisdiction's staff.

Construction Management

Construction management involves both identifying the most appropriate method of selecting contractors to meet the scope of work and providing oversight of the contract to ensure contractual requirements are followed. In instances where contract terms are not followed, timely recognition by the jurisdiction and establishment of corrective action measures will prevent small issues from escalating and impacting the project schedule and budget.

Several different approaches to construction contracting may be appropriate depending on the project and local or state restrictions. There are three common methods for managing the design and construction of capital projects: lowest bid award, construction manager/general contractor, and design/build. The method to be employed on a project must be established before the design process begins, as some methods have different procedures and schedules for selecting the design professionals. The decision may be based on the project's time sensitivity or goals, the availability of budget resources, expertise of the in-house staff, and procurement laws. Each approach has advantages and disadvantages, the most important of which are time and cost.

Lowest Bid Award

The most common method for public sector projects is the lowest bid award method, often called design/bid/build (DBB). The design professionals are usually selected through a qualifications process and construction services are selected through competitive bidding. The project is first designed by a team of design professionals, and then advertised for construction bids. The award of the construction contract is based solely on the lowest responsible bid. It is a straightforward and linear approach with separate and sequential contracts between the government jurisdiction, the design professionals, and any contractors. There may, however, be several simultaneous construction contracts, which can make the situation much more complex. If multiple bids are advertised for the project, the jurisdiction would enter contracts with numerous lowest bidders. For example, separate contracts could be issued for general contracting, electrical, mechanical, and plumbing. This creates many project management challenges, and increases the possibility of delays. With the lowest bid award, there is no contractual relationship between the design professionals and the contractor or between multiple contractors, and the contractor has no input in the design phase of the project, which may result in costly changes in materials and scheduling. This method is best suited for new projects, ones that are not time sensitive, and those that are not subject to significant scope changes. Exhibit 4.1 shows the contractual relationships between these parties. While the contractors and designers should communicate, the owner is the only party that has a direct contractual relationship with both the design team and the contractor.

Exhibit 4.1 Relationship for Lowest Bidder Award

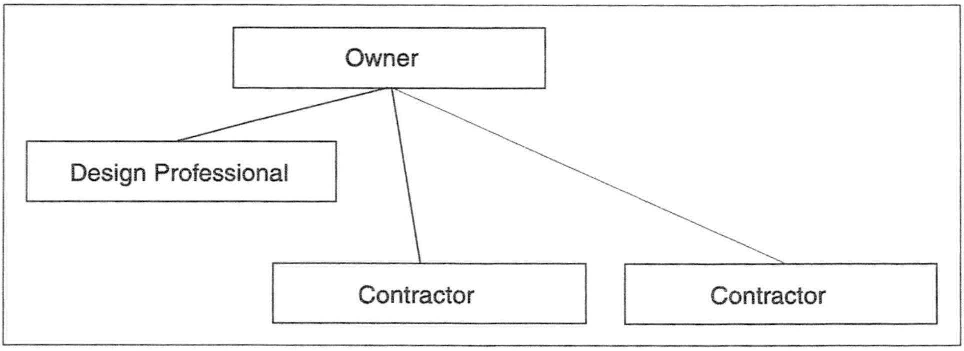

Construction Manager/General Contractor

The construction manager/general contractor (CMGC) method, also known as the "construction manager at risk," allows the jurisdiction to select a construction manager, based on a qualifications process before the design is complete. Once the construction manager is selected, all work is organized under a single guaranteed maximum price (GMP) contract and the construction manager then coordinates all subcontracted work. The construction manager is "at risk" for costs in excess of the GMP. The final price is the sum of the construction manager's fees plus all of the subcontractor bids up to the guaranteed maximum price. Exhibit 4.2 shows the relationships with this approach.

The jurisdiction has a separate contract with the design professional and the construction manager, but with this method, the design professional and the construction manager form a cooperative team. The CMGC method is often viewed as an attractive alternative contracting method that allows jurisdictions to avoid some of the drawbacks of the design/build method by allowing the jurisdiction to use its own architect. This method also may result in shorter project schedules because construction of some elements can begin before completion of entire design. Additionally, because the design professional and construction manager are able to work cooperatively, this approach may decrease the possibility of legal claims.

Exhibit 4.2 Relationship for Construction Manager/General Contractor

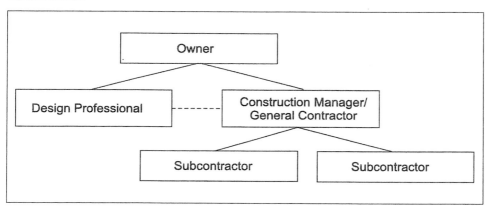

Design/Build

With the design/build method, the jurisdiction has a single contract that covers both the design and construction of the project. The selection of the "design/builder" can parallel the selection process used for a CMGC process, but with this method the jurisdiction would award the project to a firm or joint venture who would act as both the design professional and the construction manager. Working cooperatively, the builder and designer work to create a design based on the jurisdiction's specific design criteria. At the end of the design process, the jurisdiction will negotiate a GMP and schedule for the remainder of the project, similar to the CMGC model. Exhibit 4.3 shows relationships for the design/build method.

With this method, design and construction are accomplished concurrently, thus accelerating the completion of the project. The project cost is established early in the process, and the architect and general contractor are in a position to collaborate on the budget development, the project schedule, and the design of the facilities. The potential for disputes between the design professionals and the construction contractor is minimized. This team approach allows for the development of strategies which may benefit the overall project. On the other hand, because a single firm or joint-venture performs both design and construction, the design/build method may discourage competition. In addition, jurisdictions should not assume that a system of "checks and balances" is inherent within design/build relationships.

Exhibit 4.3 Relationship for Design/Build

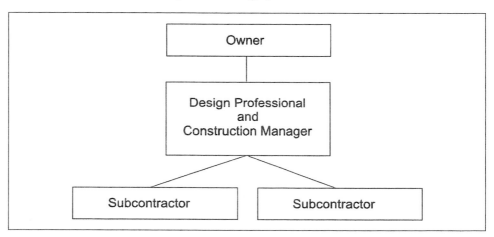

Changes to Construction Contracts

Changes to contracts are inevitable and need to be managed carefully. Changes to the construction contract can be initiated by the jurisdiction, contractor, or the design consultant if unforeseen issues are identified. When a possible change to the construction contract is identified, the design consultant is responsible for documenting the scope of the anticipated change and negotiating a fair cost with the contractor. The design consultant must continually involve the jurisdiction during the identification of changes and associated costs. Ultimately, only the jurisdiction can authorize a change in the contract when additional time or cost is involved. All changes in the scope of a project must be documented and well supported by the finance officer. If the existing project budget is not sufficient to accommodate the changes, amendments to the overall project budget must occur before authorization of a change in the construction contract.

It is vital that the jurisdiction identify and empower one person as a representative who is capable of making needed decisions. Both the design consultant and the general contractor should also identify individuals to effectively represent their interests. Throughout the construction of the project, effective communications and use of an informal dispute resolution process are essential to making timely decisions and avoiding legal actions. It is important to understand how communications must flow throughout construction process. Exhibit 4.4 presents how information and decisions flow during construction.

Exhibit 4.4 Communication Path for Construction Projects

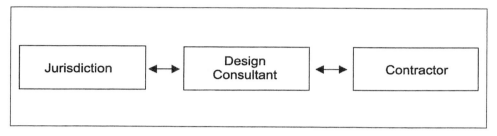

In this communication structure, the design consultant acts as the owner's agent to address issues with the contractor. The jurisdiction has communication with the design consultant about issues, the design consult then represents those issues to the contractor. In turn, issues coming from the contractor are first presented to the design consultant. Only those issues that require decision by the owner are referred to the jurisdiction by the design consultant.

Major capital projects can have complex combinations of funding sources, some of which may have restrictions on their use. When amending the project's uses of funds, the jurisdiction should pay careful attention to the project's funding sources, especially for projects that may have finite grant sources. If scope changes are nec-

Partnering

Complex projects may benefit from efforts to improve communications and clearly defined working agreements. Partnering is an approach to improve communications and develop common goals. In a successful partnering process, all parties become invested in common goals and agreements around the way difficult issues will be addressed in the future. The process is used to establish trust and problem-solving procedures well in advance of their need. Use of this approach can result in fewer contract issues ending in litigation. To make partnering successful, all parties must agree up front about the approach. Use of an outside consultant to develop the working agreements among the parties can be helpful to getting this approach off to a proper start.

essary and funding sources are constrained, alternatives, such as cutting costs elsewhere, obtaining additional funds, or deferring other projects, would need to be explored.

Project Schedule

A capital project construction schedule may range from a few months to five years or more based on the complexity of the project. Complex projects require the assistance of consultants specializing in project scheduling while smaller, less complicated project schedules may be developed by staff. It is important that one individual be responsible for development, review, and maintenance of the schedule. That person, however, should draw upon the owner's representative, design professionals, contractors, and end users.

Throughout the process, it is important to note that the level of public participation in the project will have a direct impact on the schedule. In the initial stages of a project, assessing the amount of time required for public participation may be difficult. As the public participation process continues, it may be necessary to modify the schedule.

The specific steps in a capital project will differ from project to project and based on local conditions. After a need has been established and the decision made to move forward with the project, most projects follow a typical schedule, some stages of which may occur concurrently or in a slightly different order than presented here:

Land Acquisition

Before or in parallel with design activities, the project site must be selected and acquired. Site selection is one of the most important initial steps in the project's development and has a direct impact on the overall project cost.

The location must be responsive to the service-level demands and meet the jurisdiction's current and future goals as well as fit with its surroundings. Locating government facilities in residential areas often conflicts with neighborhood interests, as government facilities are not always viewed as a desirable neighbor due to noise, traffic, and potential long hours of operations. The acquisition process requires time to identify and evaluate candidate sites from both the service-level and cost perspectives. Development costs can be significantly influenced by the proximity to utility infrastructure, site topography, current land use, and access to primary thoroughfares. It is also important to locate easements for utility companies and roads that can help determine if the facility's footprint and related structures can be configured to fit in the site.

Selecting a problematic site can become a burden on both the project's schedule and cost. A thorough investigation of any site should be completed at the earliest possible opportunity using professional consultants. The site review should include any land use restrictions and an extensive environmental assessment. Urban sites, particularly previously developed sites, may contain hidden problems that will directly impact both schedule and cost, such as underground fuel storage tanks, potential archaeological issues, and environmental contaminates.

Existing structures can also present unique opportunities and challenges. Structures warrant a thorough condition, environmental, and code assessment. All existing structures should be examined for hazardous materials, such as asbestos, lead paint, mold, PCB (polychlorinated biphenyl), and other contaminants. Understanding the magnitude of any problems and potential impacts on the project schedule and budget is critically important and may result in some sites being deemed unsuitable for development.

Design

The design phase is a sequential set of activities. It includes sub-phases, such as architectural program de-

Use of Eminent Domain

The use of eminent domain or a condemnation process is often a very public process that presents challenges for the jurisdiction. While land can be taken legally for public use, condemnation is generally a last resort after all other viable alternatives have been exhausted. In fact, some states have enacted specific limitations on the use of eminent domain. Jurisdictions should have land acquisition policies and/or practices that best position them to acquire desired land in a timely manner before beginning capital projects. For example, Hanover County, Virginia, has a policy to acquire all land sites for a capital project at least two years before beginning the project. This enables due process of site searches and time for negotiations with land owners to find a willing seller. It also prevents time pressures from influencing price negotiations. Additionally, starting early may avoid some of the reluctance that land owners may have to sell, or to sell at fair market value, once opponents to a project become engaged and try to exert their influence in altering the project.

velopment, schematic design, design development, and construction documentation. Throughout each stage, the design is re-worked in increasing detail, ending with the production of plans and specifications for facility construction that will form the basis of contractors' bids and the plans and specifications for facility construction. Cost estimates should also be produced periodically during the design phase, either by the design professionals or by third-party professional consultants. It is highly recommended that the jurisdiction receive estimates from third-party consultants to verify any cost estimates provided by the design team. Depending on the project's scope, the design phase may also include a variety of specialty work that may relate directly to the design documents, such as traffic or parking studies, feasibility studies, or marketing plans.

Architectural Program Development

During this stage, the design consultant verifies the accuracy of any initial needs assessment and develops an architectural program. The architectural program is a document that establishes functions to be included in the facility, overall land needs, program space required for the current needs, and future expansion possibilities. For example, this is the stage at which the owners should decide whether a commitment to achieving LEED[2] certification for the project should be made. The architectural program should be provided in sufficient detail so that the project team can determine the initial estimate of construction cost and anticipated project schedule. It is important that the cost estimate be prepared by a professional consultant who is only responsible for construction cost estimates in order to avoid any conflicts of interest. Construction cost estimates at this stage are typically based on national square foot cost norms for similar facilities and may not include any unique aspects of the project. Therefore, cost estimates should include a sizeable contingency for unknowns. It is not uncommon that such contingencies at this stage could range from 15 to 25 percent of the estimated project cost.

Schematic Design

During the schematic design phase, bubble diagrams describing the relationship between spaces progress into drawings that begin to look more like actual plans. At the end of this phase, the design team should provide any revisions to the estimate of time required for actual construction. At this stage, construction cost estimates are a refinement of the previous estimates and begin the shift from square foot costs based upon national norms to costs based on specifics of the project. Project cost estimates should include a careful review of the construction contingency, recognizing that significant unknowns still remain. Similar to earlier phases, the contingency could still range from 15 to 25 percent depending upon the extent of the unknown information.

> **Environmental Clean-up**
>
> It may be advantageous to pursue clean-up of environmental conditions at the earliest possible opportunity. Often such clean-up activity is undertaken during the project's program development and schematic design phases. This approach identifies and removes some of the most significant unknowns associated with site selection.

Design Development

Design development provides plans, elevations, and other information that clearly defines the nature of the project. In this stage, the design team begins to develop requirements for construction documents, as-built documents, and warranty documentation. Generally, design development will involve the most end-user participation. End users need to be prepared to provide input and make decisions on issues such as location of staff spaces and details such as the placement of data connections. The level of detail required may become overwhelming for staff unless the process is well managed. The estimate of probable construction cost is again updated, but this time the basis of the estimate is on the quantity and price of materials that will be used in the project. Like the two previous phases, the overall project cost estimates at this stage should be verified by third-party consultants. At this stage, fewer unknowns remain, so the construction contingency can generally be reduced to between 10 and 20 percent, depending upon the extent of the unknown information. Maintaining a realistic construction contingency at this stage is a necessity.

Development of Construction Bidding Documents

The final construction bidding documents include the drawings and the specifications used for the solicitation of bids from general contractors and subcontractors. These documents are eventually given to the contractor to begin construction. They are also used for the monitoring and administration of the actual construction activity. Depending on complexity or unique characteristics of the project, plans may include:

◆ Site details;

◆ Grading and drainage infrastructure;

◆ Utility service infrastructure;

◆ Landscaping;

◆ Elevation view of structures;

◆ Sections through structures, showing walls, finishes;

◆ Structural details;

◆ Electrical details;

◆ Plumbing equipment;

◆ Mechanical equipment;

◆ Heating, ventilation or air conditioning (HVAC) equipment; and

◆ Furniture, fixtures, and other equipment.

Careful consideration should be given to the specifics of how bids are structured. It is common to request only a base bid, which results in the owner receiving a single bid from each bidder. To augment the base bid, a series of alternate bids are often included. Alternate bids allow the jurisdiction to request and obtain prices for either adding or deducting specific pieces of work or changes in the project schedule. For example, alternate bids may be requested for project completion based on an eight-, twelve-, or fourteen-month construction schedule. Through consultation with the design team and careful analysis of the political risks, the jurisdiction should then decide which approach best meets the needs of the project at the most appropriate cost. The use of multiple alternative bids and how each will be evaluated may be affected by law and should be stated in the instructions to bidders as it may have an impact on the lowest responsible bid.

Pre-Construction

Parallel with and/or subsequent to design activities, there should be a process underway for understanding what federal, state, or local regulatory approvals are required and the appropriate steps to obtain them. Examples of possible approvals include building permits, zoning changes, or environmental permits. It is important to anticipate and complete approval steps promptly so as not to delay the project schedule. Often this is a responsibility of the design team.

> ### Unit Price Bids
>
> Unit prices are a useful bidding tool when the exact quantity of a particular item cannot be determined at the time of bidding. Furniture, fixtures, and equipment (FF&E) items are often suitable for bidding on a unit price basis. Such an approach requires the bidders to provide a set price for each item and hold that price valid for a specified time period. Depending upon the item and bidding approach selected, unit prices may not be part of the criteria used for the determination of the lowest responsible bid.

The project schedule should also include time to demolish and remove any existing structures. The time required for demolition and the costs associated with it will vary depending on whether the structures can be imploded or whether they must be de-constructed. Environmental problems, such as underground storage tanks, chemical contaminants, or asbestos, must be mediated before demolition. Other site work might involve dealing with underground utilities, soil cutting and filling, and other activities required to prepare the site for the structure of the building. It is often necessary to begin excavation and preparation of the site as a separate contract. This approach is particularly appropriate when there is a high degree of uncertainty about underground conditions. If there is suspicion of any potential environmental or archeological issues, it is important to begin site work early to avoid potential delays.

Construction

Construction is the most recognizable phase of project development and includes all work to build the facility. During the construction phase, regular meetings should be scheduled to track both the project's schedule and budget. Using a professional consultant in the role of owner's representative can add needed construction expertise that may not be present on staff and can provide project oversight. The owner's representative should provide regular updates to the project oversight team on construction progress, schedule, and any financial issues. Construction contracts should include milestones, from which partial billings can occur. During construction, the project manager and finance officer should review and authorize invoices to ensure compliance with contract terms. Responsibility for processing and approving payments also should be clear between the finance officer, the project manager, and any other involved individuals or departments to ensure there are no financial oversights.

Close-Out

When the project is substantially complete, the project manager and contractor will walk through the building and create a "punch list" of items that need to be completed or corrected. The contractor then has a specified period of time to correct the deficiencies before final payment is made. During close-out, contractors will also provide as-built drawings, comprehensive binders of equipment manuals, and warranties to the owner as well as any required extra materials, such as ceiling or carpet tiles. Additionally, facility managers will receive training on how to operate equipment in the building.

Commissioning

The process of ensuring that the facility and related systems, particularly the electrical and HVAC systems, operate as planned is called commissioning. Buildings have become so complex that it is difficult to guarantee that the owner receives a building that is functioning according to specifications without the involvement of an independent agent acting for the owner. Early involvement by a commissioning agent can help to minimize any conflicts in building systems that might occur during the design and construction process. The commissioning agent will also be involved in testing building systems to make sure that they perform as they are supposed to. In areas with different seasons, this may take time to ensure, for example, that both heating and air conditioning systems work properly. The cost of commissioning generally amounts to 5 to 15 percent of professional fees. As the complexity of the facility increases, the commissioning fees should also be expected to increase. Upon completion of the commissioning process, a final report that identifies the systems that are not performing as intended will generally be produced so that the jurisdiction can get contractors to fix any problems.

Warranty Period

Projects usually include a requirement that the contractor be responsible for repairing defects during the first year following substantial completion of the project. During this period of occupancy and operation, the owner should document problems with the project and direct them to the contractor for correction. To fully protect the owner's interest, the contract with the design consultant should include the requirement for a warranty review of the project by the design consultant. This review should be completed jointly with the owner and the design consultant one month before the end of the warranty. The resulting list of items requiring correction is then provided to the contractor for correction. This process insures that the owner does not assume costs for corrective actions that are the contractor's responsibility. Without preplanning, this activity is often overlooked, resulting in additional unnecessary costs to the owner.

Conclusion

The finance officer should be an integral part of the project oversight team for any major capital project. By participating in oversight activities, the finance officer can provide expertise to assist the project manager in preparing for projects or responding to a variety of financial opportunities and challenges that occur as the project progresses. Lack of proper project oversight can have significant impacts on both the schedule and budget, which could significantly affect other areas of the jurisdiction.

Notes

1. Nicole Westerman, "Managing the Capital Planning Cycle," *Government Finance Review* 20, no. 3 (June 2004): 26-31.

2. Leadership in Energy and Environmental Design (LEED) Certification is awarded by the U.S. Green Buildings Council. LEED is a voluntary, consensus-based national standard for developing high-performance, sustainable buildings. More information is available at www.usgbc.org.

| 5 |

Common Funding Options for Capital Projects

By Eric Johansen and Julia H. Cooper

The development of funding strategies to meet long-term capital plans is an integral component of a well-managed jurisdiction. The finance officer has traditionally played a key role in identifying funding options available for capital projects, especially those involving the issuance of debt. While borrowing is essential for most local government jurisdictions, an effective capital funding strategy requires consideration of a broader mix of funding tools. Finance officers need to develop an understanding of project-specific capital funding resources that may be appropriate for some projects but not for others and that may not involve the issuance of debt.

This chapter will address funding options commonly used by local government jurisdictions. While this chapter attempts to provide an overview of the more common capital funding sources used to pay for capital projects, individual project chapters provide further detail on project-specific funding approaches.

| Questions to Ask About Funding Options |

Jurisdictions can choose from a wide variety of funding options for capital projects. However, not all of these options are appropriate for every jurisdiction or for every project. Each jurisdiction will face constraints that will determine if certain options are feasible for inclusion in the capital funding portfolio. Examples of constraints include the economic environment of the community, the jurisdiction's financial situation, other projects in the capital plan, staffing levels, available resources, and any applicable policies regarding taxation, indebtedness, or amount of risk.

Initially, funding methods should be reviewed in the context of their suitability for projects in the capital plan. Among the factors a jurisdiction should consider are the following:

- ◆ **Legality.** Is the funding method legally authorized to be used as planned? Has the jurisdiction taken all necessary legal actions to use this tool?
- ◆ **Equity.** Does the funding method ensure that those benefiting from the project pay for it? For example, does the useful life of the project equal or exceed the life of the bonds?
- ◆ **Effectiveness.** Does the funding method produce sufficient resources to undertake the capital project?
- ◆ **Acceptability.** Is the funding method politically acceptable? Has it been chosen to circumvent lack of popular support for the project being funded? Does it entail greater risk than the government is willing to undertake?
- ◆ **Affordability.** Can the entity afford the financing method, now and in the future?
- ◆ **Ease of Administration.** Does the funding method result in undue burden on the staff in administering it? Are staff resources and expertise sufficient to properly administer the debt?

Funding Methods

There are two approaches to financing capital projects: pay-as-you-go and pay-as-you-use. With a pay-as-you-go approach, the jurisdiction uses available cash to pay for projects. Funding sources for a pay-as-you-go approach can include revenues derived from general fund resources, user charges, impact fees, fund balance, or designated capital replacement funds set up specifically to pay for capital improvements/replacements. To the extent available, grant funds and private contributions also fall into this category. With a pay-as-you-use approach, jurisdictions issue debt or borrow money and then pay back funds as the project is used. Pay-as-you-use financing options include debt, such as low interest loans and bond financing that allows a jurisdiction to make debt service payments after the project is complete.

| Pay-As-You-Go Financing |

Relying on a pay-as-you-go (cash) funding approach has certain advantages. Paying with cash, rather than through debt financing, avoids any borrowing costs (e.g., interest costs and bond issuance costs, underwriter's discount, bond counsel and financial advisor fees, and rating fees). Additionally, because resources are not committed to ongoing debt service expenditures, the jurisdiction will have greater flexibility to address unexpected changes in its financial position. If a major project emerges in future years for which cash resources are not sufficient, the jurisdiction's debt capacity can then be utilized to finance the project. Rating agencies also look favorably on communities that are not overburdened with debt.[1] Fitch Ratings' criteria report, *The 12 Habits of Highly Successful Finance Officers,* notes that any capital improvement plan should include pay-as-you-go financing.[2]

Identifying current revenues (cash) to pay for portions of projects can assist in reducing the debt burden. Even if a project will be debt financed, budgeting current funds to pay for project feasibility studies, preliminary design work, and environmental studies can assist in expediting evaluating the project. Cash then can be later reimbursed from the proceeds of a bond sale in some circumstances; using current-year revenues to pay for these costs reduces the overall size of the bond issue.[3]

Current revenues can also be used to cover costs for portions of a capital project that may not be eligible for tax-exempt bond proceeds. To the extent that there is private activity, the use of tax-exempt bond proceeds to finance those portions of the project is prohibited. The use of pay-as-you-go revenue sources to pay for these aspects of the project where tax-exempt debt is not allowed eliminates the need to potentially issue a portion of taxable debt for the project. Finally, to the extent that a portion of the capital improvement plan includes expenditures with relatively shorter useful life, such as furniture, fixtures, and equipment, it is often more cost effective to finance these capital improvements on a pay-as-you-go basis, rather than borrowing money.

A major disadvantage of pay-as-you-go financing is that most jurisdictions do not have sufficient cash on hand to pay for the many capital needs that must be addressed each year. Fleet, facilities, or equipment replacement plans could be compromised as a result, resulting in higher long-term maintenance costs, service interruptions, or more costly asset replacement in the future. Another disadvantage is that pay-as-you-go financing violates the "intergenerational equity" principle of paying for capital improvements, which states that those benefiting from the project should pay for it. Capital projects tend to have long useful lives, benefiting taxpayers many years into the future. Using cash on hand means that one group of taxpayers may pay for a project that benefits future taxpayers.

While pay-as-you-go funding has an appropriate place in an overall financing plan, relying only on this approach is usually not adequate to address the full range of capital needs for most jurisdictions. Capital facilities and equipment are costly, and borrowing is a practical reality that ensures that the capital needs of a community can be met in a timely manner. Many jurisdictions develop policies or practices as they pertain to cash funding for the CIP. Policies may establish a project cost threshold for using pay-as-you-go financing or identify an amount to be contributed from the general fund that will grow over time in proportion to overall budget growth. For example, a jurisdiction could set a policy that transfers 5 percent of the general fund to the capital budget each year.

Other Funding Sources

Along with current revenues, the use of other funding sources is also considered a pay-as-you-go strategy. Grant funding, the use of impact fees, or public/private partnership agreements provide opportunities to achieve the benefits of pay-as-you-go financing without using current taxpayer revenue.

Grant Funding

Grants are often considered the most favorable financing vehicle for capital projects since they do not require repayment. However, the use of grant funding does involve administrative costs, and jurisdictions should not pursue grant-funded projects solely because money is available, making the project appear to be "free." Sources of grant funding generally come from federal and state governments. In recent years, availability of some grant funds has significantly declined, but many programs still exist. For example, the U.S Department of Housing and Urban Development (HUD) has several programs that allow local communities to leverage federal resources, such as the Community Development Block Grant (CDBG) funds, into low interest loans and grants. One program, the HUD Section 108 Loan Guarantee Program, provides communities with a source of financing for economic development, housing rehabilitation, public facilities, and large-scale physical development projects. The program requires local agencies to pledge their current and future CDBG allocations to cover the amount as security for the loan.[4]

Along with the Section 108 Loan Program, HUD also manages the Brownfields Economic Development Initiative (BEDI), which is a competitive grant program used to stimulate and promote economic and community development. The BEDI is designed to assist cities with the redevelopment

> **City of San Jose, California**
>
> The City of San Jose, California, leveraged several funding sources to facilitate the acquisition of a strategically important piece of real estate. In 2005, the city used funds from the proceeds of bonds, Section 108 Loan funding, and BEDI grant funds to purchase nearly 75 acres of contaminated land adjacent to the Norman Y. Mineta San Jose International Airport. While the purchase presented many challenges, grant funding allowed the city to achieve two strategic goals: 1) begin improvements to the airport and 2) encourage private sector development of three million square feet of office space and research facilities by proving land.
>
> *Source:* For more information on this financing plan, please refer to staff reports "Acquisition of the FMC Property," August 12, 2004, and Lan Acquisition Project Lease Revenue Bonds," January 12, 2005. Both are available on the City's Web site, http://www.sanjoseca.gov

of abandoned, idled, and underused industrial and commercial facilities where redevelopment and expansion is inhibited by real or potential environmental contamination. As a condition of BEFI funds, projects must increase economic opportunity for persons of low- and moderate-income or stimulate and retain businesses and jobs that lead to economic revitalization.[5] Many other federal programs exist to provide funding for specific projects. In addition, states also generally have many programs to provide funding. Often programs will provide matching funds, where the state contributes funding in proportion to local funding for the project. Matching fund grant programs are especially common for transportation projects.

Impact Fees

In some cases, local jurisdictions can obtain capital funds from private sources to pay for public improvements. Impact fees or development fees are charged to compensate the government for costs associated with new developments, such as water/sewer infrastructure, roads, additional fire/EMS protection, or schools and allow jurisdictions to use a pay-as-you-go financing arrangement for development. In lieu of or in addition to these fees, developers may be required to provide the land necessary to construct a public facility such as a park or school. Impact fees should be set to provide funding for the financial impacts of growth to prevent current residents for subsiding construction of infrastructure and facilities needed to support growth.

Joint Ventures/Privatization

In some cases, publicly financed projects have sufficient cash flow to generate interest from the private sector. Joint public/private ventures can also include cooperative agreements between two public organizations. For example, the construction of a swimming pool that is used by both members of the public as well as physical education classes and athletic teams could be the result of a joint effort between a local municipality and school district. Other joint ventures are common in refuse collection where private sector participation may bring large efficiency gains from economies of scale. More information on joint venture or public/private partnership agreements is available in chapter 6.

Pay-As-You-Use Financing

The issuance of debt, sometimes characterized as "pay-as-you-use" financing, allows a jurisdiction to obtain funds to acquire and construct capital assets and then to repay funds over time with a tax levy, user fees and charges, or other designated source of repayment. Because of its importance as a means to pay for capital improvements, the remainder of this chapter is devoted to types of debt instruments and considerations for issuing debt. Before shifting to this topic, it should be pointed out that borrowing is not appropriate for all capital projects.

Projects with short useful lives, such as police cars, fire trucks, or other vehicles, and projects that will quickly become obsolete, such as computers or other technology, should be paid for on a pay-as-you-go basis or leased-financed over a time period corresponding to the useful life of the asset. Paying for short-term assets with long-term debt violates the equity principle described earlier. Future generations paying ongoing debt service for these projects would receive no benefit from them. Conversely, borrowing is appropriate for projects with long useful lives, such as buildings, land acquisition, and major infrastructure improvements. Thus, an important task in preparing the capital plan is to identify and categorize funding options and to allocate pay-as-you-go and other debt resources appropriately to each project.

Characteristics and Types of Debt

Most state and local governments rely on debt to pay for a portion of their capital improvement programs. Unlike debt issued by private companies, interest income on debt issued by governmental entities is generally exempt from federal income taxation and may also be exempt from state and local income taxes. This allows governmental issuers to finance capital expenditures at a lower cost relative to the private sector, as investors will demand lower interest rates on bonds whose interest income as tax-exempt.

In order for bonds to qualify for tax-exempt status, they need to be issued to finance "governmental purpose" projects such as administrative facilities, parks, libraries, or schools and be used to benefit the entire community. Other projects that may qualify for tax-exempt financing are bonds issued for governmentally owned and operated water and sewage facilities, airports, mass commuting systems, solid waste disposal facilities, and other projects identified in the Internal Revenue Code. Certain bonds issued by Section 501(c)(3) non-profit organizations also may qualify for tax exemption. Jurisdictions planning to issue tax-exempt bonds should consult with their bond counsel early to ensure projects will qualify.

The types of debt most commonly issued by state and local governments fall into two broad categories: general obligation bonds or revenue bonds. Other types of debt and different lease arrangements may also be considered.

General Obligation Bonds

General obligation bonds fall into two broad categories: unlimited tax general obligation bonds and limited tax general obligation bonds. Unlimited tax general obligation bonds are secured by a pledge of the jurisdiction's full faith and credit and unlimited taxing power. The jurisdiction promises to use its power to levy an unlimited ad valorem property tax to pay the debt.[6] The strength of this pledge provides strong market acceptance, generally high credit ratings, and favorable interest rates. Because bonds are repaid with tax revenue from all property owners in the community, this financing tool is appropriate for projects benefiting the community as a whole.

In many states, the amount of outstanding general obligation debt is subject to constitutional or statutory limitations. For example, property tax-supported general obligation bonds may be limited to a certain percentage of the jurisdiction's property value. Additionally, voter approval is often required before these bonds can be issued. The administrative process of placing a bond referendum on the ballot and generating voter support takes time and financial resources, which can be a disadvantage if the improvements to be financed are urgently needed. Voter resistance to increased taxes has been an important factor in discouraging many jurisdictions from relying on unlimited tax-supported general obligation bonds. In order to avoid these impediments, some governments choose to issue limited tax general obligation bonds, secured by legally available general fund revenues or by a property or other tax levy that may not exceed a certain rate or amount. These bonds do not pledge the unlimited taxing power of jurisdictions as unlimited general obligation bonds do. The limitations on the pledge of revenues for these bonds mean that they are issued at higher interest rates relative to unlimited tax general obligation bonds.

Revenue Bonds

Revenue bonds are secured by funds generated from fees and charges paid by users of the financed facilities or from a dedicated revenue stream such as sales taxes, hotel occupancy taxes, or lottery revenues. Revenue bonds are commonly issued to finance infrastructure improvements for water, sewer, mass transit, and other projects that benefit a specific user group.

While generally there are no voter approval requirements as with general obligation bonds, other requirements effectively limit how much debt can be issued, including rate covenants and additional bonds test. A rate covenant is a promise made by the jurisdiction to set rates so that net revenues, after meeting operating expenses, provide a certain level of debt service coverage (e.g., net revenues divided by debt service is at least equal to 1.50). Additional bonds tests limit the ability of a government to issue future revenue bonds unless certain conditions are met, usually similar in nature to the rate covenant. Because a specific revenue stream is pledged to repay the debt, it is usually necessary for a government to create a debt service reserve fund (DSRF) to be used to pay debt service in the event revenues are not sufficient to repay the debt. The DSRF is usually equivalent to one year of debt service and budgeted as part of the bond proceeds.

Other Types of Debt

In addition to general obligation bonds and revenue bonds, jurisdictions also commonly use other debt instruments, depending on the type of project, such as special district bonds, tax increment financing bonds, low interest loans, or leases.

◆ **Special District/Assessment Bonds.** Special assessment or special district bonds are issued to finance improvements benefiting a specific geographic area smaller than the entire jurisdiction, such as the downtown business district. Bonds are secured by a special assessment or tax on properties in a defined area and are often used to pay for sidewalks, streets, sewer and water projects, and other projects that would only benefit the geographic area paying the special assessment. The strength of the revenue pledge for these bonds depends on the composition of properties paying the assessment and the market value of properties in relation to assessments. Governments often have separate policies governing the formation of special districts, including acceptable value-to-assessment ratios and diversity characteristics. To enhance the security of special assessment bonds, some governments will pledge their full faith and credit in addition to assessment payments.

◆ **Tax Increment Financing Bonds.** Tax increment financing (TIF) bonds are issued as part of an economic development strategy to promote development in a particular geographic area. Debt service on TIF bonds is paid from property tax revenue on the additional property value in the TIF district resulting from economic growth. A fundamental risk of TIF bonds is reliance on forecasted property tax revenue needed for debt repayment and the possibility that property values and tax revenues may not grow as expected. As a result, tax revenues may not be sufficient to pay the debt. More information on tax increment financing is available in chapter 6.

◆ **Low Interest Loans.** State and federal government operated loan programs also provide low-interest loans to local jurisdictions. For example, the Federal Water Pollution Control Act (Clean Water Act)[7] allowed for the establishment of state revolving fund (SRF) loan programs. The programs are funded by a combination of federal grants, state funds, and revenue bonds to provide low-interest loan funding for the construction of publicly owned wastewater treatment facilities, sewer facilities, and water reclamation facilities.[8] For projects that meet the established criteria of the SRF loan program, these low-interest loans are generally more favorable than the tax-exempt bond market for projects that meet the loan programs' requirements. Finance officers may want to investigate whether similar programs for other types of projects are offered by federal government agencies and state governments.

◆ **Leasing.** Another option by which local governments acquire capital assets is through a lease. Leasing is appropriate for assets that are too expensive to fund with current receipts but with useful lives too short to finance with long-term debt. Leases are most commonly used to acquire assets with relatively short useful lives, such as vehicles, equipment, or communication systems.

Leases can be structured as a "true lease" in which the jurisdiction (the "lessee") makes payments to a vendor (the "lessor") for use of an asset over a period of time.[9] At the end of the lease term, the asset is returned to the lessor. Alternatively, a lease can be structured as a capital lease. With a capital lease, the jurisdiction enters into a lease with a vendor to acquire the use of the asset for a period of time. At the end of the lease, the jurisdiction will purchase the asset for a minimal price. The interest component in a capital lease is generally federally taxexempt for state and local governments and may also be exempt from state and local income taxation, which lowers the annual lease payments relative to a private lease agreement.

In general, capital leases may be structured in a manner similar to long-term debt in which the jurisdiction agrees to make lease payments over the term of the lease. A lease may also be structured such that jurisdictions are required to appropriate funds to pay the lease annually. The non-binding nature of this structure allows jurisdictions to not count leases as "debt" under technical or legal definitions. Because of the risk to the lessor with this arrangement, vendors will typically require that the asset be essential to the operations of the government. Rating agencies, credit enhancement providers, and others generally will include leases in evaluating a jurisdiction's outstanding debt and debt burden. A prudent approach to entering into capital leases is to include leases when reviewing measures of debt burden and affordability.

Timing for Debt Issuance

Several factors impact the timing of a bond sale. The CIP and capital budget should be used as a planning tool to assist the finance officer in making this determination. The CIP is a financial planning, budgeting, and management tool that identifies the organization's facilities and equipment requirements, places them in priority order, and schedules the timing for funding and implementation.[10] The CIP is the multi-year plan (generally a five-year plan) and the capital budget is the spending plan for the current fiscal year. Exhibit 5.2 lists seven steps for an effective CIP based on a GFOA recommended practice.

The CIP lists each proposed capital project along with the year (sometimes month) when it will be started, the amount expected to be spent on the project each year, and the proposed funding sources. Based on these individual project details, the sum of all project needs are matched with funding availability from all sources, cash/current revenues, grants, and borrowing/bond proceeds.[11]

Using the CIP as a planning tool, the finance officer can analyze and plan for the sale of bonds to finance the various projects of the capital budget. As part of the bond sale planning process, it is important to understand the timing of the encumbrance and expenditure schedule for the project(s). This requires the finance officer to be actively involved with projects and have a close working relationship with the project managers. For capital programs that extend over several years and include multiple projects, alternative financing options are often beneficial. These alternative or interim financing vehicles assist when the ultimate project cost is unknown or project expenditures exceed three years in duration. Interim or short-term financing includes the issuance of bond anticipation notes (BANs) or commercial paper. In some cases, the jurisdiction's cash balances may be sufficient to fund normal operations and meet the project's cash flow needs. When debt is issued, the cash balances would be replenished.

Exhibit 5.1 Seven Steps for Effective CIP

- Establish capital improvement policies
- Perform capital inventory
- Adopt standards to rank project requests
- Identify projects
- Assess funding sources
- Develop capital improvement plan
- Approve capital improvement plan and budget

Source: James C. Joseph, *Debt Issuance and Management: A Guide for Smaller Governments* (Chicago: Government Finance Officers Association, 1994), 5.

Planning for a Debt Program

Debt issuance commits government resources for an extended time period, often twenty or more years, before it is finally repaid. Careful planning is needed to ensure that revenues intended to pay the debt will be sufficient over the life of the debt and that the amount of debt remains affordable. This section will address preliminary steps a jurisdiction should take when planning for a debt program, including preparing a debt policy, establishing a financial plan, setting targets for debt affordability, and evaluating the revenue streams intended to support the debt.

Preparing the Debt Policy

Before undertaking a borrowing program, the first step is to prepare a comprehensive debt policy to establish the overall framework for debt issuance and management. A debt policy serves several important functions by:

- ◆ Providing guidance to staff and elected officials on acceptable levels of indebtedness and risk;
- ◆ Placing order and discipline into the decision-making process;
- ◆ Demonstrating a commitment to sound debt management practices, thereby enhancing credit quality; and
- ◆ Limiting the role of political influence.

The Government Finance Officers Association (GFOA) has adopted a recommended practice urging governments to adopt a debt policy.[12] This recommended practice identifies elements that should be considered for inclusion in a debt policy. Among the key elements guiding the capital improvement program's recommended funding plan are:

◆ Mix of pay-as-you-go and debt financing;

◆ Limitations on indebtedness, including legal limitations and policy limitations imposed to ensure debt remains affordable;

◆ Types of debt that can be issued;

◆ Term and amortization of the debt; and

◆ Integration of capital planning and debt financing activities.

A well-crafted debt policy will reflect the overall financial management objectives of the government. Common elements of a debt policy are shown in Exhibit 5.2. In particular, the debt policy should be well-integrated with capital planning policies. Policy choices on purposes for which debt may be issued, types of debt that will be considered, and limitations on amounts and term will affect the size and composition of the capital program, and therefore should be consistent with goals for service levels and capital renewal and replacement. To further illustrate the strength of the debt policy and the ability to undertake a five-year capital program, debt ratios should be projected for all years and debt policy compliance should be noted in capital budget documents. If debt policy thresholds can not be attained, restructuring capital projects and/or their funding sources may be necessary.

Exhibit 5.2 Common Elements of a Debt Policy Statement

• Purpose and uses of debt	• Short-term debt
• Types of debt	• Sale method selection
• Refunding bonds	• Reserve capacity
• Disclosure	• Intergovernmental coordination
• Statutory limitations	• When not to issue debt
• Debt limits	• Size of issuance
• Project life	• Lease debt
• Rating agency relations	• Capitalized interest guidelines
• Bond rating goals	• Market value limitations
• Repayment provisions	• Credit enhancement
• Maturity guidelines	• Interfund borrowing
• General fund revenues	• Variable rate debt
• Expenditure limitations	• Debt service funds
• Professional services	• Derivatives

Source: Government Finance Officers Association recommended practice, "Debt Management Policy" (1995 and 2003).

Ensuring Affordability through a Financial Plan

Development of a debt policy typically includes an analysis of debt affordability. A debt affordability analysis helps ensure that the amount of debt does not exceed the ability of the tax and revenue base to support it. This analysis is incorporated into policy limitations established in the debt policy.

A financial plan is an important tool to help determine acceptable financing constraints. It assists a jurisdiction assess how much debt it can afford through an evaluation of its current financial position, its perceived need for financial flexibility in the future due to changing cost structures,[13] emerging service needs, attitude toward risk, and existing debt obligations both internally and by overlapping taxing jurisdictions. Debt affordability is also tied to the characteristics of the community as a whole, including its size and wealth, growth rate, and citizens' general attitude toward taxation and debt.

The financial planning process helps to balance projected revenues, operating requirements, and capital needs over an extended time period, usually five to ten years. In the planning process, jurisdictions should project costs for providing existing services, estimate new service requirements, and determine capital needs over the planning period. The jurisdiction will then estimate the amount of revenues that will be needed to pay for them, and the implications for taxes, fees and charges, and other revenue streams. The outcome of the process helps to guide development of acceptable targets for debt affordability, given desired service levels, capital spending, and tax and fee levels.

Setting Targets for Debt Affordability

Debt affordability is often measured against targets or benchmarks included in the jurisdiction's debt policy or set by legal limitations, such as statutory or constitutional limits or limitations imposed by bond covenants. For example, a statutory limitation might restrict a jurisdiction from issuing tax-supported general obligation debt that exceeds a certain percentage of the total assessed value of property in the jurisdiction. Jurisdictions usually have little control over statutory or constitutional limits, but may have some ability to determine bond covenants particularly for a new credit. In establishing bond covenants, the jurisdiction must evaluate the tradeoff between setting more restrictive covenants and accomplishing a larger capital program.

The debt policy will also include affordability benchmarks reflecting the financial constraints facing the jurisdiction based on community characteristics and the government's overall financial condition. These benchmarks are in the form of financial ratios. Rating agencies use these measures in evaluating the credit quality of a jurisdiction's debt. Certain ratios are designed to measure affordability in relation to the community's ability to repay the debt. The strength of the community's tax and revenue base, and consequently its ability to repay indebtedness, is influenced by trends in population and employment, property values, and income levels. Affordability ratios incorporate these community characteristics. Among the commonly measures for evaluating general obligation debt are:

- ◆ Debt per capita;
- ◆ Debt as a percentage of real market value; and
- ◆ Debt as a percentage of personal income.

Another set of affordability ratios is intended to measure the state or local government's fiscal health and its ability to pay for services and for long-term debt commitments. These include:

- ◆ Debt service as a percentage of general fund revenues and
- ◆ Debt service as a percentage of combined operating and debt service expenditures.

These measures provide an indication of the jurisdiction's ability to meet day-to-day operating needs and to respond to unanticipated changes in its financial condition while meeting ongoing debt service obligations.

As noted earlier, development of acceptable thresholds for these measures should be undertaken in the context of the jurisdiction's overall capital financial plan. Over time, jurisdictions may find it necessary to adjust their policy targets to meet management objectives. In some cases, a jurisdiction may decide to live with higher debt burden ratios in order to limit increases in taxes and fees while maintaining a desired level of services and capital spending. Over time, ongoing financial planning activities should include monitoring compliance with affordability benchmarks included in the debt policy.

Analyzing Expected Revenues for Debt Repayment

The strength of the source of revenue intended for debt repayment should guide the type and amount of debt permitted by a debt policy. Two characteristics of the revenue stream are particularly important: capacity and reliability. Capacity determines how much debt can be supported. Before leveraging any revenue stream to pay for capital improvements, the finance officer needs to consider both current collections and the ability to raise rates or charges in the future to increase capacity if necessary. Reliability refers to the variability or volatility with the revenue stream. A steady, predictable revenue stream provides more certainty for meeting debt service payments than a more volatile revenue stream.

For general obligation bonds secured by property taxes, once the bonds are approved through a referendum, the revenue stream is very steady and predictable. If property values decline, jurisdictions can raise the rate to cover the debt service payments as necessary. The revenue stream for a water or sewer utility also is likely to be relatively steady and predictable because of the essential nature of the service provided, and the fact that one only one utility supplies service to the entire community. By contrast, the revenue stream for a municipal golf course is more difficult to predict because it does not provide an essential governmental service and other golf courses are generally available in a local area competing for customers. Revenue flow will depend on trends in the golf market, the facility's fees, fees of competing facilities, and weather.

Bonds issued for services with reliable revenue streams and for facilities that are considered an essential component of the jurisdiction's service delivery objectives will be more readily accepted by the market than those where the revenue stream is less stable, which will be reflected in the credit rating, interest rate, and market acceptance. Additionally, jurisdictions will have greater confidence in their ability to repay self-supporting bonds secured by revenues that are steady and predictable than bonds that are non self-supporting or are secured with more uncertain revenue streams. Debt policies will tend to reflect this, placing greater restrictions on the types of projects for which non self-supporting bonds can be issued, amounts, revenue coverage requirements, or repayment provisions.

When issuing revenue bonds supported by less reliable revenue streams, jurisdictions may choose to enhance the credit quality of the bonds by issuing "double barrel" bonds, which are secured both by the revenues of the facility and secondarily by a general obligation pledge. Alternatively, revenue streams that are unreliable, one-time, or decreasing may be better suited for use in a pay-as-you-go program.

IRS Tax Regulations Impacting Bond Expenditures

It is critical that the finance officer work closely with bond and tax counsel during the debt issuance planning process to discuss the timing and plans for the expenditure of the bond proceeds. The federal tax code prohibits tax-exempt bonds from being issued far in advance of the time money is required to construct or acquire the assets to be financed, commonly referred to as the "hedge bond rules."

In general, bonds will be considered hedge bonds and will not be tax-exempt unless the jurisdiction reasonably expects both of the following:
- To spend at least 85 percent of the net sale proceeds (sale proceeds less any amounts deposited into a debt service reserve fund) within three years of the bond's issuance and
- 50 percent or less of the proceeds are invested in non-purpose investments with a guaranteed yield format for at least four years. Non-purpose investments are those in securities, bank deposits, or other investments that have nothing to do with the governmental purpose of the bond.

It is important to note that the IRS does not consider an encumbrance for project expenditures as actual expenditures. As with many other aspects of issuing tax-exempt bonds, there are exceptions to the IRS rules and it is critical that the finance officials consult and work with their bond and tax counsel to ensure those individuals responsible for the ongoing day-to-day management of the debt portfolio have a proper understanding of these rules and regulations to ensure compliance with the federal tax laws.

The Process of Issuing Debt

When debt financing of capital improvements is deemed appropriate, the finance officer must begin the process of assembling the team of legal and financial experts that will assist the government in ensuring a successful financing. Since most jurisdictions do not have sufficient in-house expertise to handle all of the tasks associated with issuing bonds, it is essential that finance officers know what outside parties must be brought into the financing process and when. Important members of the consultant team that must be retained include a financial advisor, bond counsel, and bond underwriter.

Financial Advisor

For most jurisdictions, the financing team member that should be hired first is the financial advisor. The financial advisor works as the jurisdiction's advocate and representative in ensuring that the proposed financing meets its needs. The financial advisor is separate and distinct from the bond underwriter and has a fiduciary responsibility to represent the jurisdiction's interests throughout the financing. In contrast, an underwriter has no fiduciary responsibility to the jurisdiction, and in fact, is financially motivated to buy the bonds at the lowest price/highest yield. Among the roles that the financial advisor may fill include:

- Advising the jurisdiction in determining whether to sell the bonds through a competitive or a negotiated sale;
- If a negotiated sale is appropriate, assisting the jurisdiction in selecting the underwriting team through a competitive request for proposals process;
- Assisting the jurisdiction in selecting other financing team members;
- Structuring the bonds;
- Preparing the official statement and other disclosure materials;
- Reviewing the bond indenture, continuing disclosure agreement, and other legal documents;
- Assist in developing the bond rating and credit enhancement strategy;
- For competitive sales, preparing the notice of sale and encouraging market participation in the bidding;
- For negotiated sales, representing the jurisdiction in pricing negotiations with the underwriter; and
- Assist in preparing for bond closing, investing bond proceeds and ensuring that the jurisdiction is aware of ongoing requirements that arise after the bonds are closed (e.g., arbitrage rebate compliance, continuing disclosure filings).

Bond Counsel

The law firm that the jurisdiction selects to work on the debt financing is referred to as bond counsel. Bond counsel's primary role in a transaction is to provide a legal opinion that states: 1) that the jurisdiction has the legal authority to issue the bonds and 2) whether the bonds are exempt from federal, state and local income taxation, as applicable. In practice, bond counsel plays a much broader role than just preparing the legal opinion. Bond counsel typically takes a lead role in preparing many financing documents, advising the jurisdiction on matters of tax law and regulations as well as state and local legal requirements for issuing bonds.

Bond Underwriter

The bond underwriter is the firm (or group of firms) that purchases the entire bond issue from the jurisdiction and then resells the bonds to individual and institutional investors. The process of selecting the underwriter depends upon the method of sale chosen by the jurisdiction. In a competitive sale, the underwriter is selected through a bidding process where the bonds are awarded to the firm that submits the bid that results in the lowest true interest cost (TIC). In a negotiated sale, the underwriter is selected in advance of the bond sale, preferably through an RFP process. At the time the bonds are ready to be marketed, the jurisdiction and its financial advisor negotiate the purchase price and interest rates on the bonds with the underwriter. Assuming that agreement is reached on bond pricing, the underwriter and jurisdiction enter into a bond purchase agreement that details the pricing of the bonds and the conditions under which the underwriter and jurisdiction agree to buy/sell the bonds. It is important for the jurisdiction to understand that the "fundamental relationship between the underwriter and the jurisdiction is one of competing objections."[14]

Other Financing Team Members

In addition to the financing team members described above, several additional parties are involved in debt financing. These may include a bond paying agent/registrar, trustee, feasibility consultant, and arbitrage rebate consultant. The financial advisor can assist the finance officer in determining the need for, and the selection of, these additional finance team members.

Structuring the Bonds

In preparing to issue its bonds, finance officers must decide how to structure the bond issue to meet the jurisdiction's financial goals and repayment constraints. Structuring decisions are a key factor in determining the market acceptability and financing cost associated with a bond issue and should be made by the jurisdiction in consultation with its financial advisor. Key decisions to consider in structuring the bonds include:

◆ **Term of the Bonds.** Over what period of time will be bonds be repaid?

◆ **Fixed or Variable Rate?** Should the bonds bear interest at a fixed rate that does not change over the life of the bonds, or should the interest rate on the bonds vary over time in response to changes in short-term interest rates?

◆ **Debt Service Structure.** Typical debt service structures include equal annual payments of principal and interest, equal annual repayment of principal (with declining annual interest payments), or other structures that are designed to match a projected source of repayment revenues.

◆ **Redemption Provisions.** After what period of time should the jurisdiction have the right to prepay the bonds? Should the jurisdiction agree to pay a redemption premium if it elects to pay off the bonds prior to maturity?

Method of Sale

One of the most important (and sometimes controversial) decisions that a jurisdiction must make when preparing to borrow money through the bond markets is whether to sell the bonds through competitive bidding or through a negotiated sale with a pre-determined underwriter. The method of sale decision should be based upon the specific facts and circumstances associated with a proposed financing. Jurisdictions have an obligation to conduct their financial affairs in an environment of openness and transparency and, as such, should elect to sell bonds through competitive bidding unless the jurisdiction and its financial advisor believe there are clear and compelling facts and circumstances that warrant a negotiated sale. Generally, if a bond issue cannot achieve a bond rating in the "A" or better category, and cannot obtain credit enhancement, then the bond issue may be better suited for a negotiated sale. Some jurisdictions prefer to issue advance refunding bonds (bonds issued to refinance other bonds) through a negotiated sale in order to guarantee that required savings targets and goals are met. The jurisdiction's independent financial advisor can assist the finance officer in making the appropriate method of sale decision based on the specific details of the proposed bond sale. Jurisdictions should not make the method of sale decision based solely or primarily upon the advice of an underwriter.

Excerpt from City of Portland, Oregon, Debt Policies Regarding Method of Sale:

"The City, as a matter of policy, shall issue its debt obligations through a competitive sale unless the Debt Manager determines that such a sale method will not produce the best results for the City."

Source: Julia H. Cooper and David Persselin, "Who are the Parties in My Deal? What are Their Roles? How Do I Sell My Bonds?" *Government Finance Review* 22, no. 3 (2001): 3, 85-88.

Preparation of Official Statement and Other Financing Documents

The primary document that provides information to investors about the proposed bond issue is the preliminary official statement (POS). The POS describes the proposed bond issue, the security behind the bonds, the use of bond proceeds and relevant financial, debt, and economic information on the jurisdiction. Underwriters, investors, rating agencies, and credit enhancers rely on the POS to provide necessary information in evaluating the jurisdiction's creditworthiness.

In the case of a competitive sale, the POS is typically prepared by the financial advisor or disclosure counsel. In a negotiated sale, the underwriter, its counsel, financial advisor, or disclosure counsel may prepare the POS. While other members of the financing team may prepare the POS, the finance officer and jurisdiction staff should be actively involved in its preparation to ensure that the POS accurately discloses all material facts necessary for an investor to determine whether or not to purchase the bonds.

In addition to the POS, several other key documents are likely to be prepared in connection with the issuance of the bonds. The bond indenture (sometimes referred to as the bond ordinance, bond declaration, trust indenture, or other such document) is a detailed description of the security, covenants, and other legal terms and conditions associated with the bonds. The bond indenture is often summarized in the body of or provided as an appendix to the POS.

While the POS provides information to investors as of the time the bonds are issued, jurisdictions are now required to prepare and file annual disclosure of key financial and operating data associated with the bond's issue. The POS is finalized after the sale of the bonds to reflect the final pricing, maturity schedule, and interest rates in the form of the final official statement (OS). The jurisdiction's agreement to provide this information is described in a continuing disclosure agreement that the jurisdiction signs at the closing of the bonds. For simple transactions such as property tax-supported general obligation bonds, the continuing disclosure agreement may only require the filing of the annual comprehensive annual financial report (CAFR). For more complex transactions, the jurisdiction may also agree to file additional relevant financial and operating data that an investor would consider in deciding whether to purchase the bonds in the secondary market.

Bond Rating and Credit Enhancement

A key factor affecting the financing cost of a bond issue is the rating on the bonds. Ratings are typically provided by one or more of the three major rating agencies: Fitch Ratings, Moody's Investors Service, and Standard and Poor's Corporation. The higher the bond rating, the lower the interest rate the jurisdiction can expect to pay on the bonds.

Obtaining a rating typically involves notifying the rating agency or agencies of the upcoming bond sale, providing disclosure information to the rating analysts, and most often, a face-to-face meeting with the rating analysts to discuss the credit characteristics of the jurisdiction and the proposed bonds. While the specific criteria used by rating agencies vary among each organization, the following four factors are fairly common to all three: assessment of the financial strength, analysis outstanding debt, an assessment of quality of management and administration, and economic/demographic factors.[15] The letter ratings assigned by the rating agencies to a bond issue are intended to assess the likelihood that a jurisdiction will pay the debt service on the proposed bonds in a timely manner.

In many cases, a jurisdiction may be able to lower the cost of its borrowing by obtaining credit enhancement, most typically in the form of bond insurance. Bond insurance provides assurance to investors that the debt service on the bonds will be paid in a timely manner as the insurer agrees to pay the bonds in the event that the jurisdiction is unable. Bond insurance typically provides a triple-A rating to the insured bonds, based upon the financial strength of the insurer. Jurisdictions that elect to insure a bond issue effectively "buy" the triple-A rating of the insurer, in exchange for the payment of an upfront premium, typically expressed as a percentage of the total debt service on the bonds.

Pricing and Sale

The borrowing cost of a bond issue is determined at the time of the pricing of the bonds. In a competitive sale, underwriters submit bids to the jurisdiction for the purchase of the entire bond issue. The bid consists of an interest rate for each maturity of the bond issue as well as a purchase price for the entire issue. The purchase price typically takes into account the underwriter's discount, or the compensation paid to the underwriter to sell the bonds. The combination of interest rates and the purchase price results in a true interest cost on the bonds. Bonds are typically awarded to the underwriter submitting the bid that results in the lowest TIC.

In a negotiated sale, the interest rates and purchase price are determined through negotiation between the underwriter and the jurisdiction, with help from its financial advisor. The underwriter and jurisdiction typically agree to a preliminary scale of interest rates at which to offer the bonds to investors. An order period follows where investors indicate their interest in the bonds at the proposed interest rates. If sufficient orders are received during the initial order period, the underwriter and jurisdiction may agree to buy/sell the bonds at the agreed-upon interest rates. If the order period results in more orders for bonds than there are bonds available, repricing of the bonds at lower interest rates should follow. Conversely, if there are few orders for bonds at the initial interest rate scale, it may be necessary to increase the yield on the bonds to attract sufficient investor interest.

Achieving a successful negotiated transaction requires that either the jurisdiction or its financial advisor have sufficient knowledge of the bond market to be assured that the interest rates and purchase price proposed by the underwriter are fair and representative of other similar issues selling in the market at the same time.

Closing

After the bonds have been priced and sold, either through competitive bid or negotiated sale, all financing team members work together to prepare and assemble final documents necessary to close the bonds. Closing typically follows the sale of the bonds by about ten to fourteen days. Bond counsel tends to be the party that ensures that all members of the financing team have provided the documents necessary to assure a successful closing. Once all parties agree that the necessary documents have been agreed to and executed, the jurisdiction can receive the bond proceeds necessary to carry out the proposed project.

Roles and Responsibilities Post Bond Issuance

A critical component of any jurisdiction's borrowing plan is the active management of its debt portfolio post bond-closing. Responsibilities not only include timely payment of debt service (principal and interest payments on the bonds), but also include full and timely compliance with all of the covenants made in the bond documents, and adherence to applicable federal laws and regulations, such as arbitrage reporting. In addition, prudent debt management includes actively reviewing the debt portfolio for refunding and restructuring opportunities.

These ongoing debt management activities are briefly discussed below and are discussed in more detail in GFOA publications such as *Debt Issuance and Management: A Guide for Smaller Governments*.

◆ **Initial Debt Management Tasks.** Tasks generally include developing online access to trust accounts with the trustee, setting up the necessary account structures in the accounting system, completing any budget actions, providing initial investment instructions to the trustee, developing an appropriate record retention process, and developing an internal "ticker system" for tracking bond covenants and reporting requirements.

◆ **Monitoring Activities During Project Construction.** The jurisdiction should develop and document the disbursement/reimbursement process for distribution of bond proceeds; monitor expenditures for tax-exempt eligibility and track working capital; track project expenditures for status of project completion, reinvestment of unspent bond proceeds; set-aside identified arbitrage in rebate funds; and track any private activity expenditures.

◆ **Regulatory Compliance Activities.** Compliance activities include rebate reporting and annual continuing disclosure reporting and material event notice disclosure pursuant to SEC Rule 15c(2)(12).

◆ **Ongoing Debt Management Tasks.** Ongoing debt management includes development of procedures for annual budgeting for debt service, planning for variable rate debt service, management of bond call and redemptions; payment for service and credit providers (trustee, letter of credit providers, rebate consultants); annual "covenant" reporting to interested parties, such as bond insurers, rating agencies, LOC providers, state agencies; reinvestment of bond proceeds; tracking and monitoring of any private activity use; and ongoing refunding analysis.

Conclusion

In summary, an effective borrowing program should include three key elements: capital planning; debt issuance, when appropriate; and ongoing debt management activities. Options are available to government agencies within the capital planning processes that include not only accessing the capital markets through long- and short-term borrowing, but also using pay-as-you-go financing. Developing a financing plan and planning how capital projects are funded are important parts of planning for capital improvements. In the end, a capital improvement plan is only as successful as the jurisdiction's ability to raise funds to support it.

Notes

1. Fitch Ratings, "The 12 Habits of Highly Successful Finance Officers: Management's and Disclosure's Impact on Municipal Credit Ratings" (November 21, 2002), 6 – 7.

2. Fitch Ratings, "The 12 Habits of Highly Successful Finance Officers" and Standard & Poor, "Top 10 Ways to Improve or Maintain A Municipal Credit Rating" (February 4, 2002).

3. Federal tax regulations outline the ability to reimburse prior expenditures from bond proceeds. Finance officers should consult their bond counsel for guidance.

4. More information is available on the U.S. Department of Housing and Urban Development's Web site http://www.hud.gov/.

5. Ibid.

6. State governments or governments that do not have authority to tax property will pledge some other unrestricted revenue stream.

7. The Federal Water Pollution Control Act (Clean Water Act) was amended in 1987 to provide for the State Revolving Loan Program.

8. California Environmental Protection Agency: State Water Resources Control Board, Water Quality, http://www.waterboards.ca.gov/funding/srf.html (last updated December 18, 2006).

9. True leases are also referred to as operating leases.

10. James C. Joseph, *Debt Issuance and Management: A Guide for Smaller Governments* (Chicago: Government Finance Officers Association, 1994), 5.

11. Ibid.

12. Government Finance Officers Association recommended practice, "Debt Management Policy" (1995 and 2003).

13. Examples of changing cost structures include changes in labor settlements, rising health care or pension costs, increased maintenance costs, and federal mandates.

14. Julia H. Cooper and David Persselin, "Who are the Parties in My Deal? What are Their Roles? How Do I Sell My Bonds?" *Government Finance Review* 22, no. 2 (April 2006): 85-88.

15. See the following rating publications for more information on the credit evaluation process and criteria:

    • Fitch Ratings, "The 12 Habits of Highly Successful Finance Officers: Management's and Disclosure's Impact on Municipal Credit Ratings" (November 21, 2002).

    • Moody's Investor Service, "The Six Critical Components of Strong Municipal Management: Managerial Methods to Promote Credit Enhancement" (March 2004).

    • Moody's Investor Service, "2006 Medians for California Cities" (September 2006).

    • Standard & Poor's, "Public Finance Criteria, Financial Management Assessment" (June 27, 2006).

|6|

Economic Development Partnerships: Public-Private and Regional Agreements

By Nancy Leavitt and Patricia A. Phillips

An economic development partnership can be defined as the investment of a jurisdiction's capital and other resources to leverage investments of a private entity or another public organization. This public investment is required in order to achieve a significant public benefit that could not otherwise be achieved. If the project could be done without the private sector or public sector, no partnership would be necessary. For some projects, however, the combined resources of the public and private sectors make the project more feasible and capable of being financed in the capital markets. The public sector and private sector partners enter the project with different needs and goals. Ultimately, through negotiations, both sides must agree on a partnership agreement that will benefit both public and private sector partners in order to make the project a success. Key to the entire process is the ability to establish trust among all partners. Without a certain level of trust, the partnership will not succeed even with the best legal documents and negotiations.

Why Do Governments Enter into Economic Development Partnerships?

Every public sector and private sector partner in an economic development agreement has slightly different goals and expectations for the project. If structured correctly, the partners involved are often able to reach an agreement that would not be possible if each acted alone. Each agreement is unique and the conditions of the agreement must be developed specifically for the situation at hand. For example, if a jurisdiction wishes to preserve its limited debt capacity, the deal could be structured so the private sector partner bears the financing risk. In another example, if the project's rate of return does not meet the private partner's required rate of return, the jurisdiction could shoulder more of the infrastructure costs or offer financial incentives such as grants, loans, or tax rebates.

Just as the private sector partner has the potential for financial returns, the public sector could experience positive financial returns with economic development projects. Property owned by a jurisdiction does not produce tax revenues and vacant private property produces very little revenue. A donation of unproductive public land or other assets to a private development project can get it back on the tax roles producing tax revenue for the jurisdiction. Additionally, providing incentives to develop unused land will increase its value and associated property tax revenues. Other economic development projects may bring additional jobs, thereby increasing economic activity and associated income and sales tax revenue or achieve other goals.

Public Sector – Public Sector Partnership Agreements

Partnership agreements do not always involve a public sector and private sector partner. Governments commonly enter into agreements with other public sector organizations. Regional public-public partnerships are very similar to public-private partnerships except that the two partners are both public entities. For example, a jurisdiction might collaborate with the local community college or higher education institution to share a library, develop a technology center, or share buildings on a campus. In these cases, social goals take precedence over the economic goals. When a project resides in and benefits more than one community, regional revenue sharing agreements may be appropriate. Of course, similar to agreements with private sector partners, a jurisdiction would not enter into any agreements if it did not believe the social and/or economic benefits would exceed the costs. The discussion for the remainder of the chapter applies to both economic development partnership agreements between public/private and public/public entities. When the term private sector partner or developer is used, it is meant to apply to another public sector partner as well.

Complexity of Economic Development Partnerships

Economic development partnerships are often difficult for the public to understand and therefore generate a lot of scrutiny. A jurisdiction's actions must be transparent and the benefits of partnership must be clearly communicated to the public. The public information office can develop a dialogue with the community to educate citizens on the importance of the project and provide a forum to hear any concerns. The larger and more important a project is to the community, the more attention it will receive and the more important for the jurisdiction to perform due diligence during the project approval stage. Failure to do so could result in negative publicity and embarrassment to the local leaders if it is found that the deal is disadvantageous to the jurisdiction. A clear and defined plan to evaluate economic development partnerships will help a jurisdiction avoid many common mistakes.

This chapter explains a process to analyze economic development partnership opportunities to determine if public funding is required, and if so, what level of public investment is appropriate.

A Process to Evaluate Public Participation in Economic Development Partnerships

Because of the complexity of economic development partnerships, it is important to proceed through the project approval process in an organized way. This not only helps to direct attention to the details of the project, but it also facilitates communication between the governing body, the private partner and the public. This chapter presents a two-tiered process[1] to: 1) determine the desirability of the project and 2) determine the significance of economic and fiscal impacts. A general overview is provided here, but the process can and should be modified to best meet the needs of the individual jurisdiction.

◆ Tier 1 Guidelines. Tier 1 guidelines are used to determine if the project is desirable. In this step, the jurisdiction should decide if the project is something that will be beneficial to the community and if it contributes to existing goals and objectives. If the project passes this desirability test, then it must also be

---

Tier 1: Determine the Desirability of a Project

1. Will the project contribute to the achievement of the jurisdiction's overall goals as envisioned in its comprehensive plan or other planning and strategy documents?
2. Will the project provide jobs that will increase per capita income, or target a sector or area important to future economic growth?
3. Will the project create a synergy that helps attract other private sector development?

Tier 2: Determine the Significance of the Economic and Fiscal Impacts

4. Will the project result in the economic, fiscal and/or social benefits greater than what would occur without public participation?
5. Will the project provide a fair and reasonable return to the private partner, commensurate with the amount of risk assumed?
6. Would the project proceed or not proceed at the desired level of quality but for public sector involvement?

evaluated based on its economic and fiscal impacts.

◆ Tier 2 Guidelines. Tier 2 guidelines are used to determine the significance of the economic and fiscal impacts. This important stage will determine the role of each partner given the details of the agreement and the existing conditions. These Tier 2 guidelines can also be used for creating the structure for negotiating with the private partner.

Tier 1 – Determine the Desirability of a Project

Governments have limited resources and before considering any details of the agreement, the jurisdiction must decide if the project's outcome is worth pursuing. Desirable projects are those that accomplish goals that the jurisdiction has already determined as priorities. Economic development partnerships could be part of the strategy to accomplish goals such as: increasing the number of high paying jobs, population growth, creating cultural attractions, developing an industrial sector, tourism, and many others. A project that works well in one community may not work well in another. Each project must be evaluated given the current conditions within the community. Where possible, the following questions should be modified to better target the specific concerns of the community.

Question 1: Will the project contribute to the achievement of the jurisdiction's overall goals as envisioned in its comprehensive plan and other planning and strategy documents?

Common strategic goals include:

◆ Diversifying the tax base by attracting more non-residential development.

◆ Providing for adequate acreage of commercial, industrial, and office land in sufficient amount and in areas where it is most likely to attract high quality jobs.

◆ Supporting the major industries in a jurisdiction or attracting targeted sectors.

◆ Generating economic growth and environmental improvement through redevelopment in blighted or stagnant areas.

It is also important to identify the social, cultural, and recreational amenities for the citizens, specifically identifying which segments of the population would be served by the project. It is appropriate to seek citizen review early in the planning process, allowing ample opportunity to provide information and to receive input. If a potential project has an impact on other goals identified in the comprehensive plan or other planning document, the impact should be clearly noted so that a full discussion and analysis of all impacts can take place.

Valuable information on the importance of a project is also gained by analyzing the impacts to the jurisdiction if the project is not completed. There should be an analysis on other potential opportunities for the site. The opportunity cost, or benefits from using the site for its next best alternative, should be considered. An economic opportunity lost to another jurisdiction or state may take years to recover. On the other hand, an agreement that provides support for a private sector development that is not in keeping with the jurisdiction's plans is irreversible, and the jurisdiction will have to live with the effects for many years.

Question 2: Will the project provide high paying jobs or target a sector or area important to future economic growth?

In order to create a more vibrant economy, the project must attract businesses that offer quality jobs that enrich the community. Some governing bodies have adopted policies to target businesses offering higher paying jobs, even if it means attracting fewer businesses. To attract corporate headquarters, high tech companies, research and development operations, and those businesses offering high quality jobs, the positive image and perception of the quality of life in a jurisdiction must be marketed at the national level. The type of jobs that the project offers can create a multiplier effect and attract further relocations and more private investment in the future.

Jurisdictions also may make the strategic decision to partner with other similar jurisdictions or special purpose public sector entities to enhance the region in an attempt to attract investment from firms. Jurisdictions may enter into agreements with other governments or non-profit organizations to develop cultural facilities such as museums, parks or libraries. People making corporate location decisions will take a long, hard look at where they will be living. How the proposed project impacts these factors is an important evaluation factor. In addition, the perceived availability of a skilled/professional labor pool often influences the relocation decisions of companies.

A company or developer that would be a candidate for a partnership with a jurisdiction should provide the types of facilities and jobs targeted in the strategic plans, including at least some of the following characteristics:

- ◆ Strengthens existing firms in targeted areas;
- ◆ Builds new industrial capacity in emerging industries;
- ◆ Stimulates other economic sectors;
- ◆ Aids targeted industry-wide development; and
- ◆ Enhances the region in a way that would attract investment from desirable firms and industries.

Question 3: Will the project create a synergy that helps attract other private sector development?

A private sector partnership is one way to induce development where the jurisdiction wants it to occur and a strategy for increasing the tax base. A strategic project will not just produce jobs and revenue directly, but will also have indirect effects as the project will itself attract more economic activity and create more jobs and revenue. The importance of this synergy to the success of an economic development program cannot be overestimated. The analysis that occurs for each partnership should identify not only the direct and indirect economic impacts of the project under consideration, but should also provide an indication of how the project supports other existing or planned projects and how it will create a synergy with other public and private investments that can further increase economic and fiscal benefits.

Tier 2 – Determine the Significance of the Economic and Fiscal Impacts

After determining the desirability of the project and if the planned outcomes of the project are consistent with other planning documents, community goals, and citizen expectations, the government must then determine if the project is feasible. A project with the potential for great outcomes could be disastrous if it places a huge financial strain on a community struggling to afford an unreasonable level of public sector support. The next three questions will assist in identifying what the role of the government should be in any economic development partnership.

Question 4: Will the project result in the economic, fiscal, and/or social benefits greater than what would occur without public participation?

In order to identify those projects that will increase economic activity and provide a return to the jurisdiction over time, the jurisdiction should perform project evaluation and analyses, including a review of the market and fiscal and economic impact analyses. An interdepartmental team involving both finance and economic development staff should lead this effort.

A project that is a candidate for an economic development partnership should show through a market-absorption study that there is sufficient demand to support a project over its expected life. This study will look at the project from the developer's perspective. Projected project revenues, based on market demand, should cover the project expenses and debt service.

Economic and fiscal impact analyses for the proposed project will show the expected net financial benefits to the jurisdiction over time. The economic impact analysis projects the direct and indirect economic impacts the project will have on a jurisdiction, such as the number of new jobs, and benefit from increased economic activity. A fiscal impact analysis projects the change in government revenues and expenditures resulting from the project.

A cash flow analysis for the jurisdiction will show if the project itself is able to generate enough positive cash flow to be self-supporting once it is up and running. The analysis will identify tax revenue dedicated to cover the jurisdiction's share of project costs and the expected increase in service costs. If debt service is associated with the financing structure, it should be covered by net project revenue. Generally, a cash flow analysis does not include indirect effects.

Question 5: Will the project provide a fair and reasonable return to the private sector partner relative to the amount of risk assumed?

In order to induce development where the jurisdiction wants it occur and with the level of quality that is desired, the private partner must be motivated by a fair return on investment and assumption of acceptable risk. While it is appropriate for the project to provide a reasonable return, it should not be greater than what would be reasonable considering the risks being taken. The same is true for the jurisdiction. One large risk for governments is the partnering private sector firm. Therefore, the jurisdiction should carefully examine the private partner's experience and reputation. In addition, evaluation measures should be included in the partnership contract to enable the jurisdiction to effectively monitor performance.

Question 6: Would the project not proceed or not proceed at the desired level of quality "but for" public sector involvement?

In assessing whether the jurisdiction should participate as a partner in a project, a good place to start is with the simple question, "Would the project take place without the jurisdiction's participation?" To find out why the private sector does not complete the project by itself requires the jurisdiction to estimate the amount of public subsidy that would be required to make the project attractive from a developer's viewpoint. The jurisdiction's participation in a project should maximize its public policy objectives while minimizing direct public investment.

It is very important that these economic and fiscal impact questions be answered in the context of where the jurisdiction is heading (or wants to head) and not just relying on where it has been. That means that recent and present-day trend data are more important than historical data. It also requires projections for the project and ensures compliance with a longer-term plan.

Information Needed to Evaluate a Proposed Economic Development Partnership

In order to determine the significance of the economic, fiscal, and social impacts as described in the Tier 2 guidelines, certain information must be obtained. The following is a list of essential information:

- ◆ Feasibility, marketing and/or absorption study;
- ◆ Market-based building program;
- ◆ Pro-forma income and expense schedules/cash flow analysis; and
- ◆ Developer resume(s)/background check.

Feasibility, Marketing, and/or Absorption Study

The primary objective of the study is to determine the local demand for the project, whether it is a new hotel, office, apartment building, retail space, or other project. The analysis considers trends in the economy at the local and national levels, demographics, planned future developments, and local and regional competitors in order to project future demand for the project. The results of the market analysis help shape the building program and become the basis for obtaining financing. An outside consultant usually performs the market absorption study.

One important piece of information is the consultants' certification or independent estimate of revenues, costs, and cash flows available for debt service. If the developer's consultant provides a market absorption study, the jurisdiction should obtain an independent estimate to verify the findings. Since any project will also involve bank financing, it is also important that the jurisdiction have access to any appraisals or studies done on behalf of the bank or other financial institution.

Market-Based Building Program

The building program should be sized to meet the market demand previously identified and should be specific enough to develop preliminary cost estimates for the total project. If the project is to be constructed in phases, each phase should be clearly identified.

The developer's proposed funding sources for the building program should be identified. This includes a description of the nature and terms of the obligations for all applicable equity, lender financing (construction related and permanent), and any other sources.

Commitment of developer financing for a portion of the project shows a high level of support. The goal for the jurisdiction is to maximize the developer's debt and equity financing so the gap the jurisdiction must fill is minimized.

Pro-Forma Income and Expense Schedules/ Cash Flow Analysis

These project reports should contain or be the basis of developer-generated pro-formas that provide the financial forecast on an annual basis over the life of the project or for the life of any bonds issued for the project. Besides revenues and operating expenses, the pro-forma should include detailed assumptions on building occupancy, fee structures, and detailed information on the ability to meet required debt coverage ratios.

Developer's Resume

At a minimum, the developer's resume should include experience, financial basis, and other disclosures such as bankruptcy and tax problems. The release of the developer's financial statements is often controversial because the developer's assets usually are not pledged to the project, but it is important for the jurisdiction to understand the financial position of the developer. It is also important to assess the developer's ability to support a project in adverse circumstances, which can usually be gauged by how successful the developer has been in the past. Depending on the process used, this information may be obtained during the RFP process.

Determining the Level of Public Participation

Analysis of the projected cash flows of the project will determine if public participation is required to make the project feasible. In order for the project to proceed, the project must meet the following three conditions:

1. The project should accomplish the jurisdiction's objectives at an acceptable level of investment and risk;
2. The project should meet the rate of return requirements of the private investor(s); and
3. The project should be supported by local market conditions so that financing can be obtained.

Taking into account the amount of debt financing and equity financing the developer can obtain, the gap that requires a public subsidy is determined. Equity financing usually is determined by calculating the net present value of expected after-tax cash flows. If a gap exists, the jurisdiction would have to determine if the anticipated benefits of the project provides an adequate return given the amount of public funding required.

Project Financing Structure:

Total cost of project - Debt financing - Private equity attracted = Gap

---

The projected cash flows for the project reveal if the proposed structure is workable for all parties, including financial markets. Sensitivity analysis on changes in interest rates, attendance, occupancy, inflation, or other assumptions should be performed on all projected cash flows. If cash flows are not adequate, changing project assumptions may show what is required to make the project work.

Ways to Close the Gap

Public participation can take various forms, depending on the gap. Some common types of public involvement for economic development projects include:

◆ Land assembly/donation of land;

- ◆ Roads/storm drainage/utilities;
- ◆ Streetscapes;
- ◆ Parking ;
- ◆ Parks and playgrounds;
- ◆ Speculative office space; and
- ◆ Infrastructure projects.

Since economic development projects are generally time-sensitive, they often require mid-year adjustments to the capital plan. If a tax increment financing (TIF) district or a special service district would be required to support appropriations, it would need to be created in a timely manner. As part of the jurisdiction's fiduciary responsibility, the TIF district, special service district, or community development authority would need to be accounted for in a separate fund.

In addition to infrastructure, the provision of land, grants, guarantees, and other inducements are other common methods used by jurisdictions to make an economic development project feasible. In some cases, surplus or under-utilized land already owned by a jurisdiction can provide an opportunity to achieve public goals through a sale or lease. Jurisdiction-owned parcels could be the focal point around which a revitalization or development project occurs. In some instances, guarantees of the developer's debt service reserve, access to special debt financing, or a moral obligation pledge can close the gap between the required and projected rates of return. These types of incentives are generally not included in the capital plan.

Economic development partnerships are entered to achieve certain strategic objectives. It is up to the jurisdiction to define these objectives during the negotiating

Memorandum of Understanding

Once it has been determined to proceed with the project, the partners enter into a memorandum of understanding (MOU), which is the vital working document that comprises the agreement between the public partner and the private developer. This document states conditions that must be met by the developer before funds are available to the project. These conditions could include: having permanent financing in place, having all required permits, securing certain level of construction contracts, filling a set number of pre-lease agreements, guaranteeing tax payments, completing various phases of construction, or assuring the acceptability of improvements. If the project will take several years to materialize, much of this may be in the form of milestones. It may also be appropriate to have the construction manager and or permanent financing provider co-sign parts of the MOU. The MOU becomes the basis for the negotiated final development agreement between the jurisdiction and developer. Generally, governing bodies must approve the final development agreement and appropriate funding.

process and put them in writing. A return or payback of incentives provided by a jurisdiction may be appropriate if the developer fails to deliver on promised objectives. For example, if a project creates only 300 jobs with salaries greater than $35,000 per year instead of the promised 600 jobs, a payback or return of half the value of incentives may be appropriate. Clauses such as this should be worked into partnership agreements.

Financing Economic Development Infrastructure

There are many techniques a jurisdiction can use to finance economic development infrastructure, which can also be used to make a project workable. General obligation bonds, revenue bonds, and tax increment financing bonds are three of the most common methods used.

General obligation bonds are the primary means by which municipal infrastructure projects are financed and can be used to finance economic development infrastructure projects as well. If sufficient revenue will be produced by a project to make it self-supporting, then public facility revenue bonds are a good alternative. For economic development infrastructure projects, these revenues could include the taxes generated by the project, such as taxes on ticket sales, hotel rooms or meals, or the actual revenue stream generated by the project, such as parking fees or rental income. A history of self-support is viewed positively by the rating agencies.

If a TIF district is created, the jurisdiction could issue TIF bonds. Taxes on the incremental increase in real estate assessed value inside the TIF district would fund the debt service. If TIF bonds are issued, minimum debt coverage, reserve funds, feasibility studies, and other legal requirements would be required. These requirements could be mitigated with additional credit support from the jurisdiction. In addition, the debt service should be structured to match the projected availability of TIF district revenues. This will provide sufficient time for the project to be developed and become operational so that the incremental revenue can cover the debt service throughout the project. [2]

Tax Increment Financing

Tax increment financing is a financing technique that segregates the incremental real estate taxes resulting from improvements in a specific geographic area. It is effective for redevelopment of blighted areas, areas with limited prospects for growth, and areas where a much higher quality of development is desired. A TIF "freezes" assessed values of real estate at current levels. Taxes on the frozen levels continue to be paid to the jurisdiction to support its general fund operations. Taxes on the increased assessed values or agreed-upon portions generated as a result of improvements to the real estate (the tax increment) are set aside to fund a project on a "pay-as-received" basis or used to pay debt service on bonds issued to finance the improvements. Exhibit 6.1 shows the flow of revenue over the life of a TIF district.

Exhibit 6.1 Tax Increment Financing: Revenue Flow

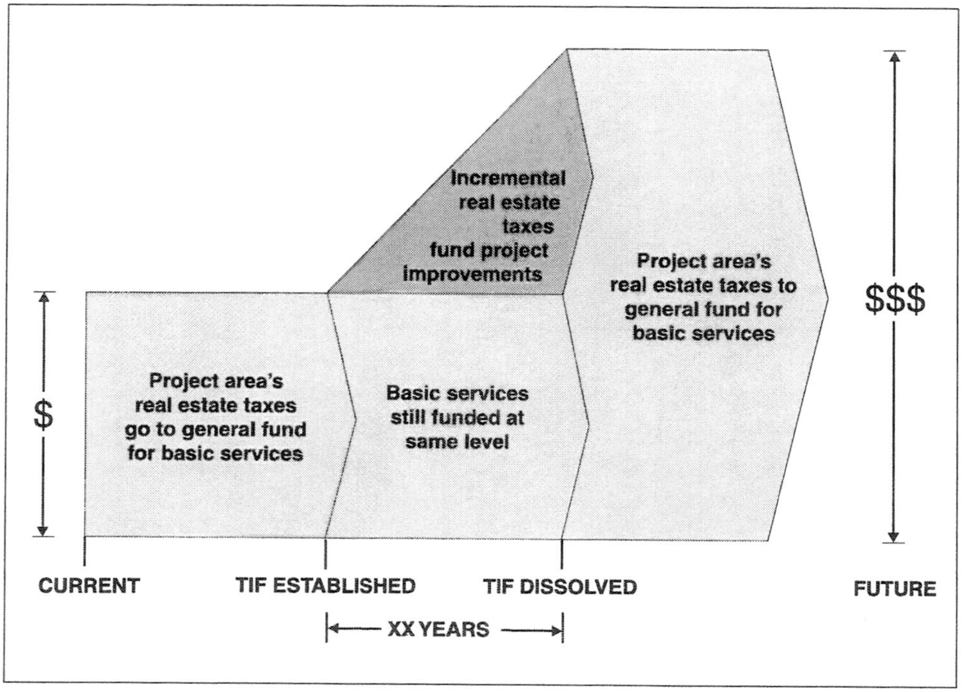

Many opportunities exist for TIF districts to provide funding for economic development projects, which are listed in Exhibit 6.2 along with important limitations. To achieve the greatest results, the TIF district should be drawn to include areas that will benefit from the new public facilities included in the project. When defining the area of TIF districts, the following points should be noted:

◆ Freezing the assessed value on which taxes are levied with the creation of the district in depressed areas with declining property values will stop the decline of revenues associated with that property.

◆ Throughout the duration of the district, the incremental revenue is used to pay for project costs, including debt service. This revenue will not be generated if there is no project. If debt is issued for a project that is not fully developed, the incremental revenue tax revenue might not be enough to afford debt service payments and the jurisdiction would need to use other "non-project" funds, depending on what funds are pledged to cover the debt.

◆ After the TIF expires or when the debt service is repaid, those incremental revenues become available to the jurisdiction, which receives higher reve-

Exhibit 6.2 Tax Increment Financing: Opportunities and Limitations

Opportunities	Limitations
• New services and infrastructure located within or benefiting from the TIF district are paid by those in that district rather than being subsidized by the rest of the areas out of general revenues. (Those outside of the district would pay for broader services like additional police protection.)	• Unless the cumulative amount of land in the community included in TIF districts is limited, the jurisdiction may lose some flexibility in its operating budget because a disproportionate amount of the increase in taxable value throughout the community is directed towards reinvestment in the districts or repayment of bonded indebtedness.
• Once the TIF district expires, the increase in tax revenue resulting from development is freed up for other general purposes.	• Unless the life of the TIF district is limited in duration, the community as a whole will never realize the advantages of increased valuations within the district.
• Property owners in the district do not pay higher tax rates than other residents. Tax revenues from the base year (that is, prior to new development taking place) remain available for general purposes.	• If bonds are issued to finance improvements and the increment does not materialize, other sources of money must be available for bond repayment to avoid a default.
• If only the TIF district revenues are pledged, the sponsoring jurisdiction's own tax and debt burdens are unaffected.	• Potential for higher interest rates than general obligation bonds (because only the incremental revenues are pledged, not the full faith and credit of the issuing jurisdiction).
• Investment in a TIF district is an effective measure to stem the decrease of property values in an area prone to decline, thus assuring that the current stream of revenue from real estate taxes to the general fund will be constant rather than declining.	• The presence of a TIF district may limit flexibility for further financing of additional development within the same district during the same time period.
• TIF districts can encourage advance developer financing of the infrastructure package on the basis that the developer will be repaid from the TIF district as the district generates sufficient income.	• As long as the district exists, and bonds remain outstanding, any increased service costs related to new development must be borne by taxpayers outside the district, unless other mechanisms are employed to cover those costs.
	• TIF debt is considered by the rating agencies in the jurisdiction's rating.

Source: Partially based on Nicholas Greifer, *An Elected Official's Guide: Tax Increment Financing* (Chicago: Government Finance Officers Association, 2005).

nues than what would have been available without the TIF project. Tax increment financing does not take a bigger piece of the taxation pie; rather, by making the project possible, it creates a bigger pie in the long term.

Special Service Districts

Special service districts (SSD), also known as special tax or assessment districts or business improvement districts (BID), may be created to provide increased services in the areas of transportation, water, sewer, public parking, refuse, infrastructure, landscaping, street cleaning, fire, power and gas systems, economic development services, and recreational and cultural activities. Generally, SSDs may not be used for schools, police, or other basic governmental services funded through standard tax levies. To pay for the improvement, a special real property tax is levied upon all property owners within the district who are subject to local taxation. The tax revenue generated by the special levy is placed in a separate fund (or is specially accounted for) to be used only within the district. Usually, property owners have control over how the special tax money is spent in the district. Basic opportunities and limitations of SSDs are listed in Exhibit 6.3.

Exhibit 6.3 Special Service Districts: Opportunities and Limitations

Opportunities	Limitations
• Allows beneficiaries/users of a specific service or facility to pay without spreading the cost across the entire community.	• Too many special service districts could lead to an unmanageable clutter of governmental units, which could cause fragmentation of local public services and confusion among citizens.
• Offers an opportunity for providing important services in areas where the financial and/or administrative capacities of the general community are constrained.	• Special service districts formed through developers may later fail if growth does not materialize.
• Can be used to expand existing system capacities to meet new demands.	• In some states, SSDs are not allowed to issue debt.
• Provides a degree of political insulation from the other concerns of local governments.	

Community Development Authorities

A community development authority (CDA) has the power to finance infrastructure and improvements in a defined area by issuing revenue bonds that are obligations of the authority. The debt created by such revenue bonds is paid from additional real property taxes or special assessments levied within the boundaries of the CDA. A CDA is a non-stock corporation that qualifies for tax-exempt financing under the Internal Revenue Service Code.

The host jurisdiction has no obligation to repay, may not repay, and may not show CDA debt as a contingent obligation on its financial statements. Also, the CDA debt shall not be used in considering the debt limit of any jurisdiction. However, CDA debt may be considered to be overlapping debt of the host jurisdiction by the rating agencies. Therefore, overuse could have negative consequences on municipal bond ratings.

Developers find CDAs attractive because CDA bonds are non-recourse and off the developer's balance sheet. They are a good source of financing, as infrastructure financing is typically hard to arrange at a bank. CDAs give the developer access to tax-exempt financing, which allows a higher return on equity by reducing the amount of equity required due to lower interest costs. CDA financing diversifies the funding mix and provides longer term financing. It is not appropriate for all projects.

Exhibit 6.4 Community Development Authorities: Opportunities and Limitations

Opportunities	Limitations
• CDAs are one more tool in economic development infrastructure financing and represent a local source contribution to the project.	• Overuse could lead to governmental fragmentation, with the potential for creating confusion regarding functional responsibility among the citizens.
• Supports the user pay concept and in some residential CDAs, the obligation is relieved upon initial sale of the residence	• There will be differential tax rates within a single host jurisdiction.
• Allows the host to facilitate priority development projects and can be used as a growth and land management tool.	• Although low risk, a CDA default has financial implications and risks to the host. Though not a liability of the host jurisdiction, its name would be associated with the default.
• In case of residential development, where CDA financing is part of the plan of finance, housing can be more affordable for buyers.	• If the assessed value of the property is based on the sale price of the property, CDA financed properties may have a diminished assessed value for tax purposes.
• Presence of CDA financing may bring about higher quality developments and in a shorter time frame.	

It is not unusual for a developer to request a TIF overlay to a CDA district. In these situations, any debt is considered direct debt of the jurisdiction by the rating agencies. Many jurisdictions develop CDA policies that place parameters on the type, scope, and aggregate amount of CDA debt that can be issued and outstanding, similar to constraints of a debt policy. Basic opportunities and limitations of CDAs are listed in Exhibit 6.4.

Conclusion

The careful analysis and evaluation of projects required before a public investment is made for an economic development partnership can be long and complex. Because of this, these projects are typically keystone projects that jumpstart or contribute significantly to the success of a jurisdiction's strategic plans. Public financing of projects lowers the cost and risk to the developer so that the project can go forward. However, care must be taken to avoid a sense of entitlement to public funds by any developer.

The challenge to the jurisdiction is to determine what level of infrastructure investment is required to make the project feasible. Before undertaking a public-private partnership, the approving body should establish some criteria or policy regarding public involvement. The methodology presented in this chapter helps a jurisdiction determine what is required to meet the investment objectives of both the private and public partners that will also be acceptable to the financial markets, while providing reasonable assurance that the project objectives will be met and can be communicated to the public.

Example of the Process in Action: The Town Center Project in Virginia Beach, Virginia

The following example describes the economic development partnership entered into by the City of Virginia Beach, Virginia, to create a "town center," in which it agreed to contribute parking as part of the public investment in the project. A TIF district was used to designate a revenue stream to fund the city's responsibilities. The Town Center Project in the central business district (CBD) was included in the city's comprehensive plan as a way to improve the overall form and quality of the development within the CBD core area and to transform mostly undeveloped or underdeveloped land into an attractive, high quality, intensive, pedestrian focused, mixed-use town center. The Town Center Project is based on a business park concept and is being developed in phases by the Virginia Beach Development Authority (Authority) in partnership with a private developer and general contractor.

Public Investment

Under the development agreements, the parking garages, plaza land, meeting space, and the pedestrian bridge were financed through revenue bonds issued by the Authority and are to be repaid through funds generated by the TIF. Though the debt service on the bonds is paid with the incremental real property taxes generated within the TIF district, the bonds were not technically TIF bonds. Credit support provided by the city was the primary security for the bonds. This was done so the bonds would receive a higher rating, a lower interest rate, and to avoid the need for a debt service reserve fund.

In addition to the TIF, the city is also using its capital improvement program (CIP), and economic development investment program (EDIP) to finance the plaza and public infrastructure. The following table summarizes the public and private investment responsibilities for phases I, II, and III.

Exhibit 6.5 Summary of the Town Center Project Financial Plan

(millions of dollars)	Phase I	Phase II	Phase III	Total
Public Investment:				
Public parking garages -TIF-funded	$ 22.5	$ 19.0	$ 17.2	$ 58.7
Plaza land - TIF-funded	0.7			0.7
Meeting space - TIF-funded			7.6	7.6
Pedestrian bridge - TIF-funded			1.5	1.5
Infrastructure - CIP/EDIP-funded	6.3	7.6	1.7	15.6
Total garage and infrastructure - public	$ 29.5	$ 26.6	$ 28.0	$ 84.1
Total private investment (projected):	$ 75	$80 - $90	$181.8	$337 - $347
Completion dates:	Fall 2003	Winter 2005	FY-2008	Public-Private Ratio 1 to 4.1
Assessed value of taxable private investment as of July 1, 2006:	$104.6	$ 92.7	$ 6.5	$203.8

Private Investment

Under the development agreement, the Authority was to fund parking garage structures after private sector investment benchmarks were hit. The Authority was required to build the parking garage for phase I after private sector investment for phase I. The Authority was then required to build the parking garage structures for phase II and phase II after private sector investment during phases II and III. Staggering public investment shielded the city from some of the project risk. With this type of agreement, if private sector development did npt occur, public investment could be reduced.

Assessed Values

Exhibit 6.6 shows the base year value and increase in assessed value within the TIF district since inception in 1999. As private investment occurred, the total

Exhibit 6.6 Total TIF District Assessments

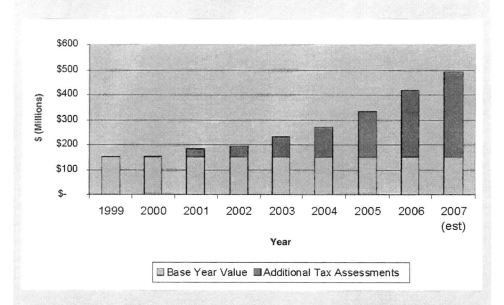

value of taxable property increased, which the city was then able to tax and use revenues to support the project. From 1999 to 2007, the total value of assessed value increased over 300 percent.

Exhibit 6.7 shows the increase in assessed values and the resulting revenue that was generated in additional property taxes. In 2007, it is estimated that the city will receive over $3.3 million in additional revenue that can be used to support the project.

Town Center Special Service District

The town center special service district (SSD) was created in May 2002, effective July 1, 2002, to cover the costs associated with the maintenance of the garages, providing streetscape enhancements, and building a long-term maintenance reserve. In addition, if there should be a debt service shortfall in the TIF, revenue from the SSD would be used to make up the difference, thus reducing the risk to the city. Currently, the property owners within the SSD pay an additional $0.57 for every $100 in assessed value to cover these costs and to build the debt service reserve fund. The rate can be adjusted to meet actual and projected expenditures, as necessary. Revenue from the SSD is shown in Exhibit 6.8.

Exhibit 6.7 Additional Revenue from TIF District

Year (As of June 30)	Base Year Value	Total Taxable TIF Assessments	Increase in Assessed Values	Annual % Change in Assessments	Total % Change	Incremental Revenue
1999	$ 151,894,230	$ 151,894,230	$ -	0%	0%	
2000	$ 151,894,230	$ 153,401,358	$ 1,507,128	1%	1%	$ 14,944
2001	$ 151,894,230	$ 182,000,836	$ 30,106,606	17%	18%	$ 353,013
2002	$ 151,894,230	$ 191,661,105	$ 39,766,875	21%	38%	$ 490,995
2003	$ 151,894,230	$ 230,438,402	$ 78,544,172	34%	72%	$ 905,331
2004	$ 151,894,230	$ 271,384,606	$ 119,490,376	44%	116%	$ 1,503,178
2005	$ 151,894,230	$ 331,957,379	$ 180,063,149	54%	171%	$ 2,142,072
2006	$ 151,894,230	$ 417,805,523	$ 265,911,293	64%	234%	$ 2,722,666
2007 (est)	$ 151,894,230	$ 491,480,663	$ 339,586,433	69%	303%	$ 3,361,906

Source: Information was gathered from a variety of sources, including the City of Virginia Beach City Assessor's Office, committee reports on the central business district TIF, and comprehensive annual financial reports for the years 1999 through 2005.

Exhibit 6.8 Revenue from the Special Service District

Town Center SSD as of June 30 Each Year	
Fiscal Year	**Actual Revenue**
2003	$261,936
2004	$435,982
2005	$656,768
2006	$890,205

Source: CAFRs (excludes interest earnings)

Throughout the project, the city mitigated the amount of risk it assumed for the town center project in the following ways:

- **Front-end Financing by the Developer for the Public Improvements.** The developer built and financed the construction of the public garages. The city issued debt through its Development Authority to purchase the garages from the developer, but only after the private investment was substantially complete.

- **Developer Guarantee of TIF Assessments.** The town center development agreement required the developer to make up any shortfalls in revenue due to assessments coming in lower than projected. This protects the city in the event that the construction of the private investment is delayed.

- **TIF Fund Reserve.** The town center TIF was in place throughout the construction period and before the beginning of debt service payments. This allowed the fund to build up a reserve in case the project did not go as planned.

- **Reimbursement Amounts.** The town center development agreement requires the developer to reimburse the city if any changes in project components result in less assessed value than that of the original components. This gives the developer flexibility to react to market conditions, but protects the city against changes in scope of the project.

- **Town Center Special Service District.** The town center special service district was created to cover the cost of maintenance of the garages and to create a long-term maintenance reserve.

Project Reflections

Projects of this type are not simple and routine, so it is important not to underestimate the complexity of economic development partnerships and to be prepared to bring expert advisors in where needed. Outside legal expertise in real estate was an important resource for this project. Along with using outside consultants to provide information to make solid decisions, getting financial and background information on the developer is important, but can be difficult. Once the jurisdiction has a developer's financial statements, they can be made public through the freedom of information process, making developers reluctant to provide this information. The city solved this problem by visiting the developer's offices and reviewing their financials, the project pro formas, and other project-related documents. A portion of the financing came from a bank loan and the city was able to gain an understanding of the bank's lending criteria and release of funds. Since the bank had strict lending policies and was willing to make the loan, the city was comfortable with the developer's financial position.

Additionally, resources must be devoted to managing the project after construction. In an effort to bring transparency to the performance of the TIF districts, the City of Virginia Beach developed an annual report covering the performance of all its TIF districts. In the report, promised private investment is compared to the actual investment, and the change in assessed property values over time is also tracked to determine if the TIF is fulfilling its expectations. Tracking the other taxes generated within the TIF district helps to show some of the spin-off effects of the project. Most importantly, the continued focus on providing due diligence for each decision and monitoring the success of the project demonstrated to the public that "but for" the public investment, the town center project would not have been accomplished at the level of quality the city desired.

Notes

1. The process for evaluating public participation in economic development partnerships was based on recommendations from the report, *Guidelines for Evaluation of Investment Partnerships for Economic Development* (City of Virginia Beach, Virginia, 1999).

2. GFOA Recommended Practice, "Tax Increment Financing as a Fiscal Tool (2006)."

|7|

Emergency Communication Centers

By Michael J. Daun

Due to civil disruptions occurring in a number of urban areas in the United States in 1967, President Lyndon Johnson's Commission on Law Enforcement and Administration of Justice recommended that police departments establish a single emergency number. The code 911 was chosen because it is brief, easily remembered, and unique, having never been used as an area code or service code.[1] In 1972, the Federal Communications Commission (FCC) recommended that 911 be implemented nationwide. Various patents were issued throughout the 1970s and 1980s for newly devised switching devices, specialized caller databases, and call handling capabilities, all aimed at implementing improved emergency system features. In 1999, President Clinton signed Senate Bill 800, designating 911 as the nationwide emergency telephone number. According to the National Emergency Number Association (NENA), as of January 2000 about 93 percent of the total U.S. population was served by some type of emergency 911 service.

The United States was not the first, however, to implement an emergency system or make such a nationwide designation. Winnipeg, Canada, had initiated a 999 system in 1959, and many developed countries have established three digit emergency phone numbers. The European Union requires the use of a single emergency number (112) for all countries.[2]

| Emergency 911 Systems |

Emergency 911 systems used by local jurisdictions can be divided into the following four components, each of which is essential to its operation:

- ◆ Phone subsystem including mapping/addressing data base;
- ◆ Computer-aided dispatch subsystem;

◆ Radio subsystem; and

◆ Building and other equipment/facilities.

Phone and Related Subsystems

The phone and related subsystems comprise the "call" side of the emergency communications system. These subsystems allow the caller to communicate the emergency event to a dispatcher and the dispatcher to relay the information to the first responder (fire, EMS, police). The receiving side of the call is known as the public safety answering point (PSAP), or 911 call center. A jurisdiction will contract with a local telephone company and/or subcontractors, sometimes referred to as the incumbent local exchange carrier (ILEC), to provide both landline and wireless phone service. Under this arrangement, the ILEC is responsible for providing the required phone system infrastructure, including automated caller location (usually with the aid of GPS technology for wireless phone companies) and phone number identification, switch system, signaling protocols, and selective routing to the proper 911 center or PSAP. Selective routing capability is critical to assure the fastest possible response to an emergency. At the 911 center, software is able to receive, queue, process, and display this information for the call taker.

Basic 911 vs. Enhanced 911

Basic 911

With Basic 911, the local land line telephone company maintains a carrier switch and 911 tandem for priority transmission and routing of the call to the nearest PSAP. The PSAP call taker answers the call, obtaining the necessary information about the emergency, caller location, and phone number. The call taker relies entirely on information provided by the caller. NENA indicates that about 4-1/2 percent of the U.S. population is still served by such Basic 911 systems.

Enhanced 911

With Enhanced 911 (E911), the phone system tandem relays a signal identifying the ten-digit telephone number of the caller, which is automatically displayed at the PSAP. Once the telephone number is supplied to the PSAP, the system will query the address database maintained by the local telephone company. This allows the call taker to focus on helping the caller while instantly passing on (or having a separate dispatcher pass on) the needed information to the proper responder in the field. E911 has operated successfully for over twenty years and continues to do so in many locations. According to a NENA report, about 88 percent of the population is served by E911 service.

One issue of concern for local PSAP operations is voice over Internet protocol (VoiP) technology. A number of broadband, high-speed Internet providers now offer services that include "telephony" Internet communications. With this innovation, the ability of PSAP systems to determine the location of the VoiP caller in an emergency became a concern. As a result, in May 2005, the FCC issued an order requiring all VoiP providers to include E911 service and enable automatic caller location information to be transmitted the PSAP.

Source: Information was compiled from the National Emergency Number Asso- ciation Web site, http://www.nena. org.

Computer-Aided Dispatch

A computer-aided dispatch (CAD) subsystem is the foundation of the emergency response side of the emergency communications system. Upon receipt of a 911 call, the CAD subsystem generates pre-programmed information to the dispatcher to recommend appropriate first response units. Additionally, a CAD system can be integrated with an automated emergency medical dispatch protocol system to assist the call taker with classifying the call (i.e., cardiac arrest, breathing difficulty, choking) and provide pre-arrival medical instructions. Most advanced 911 systems utilize direct dispatch, where both essential call answering and radio dispatch information is transferred automatically at the PSAP. The CAD system is the hub of the PSAP and usually integrated with all of the other technologies that support call taking and dispatching functions such as mapping, phone, radio, and records management systems.

Radio Subsystem

The radio subsystem supports timely, accurate, and reliable communication with required emergency responders. Components of the radio subsystem include both the system infrastructure and radio subscriber units. When planning for changes or upgrades to the radio subsystem, the jurisdiction should evaluate system design options as well as the systems interoperability with other jurisdictions' systems.

System Infrastructure

System infrastructure includes tower sites and any in-building amplifiers or bi-directional amplifiers (also called signal boosters) to ensure communications through thick steel or concrete structures such as parking garages and shopping malls. Specific requirements for the infrastructure will be driven by geographical conditions and the jurisdiction's terrain. The infrastructure is also traditionally built to a 99.999 percent level of reliability, which increases costs above what would be normal for communication systems serving other industries. Site location for infrastructure not only involves essential technical considerations, but also requires a sensitive process to gather public support. If proven feasible, possible co-location on an existing tower may help minimize citizen opposition.

Subscriber Units

Subscriber radio units include both mobile (vehicle-based) and portable (person-based) radio units. These are powerful, shock rated, heavy-duty radios and are typically much more expensive than the standard two-way radio found in an electronics store. These radios have a useful life of five years or less, but this may be extended via timely parts replacement. Large systems also may utilize mobile data workstations that allow data transmission to the first responder vehicle, usually using "rugged-ized" laptop or proprietary mobile data terminal. Each vehicle will also need to have a vehicle radio modem that will gain access to the mobile data network and will provide interfacing into the dispatch system and message capability with the dispatcher.

Building and Equipment

An effective emergency communications center must provide a 24/7 high technology facility equipped to receive vital event information and expedite a real-time first response specific to the situation, location, and scale of the emergency. This facility also becomes an essential "clearinghouse" or command center for a coordinated public safety response in the event of a widespread natural or manmade disaster. The 911 center building must be structured so as to eliminate all radio weak spots to and from the facility. From a public service standpoint, the life-and-death, high stress environment dictated by 911 emergency dispatch will increase physical facility and equipment costs far beyond what would be expected for normal office space construction. Back-up emergency electrical generators and information security system and disaster recovery procedures, including off-site data service, are mandatory in this environment.

Wireless Emergency Calls

When older 911 systems were implemented, nearly all calls were made from landline phone networks, but this is no longer true. Currently, approximately 82 million 911 calls, or 30 percent of all 911 calls, are now made from wireless phones. Current trends indicate that number will be even greater in the future.*

For wireless calls into a basic 911 system, the dispatcher must rely on caller-provided verbal information. With E911, the system automatically identifies the wireless tower receiving the call signal, but cannot identify the caller's exact location. Phase 2 E911 has the capability to provide the system the exact longitude and latitude coordinates of the caller and plot his or her location using mapping software, assuming wireless carriers and phones are equipped with the technology. In 2006, it was estimated that 80 percent of local PSAPs had implemented Phase I wireless E911 service, but only 57 percent had implemented Phase 2 wireless service.**

Implementing a Phase 2 E911 system may not identify all callers, however. The system requires the cell phone carriers to supply global positioning

Needs Assessment

The success of projects to improve emergency communication operability depends on the completion of a thorough performance and needs assessment of the current 911 system. The assessment will enable the development of a multi-year capital improvement program to invest in any of the system components described in this chapter. The assessment should begin with a full discussion of fundamental community emergency response needs and service gaps. Discussion should include individuals beyond public safety officials to include communications and technology professionals, wireless and land line phone carriers, finance officers, elected officials, state and federal officials, and even representatives from neighboring communities. Often a committee, representing all involved stakeholders, is used to develop recommendations. The following section describes some functional requirements that should be considered for an effective modern 911 system. In addition, many system design questions need to be resolved.

system (GPS) enabled phones or provide a network that identifies the caller's location. The consumer needs to be made aware that until all cell phone companies comply with the FCC Phase 2 requirements, even if a PSAP can receive Phase 2 wireless calls, the cell phone they carry may not be able to transfer the specific location information.

While wireless providers work to upgrade their systems to provide specific caller number and location information, the initiative and much of the related cost of addressing these limitations falls on local government. The technical challenges and financial burdens to both wireless and public entities are substantial. NENA estimated that the cost of bringing current 911 systems into full compliance with FCC standards for phase 2 E911 would cost around $8 billion.

---

* U.S. Government Accountability Office, "States' Collection and Use of Funds for Wireless Enhanced 911 Services" (Washington, D.C.: U.S. Government Accountability Office, March 2006).

** Ibid.

System Design Issues

As part of the needs assessment process, a jurisdiction needs to resolve many system design questions that will impact operability of the new system. For new or growing communities, local government 911 designers may wish to establish plans with adjoining jurisdictions and federal/state government to reserve additional radio frequencies to assure interoperability and serve future needs. Before making decisions, an evaluation of the current system can reveal specific strengths and weaknesses. Exhibit 7.1 shows major design elements of radio system and some key strengths, weaknesses, and features.

Exhibit 7.1 Radio System Design Options

	Characteristics	Features			
		Speed	Reliability/ Performance	Efficiency	Cost
Radio frequency selection					
Very High Frequency (VHF)	• 30 - 300 MHz • Used for shorter distances	Good	Good/ Excellent	Fair	Low
Ultra High Frequency (UHF)	• 300-3000 MHz • Used for long distances	Excellent	Good	Excellent	High
Allocation of available frequencies					
Conventional	• Dedicated frequency to each user group (example: police)	Good	Excellent	Fair	High
Trunked	• Shared frequencies to many user groups	Good	Good	Excellent	Low
Digital vs Analog signal					
Analog	• Continuous, variable signal	Good	Fair/Good	Good	Low
Digital	• Discrete groups of signals	Excellent	Excellent	Excellent	High

*More efficient use of available spectra.
**Assumes adequate frequencies are available to handle peak load call volume.

Preparing an RFP

Because of the complex nature of these radio subsystems and the unique industry practices and standards to be applied, technical assistance from the appropriate state government coordinating entity or from professional consultants should be used to assist in designing and implementing new systems. Because a limited number of relatively large, sophisticated vendors exist, a carefully prepared RFP is necessary to identify the

Analog vs. Digital

The FCC is promoting digital-based radio systems because of their capacity to transfer large volumes of data (including video and voice signals) accurately while limiting the use of available radio spectra. However, many current systems remain analog-based and may eventually need to migrate to a digital-based system. Important decisions include radio frequency selection, allocation of available frequencies, and analog- versus digital-based signals.

most suitable, cost-effective response. If significant hardware and software components are required, vendors selling a total package solution including hardware, software, installation, training, and support services may be appropriate. While there are well over 100 or more advertised CAD vendors, a major trade magazine recently identified 13 "top tier" CAD software vendors that could form the basis for an RFP bidders' list.[3]

Interoperability

As 911 systems have matured, the need for interoperability, the ability of radio operators from different departments and different jurisdictions to communicate real time in an emergency, has become a major issue. Whether in a rural or large urban district, two or more adjacent jurisdictions may cooperatively respond to an emergency only to discover that their respective radios cannot communicate with each other, hampering an effective response. For example, The Federal Department of Homeland Security has worked with leading industry professionals and the Commonwealth of Virginia to establish nationwide industry standards for wireless communications. These standards are known as "APCO 25" or "P-25" standards.[4] This effort has also produced a statement of requirements for interoperability and a statewide communications interoperability planning methodology (SCIP).[5]

Emergency Response System Integration

Enhanced emergency communications systems should eliminate manual intervention in the transfer of emergency calls for service between different 911 systems in an area. Related government agencies (fire, police, health, etc.) and surrounding jurisdictions should also assure that their respective PSAPs are efficiently mapped to the caller's location and their radio systems communicate with each other in area-wide emergencies. This interoperability requirement is a major focus of FCC compliance.

Consolidation

The initial 911 improvement phase should address the basic question of what, if any, jurisdictions and functions could be initially consolidated in the new 911 system. The result of this effort may be the most important single decision affecting ultimate 911 system cost and performance. As the prospect of large 911 enhancement investments loom, many local governments consider consolidation of the call-taking and dispatch functions between multiple jurisdictions to help control costs and assure a seamless response to calls throughout the largest possible service area. This could also involve consolidation of an individual jurisdiction's fire, police, and EMS systems into a single municipal call-taking and dispatching function. In large urban counties, consolidation could take the form of a single countywide 911 system. Many counties still retain multiple 911 systems though, often delaying emergency response and increasing taxpayer and telephone user costs. In many areas, multi-county consolidation should likewise be explored. While such consolidation may pose bureaucratic and political obstacles and resistance, real economies of scale can be achieved.

Arrival-time Standards

Regardless of the investment in computer hardware and communications software, ultimately, the success of any emergency communications system is measured primarily by emergency response time. Most large cities/counties closely monitor their response time trends for police, fire, and EMS services. Historic response time trends should be used to establish improved response time standard(s) with the help of new system capabilities.

Failsafe 24/7 Operation

Priority-one calls should desirably achieve zero lost CFS. System down time should likewise be zero. Back-up and recovery systems should assure 0 percent lost CFS, and 100 percent up time. Monitoring capability should accurately record and validate existence, response time, and disposition of all incoming CFS.

Real-Time ANI and ALI Functionality

The system should automatically provide the wireless caller phone number (ANI) and caller-specific location information (ALI). Also, local governments should verify that all VoIP Internet service providers are including E911 automatic caller location information to all of its area subscribers.

Federal and State Standards for Emergency Communication Systems

The FCC establishes standards for emergency communication systems in all areas of the United States, however, many current 911 systems fail to meet FCC requirements. An essential FCC requirement states that jurisdictions must implement automated, location-specific, inter-operable wireless caller information to the PSAP. Beginning in 1996, the FCC established deadlines for wireless companies to implement enhancement of all 911 phone systems to provide both automated caller phone number and specific location information for all wire-line and wireless systems. Unfortunately, the FCC requirements initially applied only to those systems where the local government PSAPs had formally requested such functionality of specific wireless providers. These deadlines have also been repeatedly challenged by wireless carriers and subsequently extended by the FCC. The current status of local 911 systems relative to FCC requirements leaves much work to be done. Evidence of federal enforcement in instances where FCC standards are not achieved is slim to non-existent.[6]

Other important FCC requirements address the ability of systems to serve the hearing impaired. Also, Title II of the Americans for Disabilities Act requires that all telephone emergency service providers assure direct access to emergency services for the deaf on a par with what is offered to all others serviced within the jurisdiction. Among these requirements is that each emergency call taker must have its own teletypewriter (TTY-TDD) compatible equipment.[7]

Many states have also established compliance standards for local 911 systems. The most basic state government requirement is state approval of a multi-year 911 development plan. State standards also commonly include requirements for governance structures, E911 Phase II status, call taker training, and call response times. Continued compliance with these standards is normally a prerequisite for state funding and enforced by state-created board or commission. Numerous state governments provide technical assistance and coordination of local efforts and provide state grant funds for this purpose. Other states have taken the lead in actual development of a statewide 911 system, including a phased roll-out of a statewide system over a period of years.

> ### State-Led 911 Development in Minnesota
>
> Minnesota is one example of a state that is leading 911 development. The Minnesota Statewide 911 Program provides technical assistance to cities and counties implementing, maintaining, and improving 911 systems. It also enforces rules that set system standards and distributes funds collected through a statewide telephone surcharge. An enhanced 911 fund, supported by the 911 fee, distributes funds to local governments to implement, improve, and maintain E 911.
>
> *Source:* Information taken from the State of Minnesota Statewide 911 Program Web page, http://www.state.911.mn.us.

Project Management

Most extensive 911 efforts utilize a multi-year phased approach to project completion. In addition, considering the many 911 system components, there may be more than one project underway at the same time. Therefore, the overall management and coordination of 911 projects by a 911 development manager is essential to bring the facility functions online in a timely fashion. For example, the design of a CAD system could be underway concurrently with the construction of the communications facility. The use of project status reporting by the individual project manager and both the 911 steering committee and development manager is important to keep each informed on the current situation and prevent any unnecessary delays. For example, in the 911 effort undertaken by the City of Milwaukee, Wisconsin, difficulties in resolving CAD development issues led to a situation where the city's communications center building was completed over a year before implementation of the new police and fire departments' CAD systems.

Given the considerable financial, technical, and service-level challenges involved in a 911 improvement project, an effective project management and control system is essential. This system must be in place at the start of the first project. The foundation for effective project management is a sound project plan committed to by the major funding sources and system users. Essential components of a sound plan are:

◆ A 911 steering committee of major funding and user organization executives.

◆ A 911 capital improvement plan agreed upon by the steering committee.

◆ An experienced, competent, and dedicated 911 development manager having overall responsibility for the success of the 911 enhancement effort. This position would report to the 911 steering committee. All project managers would report to the development manager.

◆ An initial project definition and scope that is achievable within the budget and timeframe.

◆ Individual project budgets should not be suspended or changed for non-project reasons.

◆ A work plan for the initial project detailing all expected work products/results, work tasks, the staff and other resources required for each task, and a schedule for overall project completion.

◆ A staffing assignment schedule for the approved project that fulfills the staffing needs indicated in the work plan.

◆ An experienced project manager for each major 911 subsystem project who is responsible for bringing his/her project to completion on time and on budget.

◆ A memorandum of understanding between all outside and internal organizations involved in the initial project describing how project disputes, requested change orders, and other issues will be resolved.

◆ A procedure and format for formally reporting project status and progress to the project manager, development manager, and 911 steering committee. Ideally, this report would address not only financial status but also physical completion status. Comparisons to budget and the work plan schedule should be included.

Finance Options for
Emergency Communication Centers

The substantial cost, variety, and complexity of emergency communication centers normally require a phased development approach that spans multiple years in the capital improvement program. Each 911 enhancement phase would be defined in terms of one of the major 911 components described above. A common financing source for emergency communication facilities, like other essential government infrastructure and facilities, is general obligation debt. For example, the $65 million police district station-communication center project in the City of Milwaukee, Wisconsin, was entirely financed through general obligation bond issuance. Additionally, many jurisdictions use dedicated 911 taxes, fees, or grant funds to finance emergency communication centers.

Dedicated 911 Tax or Fee

Numerous states have passed legislation authorizing various forms of a 911 tax. These taxes and fees take the form of a surcharge added to landline or cell phone monthly charges and generate ongoing revenue sources that can be used for current year (cash) financing of needed 911 capital improvements or satisfying debt service requirements. For example, in San Francisco, California, an emergency response fee is assessed to phone charges. Oklahoma City, Oklahoma, initiated a ½ percent police and fire general sales and use tax program to fund a variety of public safety needs, including many of Oklahoma City's 911 enhancements such as a citywide trunked radio system, police and fire joint CAD system, and construction of an emergency communications center.

Some jurisdictions, however, have experienced problems with 911 fee revenues falling below expectations. If fees are only assessed on landline phones, the transition from landline phones to wireless or VoIP may have a significant impact on revenue. There is also a concern that federal and/or state legislation may limit local governments' ability to collect these fees or taxes in the future.

Federal and State Grants

Federal and State grant programs provide valuable funding, which in many instances is essential to 911 project feasibility. The federal government provides several funding sources, such as FEMA grants, Homeland Security grants, and Rural Domestic Violence and Child Victimization Enforcement Discretionary grants that can be applied to 911 system improvement projects. In 2004, President Bush signed into law a federal grants program to establish a national coordination center and provide funding for 911 system improvements.

State government often plays an important role in local improvement efforts, and many states also offer local government grants for 911 enhancement efforts. Where state government performance standards for PSAPs have been established, these would likely form the foundation for local 911 enhancement and funding efforts. For example, the State of Minnesota provides financial assistance to local government 911 efforts with the aid of a monthly 911 fee assessed statewide to all wired and wireless telephones, but also requires that local jurisdictions have a plan for E 911 service.

Operating Issues

Some 911 facility improvements have somewhat limited useful lives. Computer-related components such as workstations and computer software replacement may reach functional obsolescence within six to ten years. Equipment such as mobile and handheld radios have even shorter useful lives. Fee revenues not only provide a needed source of 911 capital financing, but are more suitable methods of funding these rapidly depreciating, short-lived asset classes.

A 911 system expansion is likely to result in substantial operating cost increases. To the extent that fire, police, and EMS departments can consolidate their emergency response operations, some cost savings can be achieved, but finance officers should expect increased operating costs and pay attention to the following areas.

Personnel

The professional call takers, dispatchers, and line supervision are at the heart of the 911 operation and their compensation generally reflects the importance of these positions. The average cost to train an employee can exceed $50,000.[8] In addition, substantial regular training to keep abreast of recent technological changes in the field is required and often occurs every two years. Dispatchers and call taker positions also tend to incur turnover rates well above the average of other similar telecommunications positions due to the inherent high stress levels associated with these positions.[9] Turnover rates can directly affect operating cost as each resignation and hire triggers a new recruitment and training expense.

Phone System Support Services

Jurisdiction PSAPs often contract with a telephone company to provide equipment and maintenance services critical to reliable system operation. These include the necessary "customer premise" equipment to support proper routing of phone calls to the correct PSAP. The telephone company could also lease the necessary 911 trunk lines and address location information (ALI) and provide network support for automated caller phone number and location information.

These services may be charged through a fee per telephone number in the database, fee per call, a base fee plus charge per call, or a fee per data base access. In total, costs may exceed $500,000 for larger systems.

Radio System Maintenance, Repair, and Upgrade

The quality and extent of deployment of radio units in the field is a major determinant of emergency response. As the tragedy of the September 11 terrorist attacks clearly demonstrated, clear communication with first responders throughout the emergency response period is vital. This means a substantial and continuing investment in the both mobile and portable units. These are sophisticated units requiring periodic maintenance, reprogramming, and testing by qualified technicians. At the other end of the responder communication, the dispatchers' computer consoles must operate in a flawless manner in a 24/7 environment. This may mean a short replacement cycle for these units, further increasing costs.

Dispatching and Related Software Support

Most local governments own their own 911 dispatching hardware/software system. Once a CAD system has been successfully installed, it must be periodically maintained and enhanced. This could involve a series of minor CAD enhancements as well as full system upgrades every two to three years. Depending on the complexity of the CAD system, such full software upgrades can easily exceed $100,000 to $200,000 for smaller jurisdictions or millions of dollars for large systems. As is true for the radio subsystem, joint development and use of a dispatch system by affiliated public safety departments within the same jurisdiction or among neighboring jurisdictions can result in substantial economies of scale and savings if competing user needs can be accommodated.

Building Operation, Maintenance, and Overhead

As the center of emergency response, building security is normally one of the highest priorities for a 911 emergency response center. This adds not only to the cost of construction, but also ongoing security-related operating costs, such as additional security personnel, surveillance cameras, and extra lighting. Because of the need for an uninterruptible power supply, generators large enough to handle the entire building must be regularly inspected and serviced. Some jurisdictions even provide a backup facility in case the primary facility is made inoperable by storm or other disaster.

While having less of an ongoing cost impact than the above, equipment at the 911 emergency response center must meet extraordinary performance standards. To promote peak performance, the workstations, HVAC controls, lighting, and other building features must all operate at levels far beyond that of a normal office setting. Maintenance and repair standards must also be higher for 911 centers. Equipment failures could interrupt 911 functionality and increase response times, so maintenance and repair of 911 facilities should be given high priority.

Conclusion

Over the past decade, local governments have made substantial advances in their emergency response capabilities. It could be argued that these advances have contributed in some way to the nationwide decline in crime rates. With the reality of terrorist threats, the ever-expanding use of wireless phones, and continuing telecommunications advances, local governments will be further challenged to meet increasing demands for a timely and effective response to emergency calls. Projects designed to expand or enhance existing 911 systems are among the most technically, organizationally, and financially difficult system improvement efforts. While challenging, the finance officer must be aware of the unique system requirements and features to properly plan for and finance these essential facilities.

Management Audit by the City of Milwaukee, Wisconsin

In 2003-2004, the City of Milwaukee Comptroller's Office performed a management audit of the implementation of a joint police district station - data communications center building and related facilities on the city's northwest side. The audit covered design and construction processes, budgeting for the project, and ongoing project monitoring and reporting and examined both the building and internal components of the facility including the dispatching, data communications, and related IT aspects of the project. The central problem identified was a massive project cost overrun. A project begun as a $21 million effort ultimately totaled over $64 million upon completion.

The major underlying problem was uncontrolled expansion of project scope, including the addition of offsite facilities, a parking ramp, and other additions. Little was done to control scope or monitor and report costs and progress. Also, a joint police-fire dispatching system was originally envisioned, but was replaced by separate police and fire dispatching systems, adding millions of dollars to project costs. The complete audit also examined the details of the dispatch system planning, design, and implementation effort, as well as certain aspects of the supporting radio system upgrade.

Source: A summary of the audit can be found in Michael Daun, "Managing Major Capital Projects: Lessons Learned from Milwaukee's 3rd District Police Station and Data Communications Center," *Government Finance Review* 20, no. 3 (June 2004): 33-38.

Notes

1. National Emergency Number Association, "The Development of 911" (April 2006), http://www.nena.org.

2. Unfortunately, many EU countries complied with the 112 requirement, only to retain their previously established emergency number. For example, Spain retains its 532 emergency number as well as 112.

3. The list of top tier CAD firms was identified in *Dispatch Monthly* accessed at http://www.911dispatch.com. Top tier CAD firms are: GEAC Public Safety, Intergraph Public Safety, Logistic Systems Inc., Motorola, NewWorld Systems, Northrop-Grumman Corp., Positron Public Safety Systems, Public Safety Systems, Inc., Spollman Technologies Inc., Sungard THE/OSSI Tiburon, Inc., TriTech Software Systems, and VisionAIR. *Dispatch Monthly* also offers a book covering all aspects of CAD system development.

4. These Association of Public Communications Officers standards are aimed at four objectives: interoperability, adaptability to a variety of conventional and trunked systems, ability to migrate smoothly from existing to next generation radios, and efficient use of limited radio spectra.

5. See www.safecomprogram.gov.

6. In research for this chapter, the author could not find any examples of federal enforcement of FCC standards.

7. U.S. Department of Justice, "ADA Homepage," http://www.ada.gov.

8. *Dispatch Monthly* (January 2004).

9. Based on many interviews and experience with multiple local jurisdictions.

| 8 |

Fire/EMS Stations

By Allan M. Carmody and Michael J. Mucha

The first volunteer fire company was formed in Philadelphia in the 1730s, and the first full-time paid fire fighters appeared in the workforce in 1850. Over time, fire fighting agencies expanded and began responding to hazardous material (hazmat) calls and providing emergency medical services. With these changes, today's facilities are far advanced from those of earlier times. Even with advances in fire fighting technology, fire still kills more Americans than all other natural disasters combined and causes losses in excess of $10 billion each year.[1]

Most local governments either provide fire/EMS together or as separate departments using separate facilities. In 2005, there were 48,500 fire/EMS stations across the United States that responded to over 23 million calls.[2] Over the last ten years, the number of fire calls decreased by 18 percent, but calls for medial aid increased by 53 percent, Hazmat calls increased by 47 percent, and mutual aid calls increased by 77 percent. Exhibit 8.1 shows the number of calls across the United States, broken down by type for 1995 and 2005.

| Description of Fire/EMS Facilities |

Fire/EMS stations contain space for personnel and equipment to meet basic structural fire and advanced life support emergency medical service needs on a 24/7 basis. Depending on specific services provided, additional unique features may be required, but most facilities have many common characteristics.

Apparatus Bays/Storage Areas

Typical fire/EMS facilities house fire engines and ambulances along with the necessary equipment to respond to calls. Apparatus bays used to store fire equipment should be at least 50 to 60 feet deep and 18 feet high to accommodate the larger modern fire equipment, and doors may need to be up to 14 feet by 14 feet to fit

Exhibit 8.1 Number of Fire/EMS Calls in 1995 and 2005

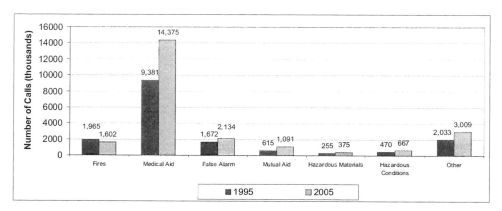

Source: National Fire Protection Association, "Fire Statistics: The US Fire Service," http://www.nfpa.org.

some equipment.[3] Drive-through bays make parking equipment easier and avoid backing up fire equipment. Special rescue and hazmat units pose more challenges for facility design and may require specialized facilities due to their size. In addition, the bays should include a hose drying tower or area and decontamination facilities such as sinks, showers, and counters. Fire departments also have very intense and rather large equipment needs, such as turnout gear, air bottles, and fire hoses, all of which must be kept in good working order. Readily available back-up equipment is also important to have, and thus storage areas must also be included.

Living Areas

While men have historically dominated the fire and rescue profession, many women have entered the profession. A facility may need to accommodate separate or special sleeping, restroom, and shower spaces for male and female occupants. Since fire/EMS personnel typically work long shifts and "live" in the station, a fully equipped kitchen should be included. Furniture and equipment budgets commonly include items to provide for comfortable living conditions such as televisions, fitness equipment, dressers, bedding, and other household items. Areas should also include quiet private spaces and workspace for administrative functions. Design should also consider the impact of a combined paid/volunteer work force, if necessary. Understanding the needs of differing work shifts and equipment ownership and care can dictate design decisions.

Support Features

Modern fire stations have special building systems intended to minimize response times and mitigate occupational hazards. For example, complex alarming systems notify fire personnel, EMS staff, or special rescue units of a call. Other systems include electronic control sequences that automatically turn on lights in certain sleeping quarters and apparatus bays while also opening overhead bay doors. Systems may also extend beyond property limits. For example, traffic signals near the facility can be controlled and force a green light to allow movement through an intersection. Many of these systems allow quicker response times and help achieve the best levels of service for protecting life and property.

Communications networks for voice and data are vital components of an efficient fire and emergency operations system. Both emergency and administrative communications must be addressed in facility design. Options include land lines, wireless devices and networks, Internet service providers and different radio frequencies. It is important to communicate in the field during emergencies with police and emergency responders from surrounding jurisdictions. It is also important to connect remote facilities to the government's support services information network for administrative functions such as procurement, human resources, payroll, and financial activities.

Training Facilities

Fire and EMS services require various physical training exercises for tactical and special rescue situations and space for training activities should also be considered in facility design. It is also important that members of the fire and life safety occupation remain physically fit and in the best of health. Fire/EMS stations often include workout space and fitness equipment within the building so staff can maintain fitness for the rigors of the job, thus reducing risks that are inherent in this work environment.

Additional Features

Modern fire/EMS stations include features to mitigate the risks of occupational hazards. Vehicle exhaust poses health threats to building occupants and many facilities have exhaust systems that vent fumes out of the building. Equipment cleaning and repair facilities may also be included in the fire station as it is necessary to keep the tools used by the occupants in good repair.

Some jurisdictions choose to install fuel pumps and fuel storage tanks for the refueling of equipment, vehicles, and large apparatus. Underground fuel storage tanks pose environmental hazards and because of this, many regulations exist for their use. Alternatively, agreements with nearby gas stations may prove more beneficial and proximity to services should be considered in location decisions.

Equipment

Depending on how a project budget is developed, certain one-time equipment expenses may be included. These items would include large items such as the fire and rescue apparatus, or less expensive items such as protective fire clothing and air tanks. Equipment costs must be considered and funded either in the capital improvement budget or the operating budget. Each of these items has a useful life and thus requires replacement in the future. Finance officials should consider such facts and develop plans that allow for replacement funding. Exhibit 8.2 shows the approximate costs and useful lives for common fire and rescue equipment.

Exhibit 8.2 Fire and Rescue Apparatus

Vehicle	Equipped Cost	Useful Life
Aerial ladder	$850,000 - $950,000	100,000 miles/ 15-20 years
Fire engine	$465,000 - $530,000	100,000 miles/ 10-15 years
Tanker	$245,000 - $375,000	100,000 miles
Brush truck	$ 60,000 - $ 75,000	100,000 miles
Ambulance (type 1, medium duty)	$180,000 - $230,000	350,000 miles/ 7-10 years
Hazmat truck	$485,000 - $600,000	100,000 miles
Scuba rescue	$160,000 - $210,000	100,000 miles
Command van	$450,000 - $650,000	100,000 miles
Note: Costs and useful life may vary.		

Source: Chesterfield County, Virginia

Needs Assessment: Planning for Fire/EMS Facilities

The modern fire/EMS station needs to be able to respond to a variety of emergencies. The fire, hazardous material, and medical risks to a community vary greatly based on the built environment, geographical and natural features of the area, demographics, and population densities. For example, urban areas will have many different needs than rural areas, industrial areas will be different than commercial or residential areas, and areas with lakes, rivers, or mountains may require unique equipment and specially trained personnel. Additionally, in an aging community, the need for emergency medical services might be greater than in a community with a younger profile. Such risks may not be constant over time and should be periodically reevaluated.

Master Planning

Each community stands to protect against different degrees of loss of life and property. The U.S. Fire Administration has long supported master planning that involves fire personnel to work closely with planners, engineers, and finance personnel to create a plan for providing fire, EMS, hazardous material, and disaster services for the community. As fire departments and EMS service providers respond to an increasing number of calls, careful planning is essential to provide quality fire/EMS services. Strategic planning for fire services has resulted in long-range approaches to improve response times, station design, and equipment along with new strategies for responding to medical emergencies, hazardous conditions, and potential terrorist attacks. Master planning with respect to fire/EMS services should include considerations for planning for station location, reducing response times, community growth, plans for aging facilities, access to water, response to natural disasters, and potential redistricting and multi-jurisdictional agreements. Any capital needs should be addressed in the jurisdiction's overall capital improvement program.

Station Location

One of the most important factors in preventing extensive property damage from fire is the ability of the firefighters to respond and get to the scene quickly. Locating fire/EMS facilities appropriately can significantly reduce response times and increase the level of fire protection services. The Insurance Services Office (ISO), a leading source of information on property and liability risk, established the standard that developed areas should have an engine company within 1.5 road miles and a ladder company within 2.5 miles road miles. Shorter distances may be appropriate for urban areas and longer distances for rural areas based on different travel speeds. Currently an estimated 60 to 75 percent of communities do not have enough fire stations to meet ISO guidelines.[4]

Response Time

To comply with National Fire Protection Association (NFPA) requirements, 90 percent of responses by the initial arriving company should be within six minutes, which includes one minute for the dispatcher to handle the call, one minute for firefighters and EMS personnel to ready equipment, and four minutes to drive. The RAND Corporation, in its extensive studies of fire department responses, developed the formula in Exhibit 8.3 to calculate response times, which is based on the assumption that equipment will travel at 35 miles per hour.[5] Continued testing and evaluation shows that the formula is accurate for distances between .5 miles and 8 miles. Proper location of fire/EMS facilities is extremely important to guarantee required response times. Regardless of the distance, firefighters should not attempt to respond at speeds that are beyond a safe level. Currently, 17 percent of on-duty firefighter fatalities occur responding to calls.[6]

The fire/EMS facility should be placed with a strategic focus to minimize response times within its service area. Convenient locations near major north-south/east-west arterial roads will maximize response coverage areas.

Exhibit 8.3 Response Time Calculations

> **Response time in minutes = .65 * 1.7 (Distance in miles)**
>
> Using the location guide stated previously and the formula, a 1.5 mile distance would result in an expected driving time of 3.2 minutes and a 2.5 mile distance of 4.9 minutes.

Source: Insurance Services Office response time considerations, http://www.isomitigation.com/ppc/3000/ppc3015.html.

To accommodate future expansion opportunities, it is important to consider many options when building new facilities. Acquiring oversized land parcels, for example, can position a site for a phased development over time. When selecting a site, long-range land development plans should be considered, as fire and emergency response facilities typically have a long useful life and would need to respond to the changing community. It is important to know the build-out potential of the area being served so that a site can accommodate long-range projected service demands. Selecting a site that allows for facility expansion is an acceptable alternative to initially building a facility to meet projected service levels in the future.

Community Growth

As communities expand, the demand for fire protection services also expands. Community growth must be met with additional fire stations, equipment, and fire fighters. In a survey of fire chiefs, 50 percent said growth occurred in areas that still needed additional fire stations.[7] It is common to find departments renovating stations after ten to fifteen years of service because growth and development in the area have outpaced what the station was designed to handle. Fire/EMS facilities need to be a part of planning efforts so that necessary service levels are maintained.

Expanding Existing Facilities

Approximately 32 percent of fire stations are over 40 years old.[8] Many older facilities do not include modern features and may no longer serve the community's needs. These facilities were often built with open sleeping areas that did not separate male and female firefighters and without many of the amenities that are common in newer facilities. Renovating or expanding old facilities may be an attractive short-term solution to building new facilities. Short-term improvements could include emergency power capabilities, on-site fuel tanks, vehicle exhaust systems, structural reinforcements, painting, and other critical improvements that will extend the facilities' life. Other improvements such as renovating living areas, training facilities, and apparatus bays may also be necessary. Some renovations may not be possible, however. For example, older facilities may not have enough existing floor to ceiling space to accommodate modern heating and cooling systems. With all renovations, the jurisdiction must decide if it will continue to occupy the station during renovation. Most often, any substantial renovations force the station to close temporarily. Firefighters must then be re-allocated to other stations or temporary facilities must be set up, and the jurisdiction must also find storage space for equipment.

Access to Water

Access to a reliable water supply is important when assessing the level of fire protection services within a community. To meet minimum requirements, the water system must be capable of providing 250 gallons per minute for two hours, although specific buildings may require flows of up to 12,000 gallons per minute depending on the type and location.[9] Planning for water infrastructure should consider any fire protection needs. If minimum water flow is not available, other alternative methods may be used including hose-relays, hauled water using tankers, and dry hydrants. A dry hydrant has piping that extends into a body of water from dry land and is used by connecting a fire engine that pumps water out of the lake or river. Dry hydrants are not pressurized and are relatively inexpensive. If water is supplied through a tanker, the water must be available within five minutes of the first responder arriving at the scene.[10] Jurisdictions prone to droughts may need special certification to ensure that water supply will be available.

Response to Natural Disasters

Fire/EMS facilities are also a potential location for an overall emergency operations command centers. While a fire station may not be the primary location for such an operation, redundant or secondary locations may prove useful in large scale incidents. Fire stations are useful as supporting hubs in a centralized emergency response strategy. The Federal Emergency Management Agency requires that essential facilities such as fire/EMS and police facilities be located out of flood plains. Additionally, facilities in earthquake prone areas are now being constructed to withstand quakes and existing facilities are given seismic upgrading. Back-up power supplied by on-site generators is also important in keeping the facility operational during disasters. Site and facility design must address the location and size of generator to serve the necessary systems.

When facilities serve multiple purposes, the requirements for each of those alternate uses must be evaluated for the impact on project scope and thus financing needs. Many localities have emergency preparedness plans that describe the activation of either command centers or emergency operations centers. Such facilities must accommodate many people from various functional areas assigned to incident management tasks, usually for prolonged periods of time. Support services are vital to an operations success in such circumstances that may last days, weeks, or even longer as seen in large disaster incidents.

Redistricting

Adding a new facility also requires a system-wide evaluation that considers existing service-level gaps, projected needs based on growth patterns, replacement facilities, and the benefits of planned road improvements that may provide shorter response times when the road infrastructure is completed. New facilities can be placed to reduce overburdened existing call loading while also serving newer and growing developments. The task of locating facilities requires that existing facility service boundaries are analyzed and most likely reconfigured. Locating facilities in areas that serve newer and planned development will minimize the reconfiguration efforts, but anytime a new facility is added, the entire system should be analyzed.

Multi-Jurisdictional Agreements

Two different types of interjurisdictional agreements are often used to compensate for deficiencies within a jurisdiction's fire protection capabilities. With automatic aid, assistance is dispatched automatically by a contractual agreement between two jurisdictions. Aid is provided 24 hours a day, 365 days a year, just as if the responding unit was part of the jurisdiction's fire department.[11] Automatic aid is used to offset service not provided by a jurisdiction's own department. For example, if one jurisdiction does not have hazmat capabilities, any hazmat call would automatically dispatch a hazmat team from the other jurisdiction through the contractual agreement. With mutual response agreements, jurisdictions agree to respond to emergencies across jurisdictional borders if neighboring jurisdictions need additional resources. An example of mutual aid is when neighboring jurisdictions respond to help with large fires or emergencies. In some cases, a fee may be paid to the jurisdiction providing the service, especially if there are not opportunities for a reciprocal return of service.

When planning facilities that serve a jurisdiction's borders, location decisions should consider the current and planned needs of the coverage area, including the area outside of one's own jurisdictional boundaries. This information should be evaluated in context with the terms of such agreements that specify each bordering jurisdiction's response requirements.

Co-Locating Facilities

Co-location with other uses is also something that should be considered in the planning stage. Economies of scale can reduce costs, particularly in the land acquisition and land development activities. Police operations may be a compatible use to co-locate with fire and EMS facilities as both are 24/7 operations, both have similar support service needs in the way of fueling, and periodic in-service training and physical fitness requirements. On the other hand, finding a location that best serves both operations' demand for service and response time goals may prove challenging. Fire and EMS demands may not coincide with ideal locations to be in proximity with police service areas.

Alternate Uses

When programming a facility, it often makes sense to include alternate uses within the structure. Public meeting spaces or using the facility as a polling location are both common uses for fire/EMS facilities. Other infrequent uses can also be accommodated with little interruption to the primary function of the facility. Such alternative uses should not be primary considerations in the design, but should be given serious consideration when evaluating overall community needs and not be afterthoughts, which can prove costly to incorporate. If a facility is also used as a voting precinct, the facility will need to comply with regulations, such as the voting act standards for facilities, not normally required for the fire station's primary use. Other uses may have additional impacts on land requirements or facility access.

Development Standards/Best Practices

Fire/EMS facilities and services are subject to many regulations and standards to ensure the safety of firefighters and the public. Before work on any new facility, the jurisdiction should consult with individuals with advanced knowledge of this industry's unique requirements.

Public Protection Classification

The Public Protection Classification (PPC), developed by ISO, provides information on local fire-protection services throughout the country for insurance companies, fire departments, insurance regulators, and others to evaluate risk. Studies have shown that excellent fire coverage and low fire losses are related. Insurance companies generally offer lower premiums to communities with better protection. To classify fire protection levels, the PPC uses a 10-point scale with 1 representing excellent protection and 10 indicating the fire program fails to meet minimum requirements. In 2006, only 46 fire districts, or 0.1 percent of the total evaluated, received the top protection classification. Exhibit 8.4 shows the number of fire departments at each level of the PPC rating scale. Ratings use recognized standards developed by the National Fire Protection Association (NFPA) and the American Water Works Association (AWWA), and depend on fire alarm and communications systems, the water supply system, and the equipment, staffing, training, and location of fire departments.[12] Communication systems are covered in chapter 7 and the water infrastructure in chapter 11.

Exhibit 8.4 Number of Fire Departments at Each Level of the PPC Rating Scale

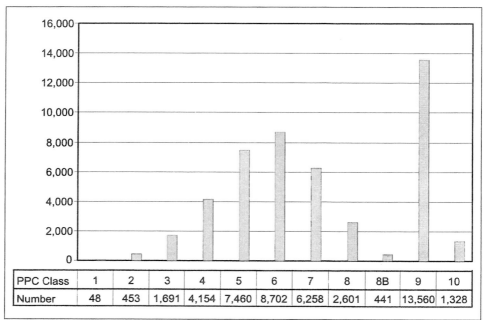

PPC Class	1	2	3	4	5	6	7	8	8B	9	10
Number	48	453	1,691	4,154	7,460	8,702	6,258	2,601	441	13,560	1,328

Source: Insurance Services Office, "Facts and Figures about PPC Codes Around the Country, http://www.isomitigation.com/ppc.

National Fire Protection Association

The NFPA works to develop and publish an extensive list of codes and standards that attempt to minimize fire risk and develop best practice requirements for fire protection services. Virtually every building, process, service, design, and installation in society today is affected by NFPA documents.

NFPA Standards #1710 and #1720 contain requirements for organization and deployment of fire operations, EMS operations, and special operations for all fire departments, including standards for response times, managing resources, training, communications, and pre-incident planning. The requirement addresses the strategic issues involved with locating fire companies and facilities.

Other Regulatory Standards

Equipment and safety regulations such as those issued by the Occupational Safety and Health Administration (OSHA) also play a large role in the fire/EMS industry. Some states also administer their own occupational safety office and set specific requirements in addition to OSHA standards. The useful life of equipment such as breathing apparatus and other dispensable supplies such as medicines are all governed by established standards. State and local design codes will dictate facility construction standards and vary based on the importance and thus classification of the building. EMS services also must comply with Health Insurance Portability and Accountability Act of 1996 (HIPAA) to maintain confidentiality of patient information and may have to set up secure storage space for such records.[13]

Design

Fire station projects are prime candidates for using a standard, or prototype design for multiple locations after adapting them to the specific parcel characteristics. Most jurisdictions will need more than one fire station and there are many development and operational advantages to having the same facility layout. Prototype designs can reduce design times by nearly one-half and can provide some savings in design costs. From an operational advantage, similar floor plans offer a familiar circulation pattern, thus minimizing response times for personnel that may move between facilities. This familiarity should also be apparent in the operating and maintenance costs of the facility, making for a more predictable operating budget. This approach can also save money through reduced maintenance costs for common replacement parts, service contracts, and so forth used for all stations. From a public safety service perspective, similar design layouts can provide more consistent locations for important equipment and supplies.

Financing Fire/EMS Facilities

Property tax levies remain the most common and appropriate funding source for fire/EMS services and for fire/EMS capital projects. Some general purpose local government jurisdictions contain fire/EMS departments and collect taxes as part of a general levy. Others have established separate fire/EMS districts that levy taxes on their own. If property tax rates must increase to fund a new facility, the increase may be subject to a voter referendum. Some jurisdictions, however, use impact fees and volunteer fire departments commonly are able to collect donations to offset part of the capital cost of fire/EMS facilities.

Impact Fees

Impact fees may provide funding for fire/EMS feasibilities in growing communities. With impact fees, developers of residential or commercial property generally pay a calculated price that attempts to estimate the costs of providing fire and EMS services to the growth area. Impact fees, in theory, allow additional stations to be developed with pay-as-you-go financing and without burdening existing taxpayers.

Donations

Occasionally, smaller jurisdictions, typically with volunteer fire departments, are able to raise funding for capital projects through fundraisers and donations. Most volunteer-initiated donations programs pertain to small capital items in the project such as fitness equipment, TVs, or furniture. With donation fundraising programs, it is important to keep the program from being overly restrictive so that use for the funding can be changed later on in the project if scope changes are necessary.

Operating Issues

Operating costs represent a large portion of total life cycle costs at most fire/EMS stations. Finance officers must work with the fire department and the department responsible for ongoing facility maintenance to develop operating cost estimates. To lower costs, fire stations are designed for functionality and to minimize maintenance costs. Using maintenance-free materials, such as aluminum doors instead of painted doors, may be more expensive initially, but should save on operating expenses over time. One important area to note is training of new firefighters. It is not unusual for firefighters to be hired four to six months in advance of the project completion in order to complete all necessary training.

Equipment Distribution

Equipment rotation and distribution is important to its operational effectiveness and lifespan. Equipment in the later years of its life cycle can be relocated to stations with lighter call loading as part of a system-wide replacement plan. Doing so will allow the timing for replacement to be extended while not exceeding useful life or mileage limitations. Caution should be taken to avoid pushing vehicles far beyond their useful life as maintenance and repair becomes less cost effective and thus could impact response rates when an apparatus is out of service for prolonged time periods.

Conclusion

Fire stations are just one of the many public facilities that governments build and operate. Often with issues concerning public safety, public participation is essential on all aspects of defining service-level goals. It is also important that the finance officer play a role on any committees that are formed to understand costs and determine proper financing strategies. The finance officer can also play an important role in effectively communicating the desired service level's impact on the operating and capital budgets and working to develop a fire/EMS station and program that the community will support.

Notes

1. U.S. Fire Administration, "QuickStats," http://www.usfa.dhs.gov/statistics/ quickstats.

2. National Fire Protection Association, "Fire Statistics: The US Fire Service," http:// www.nfpa.org.

3. Dennis Ross, "Bay of Rigs," *Fire Chief* (November 2005).

4. Insurance Services Office, *Effective Fire Protection: A National Concern* (2004).

5. Average speed of 35 miles per hour is with the siren on in normal traffic and weather, and slowing down for intersections.

6. Insurance Services Office Mitigation Guide, http://www.isomitigation.com/ppc/ 3000/ppc3015.html.

7. Federal Emergency Management Agency, NFPA, *A Needs Assessment of the U.S. Fire Service* (December 2002).

8. Ibid.

9. Insurance Services Office, Water Supply Evaluations, http://www.isomitigation.com/ ppc.

10. Based on Insurance Services Office standard.

11. Insurance Services Office, *Automatic Aid,* http://www.isomitigation.com/ppc.

12. Insurance Services Office *ISO's PPC Program* (2001).

13. More information on HIPAA can be found on the Web site for the U.S Department of Health and Human Services, http://www.hhs.gov/ocr/hipaa/.

9

Correctional Facilities and Jails

By James C. Willett

From the first recorded single occupant cells at Auburn Prison in New York in 1816, to the modern correctional facilities utilizing direct supervision and interaction with inmates that are common today, the corrections profession in the United States has changed greatly. Over the past century, there have been four significant changes in correctional thinking: the progressive era, the medical model, the community model, and the crime control model, as shown in Exhibit 9.1. The crime control model, which is currently the dominant model, helped create the idea of the regional, multi-jurisdictional jail, but has significantly increased the number of incarcerations, forcing many local government-run jails to reevaluate their thinking on the regional jail system.

Exhibit 9.1 Dominant Correctional Strategies in the Twentieth Century

Dominant Strategy	General Period	Defining Characteristic
Progressive era	1890s to 1930s	• Introduction of probation, indeterminate sentencing, and parole • Creation of the juvenile court
Medical model	1930s to 1960s	• Treat crime as a disease • Attempt to identify psychological, social, or biological deficiencies
Community model	1960s to 1980s	• Reject rehabilitation and indeterminate sentencing in favor of punishing the offense, not the person
Crime control model	1980s to present	• Strict supervision, increased conservatism • Resulted in a large increase in incarcerations

Jail governance structures are also much different than before. Private sector operation of jails is not uncommon and the concept of regional jails also offers the possibility of joining with other jurisdictions to provide jail facilities or paying another jurisdiction to house inmates. This chapter assumes that the construction of a new facility or expansion of an existing facility is necessary, but jurisdictions should also fully consider any potential alternative arrangements with other jurisdictions for their jail needs.

> **Authorizing Statutes**
>
> State laws provide an authorizing statute to build, operate, and maintain a jail. Authorizing legislation is extremely important, as it codifies what is allowed in the operation of a jail. In a regional system, it permits resource sharing across jurisdictional lines, and authorizes the creation of a jail authority to oversee operations, both essential components of a regional jail. Each state may have different authorizing statutes, which may lead to differing organizational and operational requirements for the facility.

Jail Facilities

All jail facilities, large or small, urban or rural, contain housing or living areas for prisoners. These areas may be comprised of single- or multiple-occupancy cells, as well as open dormitory-style areas. New committals are processed through an intake or receiving area. In addition, many modern jails include a drug abuse center, doctor's office, pharmacy, library, kitchen, learning/skill center, laundry area, and administrative spaces all in one facility. Most will also contain some type of medical infirmary used to treat inmates for routine as well as serious illnesses.

Newer facilities contain many electronic and integrated systems, which may include video imaging systems for booking, tracking and release of inmates, computer network systems, and electronic locks, operated by a central control center. This area generally controls access to all areas of the jail via cameras and intercoms. In some facilities, it is impossible for a person to enter or move throughout the facility without the knowledge of the officer in central control.

Locating other government offices in the jail facility may be cost effective for the jurisdiction involved. Court buildings and a magistrate's office are two of the many non-correctional uses that may share the facility.

Court Buildings

Because a jail will house offenders that have ongoing court cases, locating court buildings near or at the same location as correctional facilities has operational advantages, allowing for efficient transportation of inmates to and from court.

Magistrate's Office

In many states, the magistrate's office provides an "independent and unbiased" review of complaints brought to the office by police officers, sheriffs, deputies, and citizens. Magistrates are not police officers, nor are they in any way connected with law enforcement. Instead, magistrates are officers who serve as a buffer between law enforcement and society. Most magistrates are not lawyers, but are specially trained to issue search warrants, subpoenas, arrest warrants, summonses, and set bail. In addition, magistrates may assist the public by providing information on the judicial system processes and procedures.[1] For this reason, many new jail facilities include space for the magistrate's office. This allows convenient access for law-enforcement, the courts, and the community.

Needs Assessment: Planning for Jail Facilities

To plan for a correctional facility, jurisdictions should assemble a team composed of corrections staff, sheriff's office representatives, the district attorney, the public defenders office, court representatives, elected officials, citizen groups, and finance staff to complete a community-based corrections plan (C-BCP) and planning study. The C-BCP and planning study will present an overview of the existing and future population of the jail's service area, provide information on state-mandated jail programs, and contain an analysis of trends within the criminal justice system, historical crime rates, arrests, bookings, and average length of stay. The planning study details specific requirements for the facility, including the most appropriate design, staffing needs, and operating budget of the facility. Throughout the entire process, professional consultants should be used whenever required on-staff expertise does not exist. Essential to effective planning for jail facilities is developing responses or recommendations to the following questions:

◆ How many inmates must the jail accommodate?

◆ What type of inmates will be housed in the jail?

◆ How will inmates be supervised?

◆ What are the staffing needs?

◆ How will the jail impact the community?

◆ What other facilities will link to the jail?

◆ What are the long-term needs for jail facilities?

◆ What are the applicable standards that will guide jail design, management, and operation?

◆ How much will the facility cost?

Inmate Projections

Projecting inmate populations is essential to determine the overall project scale. Additionally the total number of inmates drives facility costs more than any other factor.[2] When considering future needs, it is important to look at past records on the number of bookings. Yearly bookings as well as average sentence length can form the base for projected inmate populations. Other factors to consider are growth trends in the overall citizen population, economic indicators, and changes in laws that may have implications on prison populations, such as minimum sentencing laws. When considering overall citizen population growth, it is important to identify demographic trends, such as age and income level. Additionally, the jurisdiction needs to pay attention to any trends that may influence the number of inmates that receive alternatives to standard incarceration, such as work release, home arrest, or the use of halfway houses.

With any inmate population projection, it is important to differentiate between pre-trial inmates and those serving out sentences, as each requires slightly different facilities. Pre-trial inmates may need additional space to consult with attorneys and will need transportation to and from court during trial. Along with this distinction, jail facilities must also be designed to handle many different types of offenders.

Type of Inmates

Jail facilities often house inmates sentenced for a variety of crimes. One of the essential priorities of a jail facility is to protect the inmates' safety. To accomplish this, it is necessary to separate inmates depending on the seriousness their crimes. For example, jail facilities separate male inmates from female inmates and adults from juveniles. In addition, Exhibit 9.2 shows potential other classifications that may be used to separate inmates.

Exhibit 9.2 Potential Inmate Classifications

• Prior arrest history	• Inmates requiring medical assistance
• Prior incarcerations	• Inmates with health problems
• Violent offenders	• Inmates with a history of medical health problems
• Drug offenders	
• Alcohol offenders	• Disabled inmates
• Sex predators	• Inmates with known enemies

Jail Design

The jail administrators will need to coordinate with the architect to determine the design elements for the facility, including the type of structure, future expansion options, and the needs of the agencies involved. Questions relating to the type of inmate supervision will enable the architects to produce a well thought out and usable design. Individuals involved in the jail design need to be familiar with the construction requirements set forth by the American Correctional Association (ACA), applicable state standards, building codes, and the requirements mandated by the Americans with Disabilities Act (ADA).

Jail design can benefit from the experience of planning team members. Sheriff's officers can suggest design elements from their knowledge of jail management and operation. Judges and magistrates can assist with views on video arrangement and prisoner transportation issues. Professional consultants should be used at this stage for input on best practices, industry standards, or state-of-the art design elements that should be included. The architectural firm's responsibility is to review all the suggestions and produce a design that is functional, cost-effective, and visually appealing.

The three predominant design configurations of jail construction used today are listed below. The impact of each design on jail operations should be evaluated during the planning process.

- ◆ **Direct Supervision.** A direct supervision environment places an officer in the housing pod among the inmates with unfettered access and sightlines to all areas of the pod. Inmates are generally out of their cells or bunk areas for the majority of the day and are able to approach the officer. Direct supervision has grown in popularity over the last twenty years and a majority of new correctional construction incorporates some form of direct supervision design.

- ◆ **Indirect Supervision.** An indirect supervision environment separates the officer from the housing pod with a barrier, such as an enclosed control booth. The officer has sightlines into the pod, but is required to move through a series of security doors to enter the actual pod. Many correctional facilities will offer a mixture of direct and indirect supervision pods, depending on the level of security required.

- ◆ **Linear.** A linear design organizes cells in rows and officers then check on inmates during roving patrols. The linear approach offers the least amount of contact between officers and inmates. This type of construction was most popular during the first half of the twentieth century, and many famous institutions, such as Alcatraz, used this design type.

Staffing Requirements

Along with the number of potential inmates, jurisdictions need to estimate the staff required for supervision. Often staffing levels are determined, at least in part, by jail design. The American Correctional Association has produced national standards that dictate that facilities operate with sufficient staff needed to oversee inmates. For example, one such standard states: "A comprehensive staffing analysis is [to be] conducted annually. The staffing analysis is used to determine staffing needs and plans. Relief factors are calculated for each classification of staff that is assigned to relieved posts or positions. Essential posts and positions, as determined in the staffing plan, are consistently filled with qualified personnel." In addition, many states also offer either guidelines or mandates relating to staff to inmate ratios.

Access to the Facility

Examining public access to a jail provides another essential component of the criminal justice system. American Correctional Association standards mandate a public lobby and other public spaces, and dictate that all spaces accessible by the public meet ADA requirements. The U.S. Department of Justice provides information on the ADA, including requirements for ground and floor surfaces, parking and passenger loading zones, curb ramps, stairs, elevators, platform lifts (wheelchair lifts), windows, doors, entrances, drinking fountains, restroom facilities, bathing facilities, and other amenities.

Jail facilities should also be designed and located to accommodate the many linkages with other aspects of the criminal justice system such as courts, law enforcement, and legal representation. A jail's location is an important decision that is likely to generate a lot of public attention. Along with standard site selection issues common for most capital projects, such as availability of land, access to utilities and other infrastructure, and acquiring necessary zoning changes, traditionally, new jail construction has been hampered by the "not in my backyard" mentality. Despite overall public support, any areas near the chosen site may present problems.

Future Expansion/Satellite Locations

Once constructed, jail facilities are expected to remain operational for an extended period of time, but may need to be expanded if inmate populations grow above projected numbers. Many localities, especially in urban areas, have physical limitations in terms of the areas of the facility that may be reasonably expanded. Some sites may be land-locked, so as to prevent any new construction whatsoever, outside of renovation. During the planning process, it is important for the jurisdiction to consider the long-term future needs and requirements of the jail, and allow for expansions if necessary. If expansion is not possible, jurisdictions often develop satellite locations. Some jurisdictions chose to use a decentralized approach and develop a master plan that allows many satellite facilities to be constructed in phases as the need arises.

American Correctional Association Standards

The ACA standards[3] are the national benchmark for effective operation of correctional systems throughout the United States and are necessary to ensure that correctional facilities are operated professionally. They address services, programs, and operations essential to proper correctional management, including administrative and fiscal controls, staff training and development, physical plant, safety and emergency procedures, sanitation, food service, and rules and discipline. Standards reflect practical, up-to-date policies and procedures that safeguard the life, health, and safety of staff and inmates.

The ACA currently publishes 21 different manuals of standards, each of which applies to a specific kind of correctional facility or program. The standards cover programs for adults and juveniles housed in correctional facilities, detention centers, and community correctional programs. There are also standards for probation and parole agencies, health care programs, and electronic monitoring programs.

Approximately 80 percent of all state corrections and youth service departments are active participants in ACA's accreditation program. Programs and facilities operated by the Federal Bureau of Prisons and the private sector are also included.

State Standards

In addition to the ACA, many states, either through their Department of Corrections or another regulatory agency, have established additional standards for the construction and operation of jail facilities. While many standards mirror those set forth by the ACA, some offer specific guidelines that go beyond what is required nationally or are unique and outline specific requirements, such as timelines for vermin/pest control or for fire and health inspections, or a requirement to provide a special purpose area for those inmates suffering alcohol or drug withdrawal symptoms. For example, the State of Virginia mandates that jail facilities have "a special purpose area to provide for the temporary detention and care of persons under the influence of alcohol or narcotics; or for persons who are uncontrollably violent, self-destructive, or those requiring medical supervision."

Facility Costs

It is important that the jurisdiction fully account for both the construction costs and the future costs of operating the facility. While planning for the facility, the jurisdiction needs to complete a feasibility study. Most often, professional consultants with unique knowledge in jail construction and operation will be required. The economic feasibility study should estimate all capital costs and operating costs and evaluate the potential for various funding sources.

Financing Jail Facilities

State and federal funds may be available to reduce the amount of local funding, but rarely will grant funding be sufficient to finance the entire facility. Financing for jail facilities will inevitably become a balancing act between what is necessary and what is politically acceptable. The importance of jail projects makes it possible for some jurisdictions to have a special purpose tax to enable cash funding, but almost always general obligation debt is required. If voter approval for general obligation debt fails, jail authorities, which would not require public approval for debt issuances, may be a possibility. Jails may also be able to recover part of the cost of a jail with "bed" charges or fees for housing inmates from other jurisdictions.

State Funds

Many states have grant programs in place to accommodate funding requests from local governments for renovation, construction, or expansion. Many state funding programs require matching funds. As a condition of receiving state funds, some states may require the facility to house state prisoners for a pre-determined length of time.

Federal Funds

Although not as prevalent as in the past, another source of funding comes from the federal government. Between 1982 and 2005, the U.S. Marshals and the Bureau of Immigration and Customs Enforcement (BICE) offered Cooperative Agreement Program (CAP) funding, which was given to localities for renovation, expansion and/or construction of jails. In exchange, local government jails agreed to house federal prisoners for a pre-determined length of time. A sum of $285 million was awarded to counties and municipalities before the program was eliminated. Most current federal programs are limited to targeted grant opportunities and are usually mission-specific, rather than for capital project use.

Bed Rentals

Per diems and bed rentals can be structured to help pay any debt service or operating costs of operating jails. Jurisdictions without jail facilities will often contract with neighboring jurisdictions to provide jail services. Debt service payments backed through bed rentals should be carefully examined to make sure the payment is a suitable revenue source into the future. Additionally, reliance on revenue streams produced by inmates from other jurisdictions should be carefully considered. Relying on other jurisdictions to supply inmates may call into question the essentiality of the project, which could be looked down upon by credit rating agencies. Additionally, if other jurisdictions find alternatives for housing inmates, the revenue stream may dry up, and additional funding may be necessary.

Operating Issues

Just as important as funding the development of a jail facility is the ability to fund operating costs. Before committing to the construction of a jail, jurisdictions should be fully aware of the long-term ongoing costs of its operation. Jurisdictions unable or unwilling to support a jail should consider alternatives, such as outsourcing all or part of the management of the jail or jail services. The operating budget is the total of many factors, including the staffing costs discussed above, food service, health service, inmate programs, transportation, direct support, and utilities. Exhibit 9.3 displays the cost breakdown of a typical mid-size jail facility over thirty years.

Exhibit 9.3 Thirty-Year Costs of Jail Facility

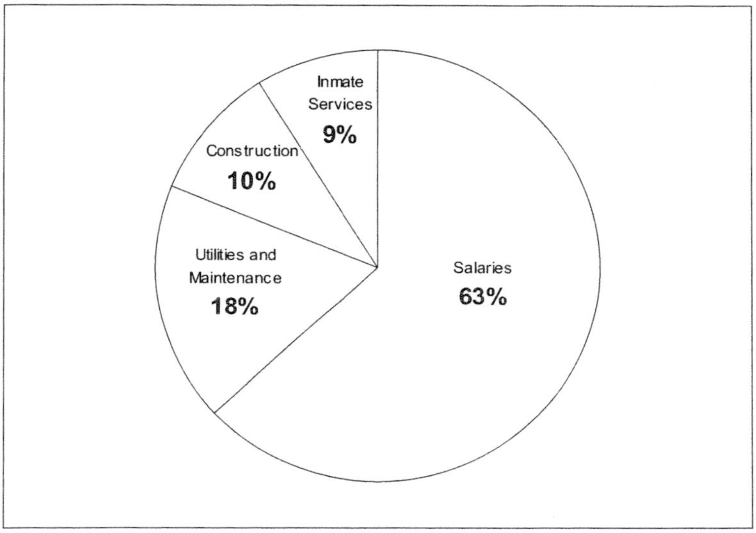

Source: Kimme & Associates, Inc., *Jail Design Guide: A Resource for Small and Medium-Sized Jails* (Washington D.C.: National Institute of Corrections, 1998).

Personnel

Staff salaries make up the largest cost component over the life of the jail facility. Some states offer assistance and may reimburse the local jurisdiction for a portion of salaries. Correctly staffing a jail facility can be a challenging task. The U.S. Department of Justice offers an excellent resource on its Web site entitled, *Staffing Analysis: Workbook for Jails, Second Edition*.[4] This publication breaks down the staffing process in detail and offers insight into the entire procedure, including staffing analysis, calculating work hours, and developing a staff coverage plan.

Privatization of Jail Services

Jurisdictions may be able to reduce operating costs in a jail facility by outsourcing management of the facility. Many jurisdictions have been able to successfully operate jails through a private firm and realize cost savings. If complete outsourcing is not a viable option, it may still be possible to outsource some jail services, such as medical and mental health services, food service, or educational programs. Primary cost savings from privatization are realized through reduced personnel costs.[5]

Conclusion

Planning and budgeting for a jail facility is more complex than most other capital facilities and takes time. The entire development of a correctional facility from planning through construction takes on average 40 months.[6] Evaluating the current facilities and estimating future needs far in advance will enable jurisdictions to prepare both the capital facilities and the most appropriate financing plan. Finance officers need to be aware of the many unique features with jail construction and operation, espe-cially how the design of the facility impacts operating costs and staffing levels, to plan a successful facility.

Furniture

Any furniture in the facility should be consistent with the custody level of inmates and should not interfere with any function of the jail. Additionally, the jurisdiction should carefully research all applicable ACA and state standards for furnishings. For example, all mattresses and linens must conform to all applicable fire ratings. Standards should be strictly adhered to in order to avoid costly errors, including unplanned replacement costs.

Furniture within a jail facility, such as chairs, tables, and other furnishings will generally wear at more than twice the usual rate due to 24-hour use. Additionally, inmates frequently abuse furnishings in the housing pods, either through neglect or vandalism. Furnishings and equipment should be evaluated on a frequent and regular basis to determine if repairs or replacement is needed.

Notes

1. Information from the Virginia Court Web site, http://www.courts.state.va.us/mag/page1.htm.

2. Kimme & Associates, Inc, *Jail Design Guide: A Resource for Small and Medium-Sized Jails* (Washington D.C.: National Institute of Corrections, 1998).

3. Taken from the American Correctional Association's Web site, http://www.aca.org.

4. Dennis R. Liebert and Rod Miller, *Staffing Analysis: Workbook for Jails* (Washington D.C: U.S. Department of Justice, National Institute of Corrections, 2004) Available at http://www.nicic.org/pubs/2001/016827.pdf.

5. Based on information in a white paper published by the Reason Public Policy Institute, www.reason.org. Geoffrey F. Segal, "Innovative Alternatives to Traditional Municipal/County Corrections."

6. National Institute of Corrections, "Jail Planning and Expansion: Local Officials and Their Roles," www.nicic.org.

| 10 |

Roads

By Soliman Khudeira

Highway and road projects can have significant impact on local and regional development and therefore should be determined through a transportation planning process that involves key government officials, including the finance officer. Before implementing a road project, program managers should identify why the project is needed, what type of improvement best fits the needs and budget, and what problems and issues need to be addressed and resolved to allow for its successful implementation. This chapter discusses topics related to a typical roadway project including roadway classification, needs assessment, project scope and schedule, project phases, cost methodologies, funding sources, and ongoing maintenance of roadway elements.

The public sector's role in planning for roads is rooted in this country's historical development from the time when horses and walking were the primary modes of travel. Planned grid designs for roads in the earliest U.S. cities provided the means to shorten travel distances; connecting trails between towns allowed for longer distance travel by horse and buggy. Securing these key transportation routes was paramount during the American Revolution and Civil War. With the advent of the interstate highway system under the Eisenhower administration in the 1950s, federal standards were developed. Land acquisition, many times through condemnation, began to further shape this country and enable increased suburbanization and automobile transportation to flourish. Through land use planning, the public sector's role in developing transportation strategies is essential for maintaining its citizens' quality of life.

| Roadway Classification |

Classification of roadways is necessary for communication among engineers, planners, and the public.[1] Roadways are commonly classified by design type, route number, maintenance and funding responsibilities, or functional classification. Functional classifications are the most important to the finance officer, as these have direct impact on funding availability.

Functional Classification

Functional classification is a common method of classifying highways and was developed for transportation planning purposes. Functional classification groups streets and highways according to the character of service they provide. Access to points of origin and destination is provided via the local road network; the through portion of the trip is via collectors and arterials. Local streets provide land access, whereas collectors and arterials are used to provide mobility. Using a functional classification, roads are classified as local roads and streets, collector roads and streets, rural and urban arterials, freeways, at-grade intersections, and grade separation and interchanges.

◆ **Local Roads and Streets.** Local streets provide direct access to residential, business, and commercial properties, with little through traffic.

◆ **Collector Roads and Streets.** Collector roads and streets connect local roads and streets with the arterial streets.

◆ **Rural and Urban Arterials.** Arterial streets generally provide regional links between cities, towns and/or higher density areas.

◆ **Freeways.** Freeways are the highest classification of arterial streets. They are defined as an expressway with full control of access to give preference to through traffic.

◆ **At-grade Intersections.** An at-grade intersection is defined as the general area where two or more roadways join or cross at the same level.

◆ **Grade Separations and Interchanges.** With grade separations, the intersecting through-traffic lanes are separated with either an overpass or underpass. This is done to attain efficiency, safety, and capacity.

Project Types

The current and expected average daily traffic (ADT) normally plays a major role in defining the project type, along with amount of available funding, condition of the current roads, and long-term plans for the area. ADT is defined as the total traffic volume during a given period divided by the number of days in that time period. The current ADT volume for a roadway can be determined readily where continuous traffic counts are available. Where only periodic counts are taken, however, ADT volume can be established by correcting the results according to factors such as the season, month, or day of week. The following sections outline the three types of roadway improvements: new construction; reconstruction; or rehabilitation, restoration, and resurfacing (3R) projects.

New Construction

Generally, new construction will connect major roadways or serve new growth areas. Projects are typically based on at least a twenty-year design period and require a significant amount of time to complete. In the United States, the most common pavement material for new construction is asphalt, but concrete is also common. Selection of specific material is generally dependent on factors including budget, climate, desired noise levels, and sub-grade conditions.

Reconstruction

Reconstruction of an existing roadway will typically include adding travel and/or turning lanes, reconstructing the existing horizontal and vertical alignment, widening the roadway, and/or flattening side slopes, but the roadway will remain essentially within the existing roadway corridor. Reconstructing an existing roadway is undertaken primarily when it cannot accommodate its current or future traffic demands, the existing alignment or cross section is significantly deficient, drainage improvements are needed, and/or the service life of the pavement has been exceeded. In addition, any intersection located within the limits of a reconstruction project will be reconstructed as needed. These projects may still require some right-of-way acquisitions.

Road Noise

Motor vehicles generate traffic noise from the motor, aerodynamics, exhaust, and interaction of tires with the roadway. Efforts should be made to minimize the radiation of noise into noise-sensitive areas along the roadways, such as residential communities. An effective method of reducing traffic noise to adjacent areas is to design the highway so that some solid material blocks the line of sight between the noise source and the receptor. Methods to reduce the noise levels on adjacent areas include installation of noise walls, depressing the roadway below the adjacent areas (if possible), and planting trees on the roadside.

Rehabilitation, Restoration, and Resurfacing Projects

Since available funds do not always permit the total reconstruction of a roadway, the Federal-aid Highway Act of 1976 amended the term "construction" to permit federal-aid funding of resurfacing and widening of existing rural and urban pavements with or without revision of horizontal or vertical alignment or other geometric features. The 1982 Surface Transportation Assistant Act stipulated that 3R projects be constructed to standards to preserve and extend the service life of the roadways and enhance safety. The scope of 3R projects varies from thin pavement overlays and minor safety upgrading to more complete rehabilitation. 3R projects differ from reconstruction projects in that reconstruction projects substantially deviate from the existing horizontal and/or vertical alignment and/or add capacity.

Project Evaluation

For a project to qualify as a 3R project, a detailed evaluation must be conducted to assess its appropriateness. The evaluation should include field review and documentation of existing geometrics; analysis of accident data; and an assessment of the pavement condition, geometric design of the adjacent roadways, physical constraints, and bridges and other structures within project limits.

Design Guidelines

Design guidelines for 3R projects have been developed to allow greater design flexibility than new or reconstruction projects. The guidelines offer sufficient flexibility to ensure cost effective design and further compliance with the program goals of preserving and extending the service life and enhancing safety. While safety may not be the primary reason for initiating a 3R project, roadway safety is an essential element of all projects. 3R projects should be developed in a manner that identifies and incorporates appropriate safety enhancements.

Typical design guidelines for a 3R projects include criteria for design speed, shoulder width, lane width, turn lane width, horizontal clearance, and bridge width. Design criteria for a typical 3R project is presented in Exhibit 10.1.

Purpose and Needs Assessment: Defining the Problem

A purpose and needs assessment helps identify problems that already exist or potential problems that could develop and establishes the case for why the jurisdiction should devote resources to the project. Any potential negative impacts expected during the project, such as increased congestion or potential environmental damage, should be explained. The purpose and need should be consistent with other plans developed by the jurisdiction concerning mobility issues, safety, new residential growth, or economic development. Defining problems and understanding the need for a project is the first step in planning effective roadway projects.

Development of Alternatives

Early meetings are an excellent way to reach agreement with stakeholders on the basic purpose and need for the project. Many factors should be considered when working to determine purpose and need, including project history; actions taken to date; agencies involved; actions pending; schedules; project location with respect to other major routes; ownership; maintenance jurisdiction; current and future land use planning along the route; adjacent sites, including historically or environmentally protected land; existing geometry; local interest; current deficiencies; safety and accidents; economic development plans; system linkage; transportation demand; relationship to any statewide plan; modal interrelationships; and citizen preferences.

After the basic purpose and needs for the project are established, several options can be developed. Vague purpose and needs statements allow for many

Exhibit 10.1 Design Criteria for a Typical 3R Project

Design Element	Design Guidelines for Rural Two-Lane Roadway		
Current average daily traffic (ADT)	0 - 400	400 -1,500	1,500 or more
Design speed	30 mph	30 mph	40 mph
Shoulder width	0 ft	1 ft	3 ft
Lane width	10 ft	11 ft	11 ft
Turn lane width	10 ft	10 ft	10 ft
Horizontal clearance	7 ft	7 ft	16 ft
Bridges: Width to be retained	20 ft	24 ft	24 ft

more alternatives, but also may make the decision and alternative evaluation process more lengthy. As the project's purpose and needs are refined, some alternatives will be eliminated, permitting a more detailed analysis of alternatives that truly address the problem. Occasionally an unreasonable alternative remains, based on another agency's request or perhaps due to public expectation. In these cases, the jurisdiction should provide a clear explanation to communicate the reasons why the alternative is not possible.

Using Data in the Analysis

The purpose and need should be as comprehensive and specific as possible. For example, rather than simply stating that additional capacity is needed between two points, information on the adequacy of current facilities to handle the existing and projected traffic should be discussed. Other information such as safety, system linkage, and social demands that the proposed project will attempt to address should be described. All of the relevant elements should provide specific and detailed data to compare the present, future no-build, and future build conditions. Data should be presented on project benefits, such as reduction in vehicle hours of travel; improvements in travel speeds on the system; reduction in traffic accidents, injuries, and fatalities; savings in cost to the traveling public; enhanced economic development potential; and improved access to public facilities. It is not sufficient to state that the project is needed to provide increased capacity and improve safety without backing this up with supporting data. Elements of a needs assessment are displayed in Exhibit 10.2.

Exhibit 10.2 Elements of Needs Assessment for a Typical Roadway Project

Topic	Items to Be Included
Project status	• Briefly describe the project history including actions taken to date, other agencies and governmental units involved, actions pending, and schedules
Project location and route classification	• Functional classification and local road name(s) • Regional location: identify the project location with respect to other major routes, municipalities, and geographical markers • Maintenance jurisdiction and ownership of the roadway • Separate classifications (e.g. truck route, national highway system)

Existing conditions	• Land use along the route and in the project vicinity
	  – Residential, commercial, industrial
	  – Historical sites
	  – Schools, parks, forest preserve, etc.
	• Existing cross section
	  – Number of lanes, parking, shoulders and/or curb and gutters, sidewalk, median type, and right-of-way, pavement composition
	• Existing drainage: description of open/close system and record of flooding

Project history	• Identify why the project was initiated and explain the need for the project • Local interest in the project • Relationship to other projects (past, current, future)

Deficiencies	• Safety concerns: Include brief accident summary (e.g., number of accidents, predominant accidents and causes). Is the proposed project necessary to correct an existing or potential safety hazard? Is the existing accident rate excessively high and why? How will the proposed project improve it?
	• Roadway deficiencies: Is the proposed project necessary to correct existing roadway deficiencies and how will the proposed project improve it? Deficiencies include:
	  – Substandard geometrics
	  – Load limits on structures and other structural deficiencies
	  – Inadequate cross-section or high maintenance costs
	  – Operational concerns/capacity
	  – Pavement deficiencies

Legislation	Is there a federal, state, or local governmental mandate for the action?
Social demands or economic development	New employment, schools, land use plans, recreation, etc. What projected economic development/land use changes indicate the need to improve or add to the highway capacity?
System linkage	Is the proposed project a "connecting link?" How does it fit in the transportation system?

Topic	Items to Be Included
Capacity	Is the capacity of the present facility inadequate for the present traffic and projected traffic and what capacity is needed? What is the level(s) of service for existing and proposed facilities?
Transportation demand	Include relationship to any statewide plan or adopted urban transportation plan together with an explanation of the project's traffic forecasts
Modal interrelationships	How will the proposed facility interface with and serve to complement airports, rail and port facilities, mass transit services, etc.?
Project purpose	General statement outlining the project purpose

Source: Adapted from Federal Highway Department, "Elements of Purpose and Needs" (Washington, D.C.: United States Department of Transportation). See the department's Web site at www.fhwa.dot.gov/environment/elements.htm.

Decision Making

The decision-making process should consider any alternatives that meet the project's purpose and need statement and the jurisdiction should select the alternative that can best achieve service-level goals with the most effective and efficient resource use. At times, it is possible that no alternative meets all aspects of the project's purpose and need. In such a case, officials must determine if the alternatives are acceptable and worthwhile pursuing in light of the cost, environmental impact, and less than optimal transportation end solution. To properly assess this, the jurisdiction should identify and give higher priority to critical elements. Critical elements are those, which if not met, would lead to a "no-build" decision. Identifying the critical elements and evaluating alternatives only on those elements may make it easier to find a viable solution.

Phases and Duration of Roadway Projects

Development and implementation of a typical roadway improvement project involves four phases: feasibility study phase, phase I preliminary engineering, phase II engineering, and construction phase. The first three phases are described below.

Feasibility Study Phase

The feasibility study is prepared only for a new roadway on a new alignment. This phase is a pre-preliminary engineering study initiated to develop the feasibility of alternatives proposed in the project's purpose and needs assessment and to estimate the project's initial cost. If resources do not exist in-house to perform such a study, then a professional design consultant is usually contracted with to undertake it. This contract may be specific to the project or it may be part of a general road consulting contract. The final deliverable is a preliminary project report.

Phase I Preliminary Engineering

The preliminary engineering phase includes project scope definition; funds allocation; analysis of the right-of-way required for the project; environmental impact studies; and identification of the type, size, and location of the roadway and structures. During this phase, the jurisdiction will review alternatives, hold public input sessions, coordinate project plans with other stakeholders, and develop a more detailed cost estimate. Again, if in-house resources are not available to perform such a task, then professional services are contracted and may be an extension of the roads consultant contract. The final deliverable is a more detailed project report, also known as a design concept report.

Environmental Assessment Methodology

In order to incorporate environmental considerations into the decision-making process, it is necessary to develop a complete understanding of the project's potential adverse impacts on its surroundings. Exhibit 10.3 outlines the required

Exhibit 10.3 Project Environmental Process for Federal-Aid Projects

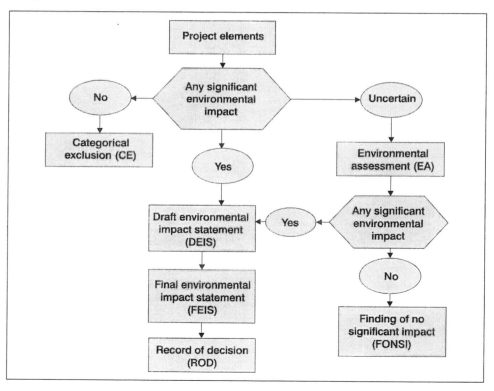

environmental process for a typical federal-aid roadway project. States may also have additional requirements.

Categorical Exclusion

For roadways developed with federal funds, projects or actions can be classified as a categorical exclusion if the project or actions do not individually or cumulatively have a significant impact on the human environment. Categorical exclusion projects do not require an environmental assessment or an environmental impact statement. For a project to qualify as categorical exclusion, it cannot include the following: 1) significant impacts on the environment, 2) substantial controversy on environmental grounds, or 3) significant impacts on properties protected by Section 4(f) of the U.S. Department of Transportation Act of 1966 (see the sidebar). Section 4(f) is applicable to the following lands: 1) publicly owned parks, 2) recreational areas, 3) wildlife and waterfowl, or 4) any historic site in or eligible for the National Register of Historic Places.

Environmental Assessment

The environmental assessment (EA) is an interim decision document prepared for an action where the significance of social, economic, or environmental impact is not clearly established. If the action is determined to have significant impact, an environmental impact statement (EIS) is then prepared. If there is no significant impact, a finding of no significant impact report (FONSI) is prepared.

Environmental Impact Statement

An EIS is a document prepared for an action that is likely to have significant impact. This document summarizes the major environmental impacts, outlines issues, examines reasonable alternatives, and arrives at a record of decision identifying the selected alternatives for the project. The record of decision also documents the method of mitigation adapted for the selected alternative choice.

Public Involvement Process

Chapter 5 of the *Federal-Aid Procedure for Local Highway Improvement Manual*[2] requires public involvement in the decision-making process, which is required by the National Environmental Protection Act of 1969 and by the federal

Section 4(f)

Section 4(f) is national policy that helps preserve U.S natural resources and is considered the strongest federal preservation law. The U.S Department of Transportation Act of 1966 included this special provision and stipulates that the Federal Highway Administration (FHWA) will not approve any program or project that requires the use of any publicly owned public park, recreation area, wildlife refuge or historic sites unless:

1) there is no feasible and prudent alternative to the use of such land, and

2) such program includes all possible planning to minimize harm to such areas.

statute and regulations for federally funded projects. The *Manual* requires newspaper notification of the proposed improvement, an informal public gathering that blends individual discussion periods with presentation of the proposed improvement, and a public hearing. The public hearing is to be conducted by a local agency to inform the public of proposed projects or programs, explain the options under consideration, and receive and document public reaction. State and local government policies may require additional public participation or participation for non-federally funded projects.

Right-of-Way Acquisition Process

The preliminary right-of-way (ROW) acquisition process starts in the phase I engineering stage to identify the approximate location and cost of the land needed for the project. The actual land acquisition starts in the phase II engineering stage. Land acquisition also includes obtaining necessary easements and relocating utilities, if necessary. The ROW process includes plats and legal descriptions, appraisals and appraisals review, negotiations with the landowners, and possible condemnation.

In certain cases, the acquired ROW represents more than is required for the new roadway, resulting in "excess land" that will need to be disposed of through exchange, legislative release, or public sale.[3]

Context Sensitive Solutions

Context sensitive solutions (CSS) is an interdisciplinary approach that seeks effective, multimodal transportation solutions by working with stakeholders to develop, build, and maintain cost-effective transportation infrastructure. The resulting projects should help improve safety and mobility for the traveling public, while seeking to preserve and enhance the scenic, economic, historic, and natural qualities of the settings through which they pass.

The CSS approach seeks to ensure that stakeholders' views are carefully considered in the decision-making process. The approach involves the stakeholders early and often, especially before major design decisions are made. The information gained from partnering with stakeholders is then used to develop solutions to the transportation issue. The federal government, through the FHWA, is encouraging states to adopt the CSS approach to transportation planning and design. Some state departments of transportation have implemented the CSS process and included guidelines on their Web sites.

Note: The Illinois Department of Transportation has information on its Web site for guidelines used in the CSS process in Illinois at http://www.dot.state.il.us/css/home.html.

Phase II Engineering

Phase II engineering studies include preparation of detailed engineering plans, specifications, and an engineer's line-item estimate of construction cost. At the end of this phase, the project is ready for bidding by contractors. The right-of-way acquisition process starts in the middle of this phase after right-of-way requirements for the project are defined. This phase normally takes between one and three years, depending on the project's complexity. The final deliverable is the plan, specification, and estimate (PS&E). For a complex project, phase II is divided into more than one contract. For each contract, a separate PS&E is prepared for bidding by contractors. Normally, the first contract is for work to prepare for the project, such as utility relocation, and the other contracts are based on specifics of the project. This way, the construction on the first contract could start while the phase II design on the subsequent contract(s) continues.

Cost Methodology of Typical Projects

To ensure sufficient construction funds are available, cost estimates are required throughout various stages of project development. As the project progresses, the estimates are refined to ensure the projects are cost effective, sufficient funds are available for construction, and the contractor's bid price is reasonable. The various estimates are outlined below.

Project Initiation Estimate

Once a project has been included in the jurisdiction's multi-year program, several years may pass before a phase I study is conducted. Consequently, the project initiation cost estimate must be updated annually until the phase I study has been conducted.

Initial project cost estimates generally are based on broad units such as cost per mile or cost per square foot and by reviewing similar, recent projects in the area. An additional 10 to 20 percent should be added to account for contingency items that may be needed. In addition, the cost for any major features that are beyond the basic assumption used to develop the estimate should be added. For example, the cost of a noise wall should be added to the cost per mile estimate. Additionally, the following factors should be considered when preparing the estimate: geographic location, inflation, reliability of historical data, changes to the price of materials, project size, schedule, construction staging relative to the previous projects, required right-of-way, railroads, utilities, and environmental problems. Below is a brief description of initial costing methodologies for different types of projects.

◆ **Roadway Projects.** For most roadway projects, a cost per mile per roadway width is used. This estimate includes the cost of earthwork, pavement, drainage, and other miscellaneous items.

◆ **Structure Projects.** For most structural projects, a cost per square foot is used based on similar structure types and length.
◆ **Traffic Signal Projects.** Traffic signal projects are estimated per intersection installation.

Exhibit 10.4 provides approximate construction costs per mile for a typical roadway project. Other methods of estimating a project cost are also shown. The range in the cost is based on various factors to be considered, such as project location.

Exhibit 10.4 Project Cost Examples Based on the Scope of Work

Project Type	Construction Cost Per Mile of Roadway	Construction Cost Per Square Foot of Roadway	Construction Cost (Other Method)	Project Scope
Roadway resurfacing (3R projects)	$375,000 to $400,000	$1.70 to $1.80		42-feet-wide pavement: removal and replacement of bituminous material, adjustment of the utility structures, minor pavement patching, minor sidewalk, curb and gutter removal and replacement, no landscaping, no change in roadway dimensions
Roadway improvement (3R projects)	$4 million to $4.5 million	$18.00 to $20.30		42-feet-wide pavement: partial removal and replacement of pavement, minor roadway widening, pavement resurfacing, street lighting, traffic signal modernization (three intersections), and landscaping
Roadway reconstruction	$6 million to $7 million	$27.10 to $31.60		42-feet-wide pavement: full removal and replacement of pavement, minor roadway widening, street lighting, traffic signal modernization (three intersections), and landscaping
New arterial roadway	$8 million to $9 million	$30.10 to $40.60		42-feet-wide new pavement: Sewer and water mains, earth excavation, pavement, curb and gutter and sidewalk, street lighting, landscaping, traffic signals (three intersections)

Project Type	Construction Cost Per Mile of Roadway	Construction Cost Per Square Foot of Roadway	Construction Cost (Other Method)	Project Scope
Roadway enhancement	$1.5 million to $2 million			Installation of: median planters, landscaping, irrigation system, minor utility adjustments, partial resurfacing of the roadway
Grade separation			$17 million to $19 million	Lower the road under railroad tracks and build one railroad bridge, retaining walls, lighting, traffic signals, utility lines, landscaping
Viaduct clearance improvement			$1.5 million to $2 million	Remove and replace 900 feet of pavement and lower the roadway by an average of two feet, water and sewer lines, small retaining walls
Bridges rehab		$136 per square foot of the bridge		New pier and abutment caps, structural steel, bearings, eight-inch concrete deck, sidewalk, and new pedestrian railing and roadway. A typical bridge is 80 feet x 350 feet ($4.2 million)
New bridge		$215 per square foot of the bridge		New bridge includes: substructure work. Either caissons or H-piles, concrete abutment, and piers
Traffic signal Modernization			$225,000 to $350,000	Modernization of traffic signals at one intersection

Source: Information was based on author's experience and many interviews with project managers within the Chicago Department of Transportation.

Phase I Cost Estimate

A phase I cost estimate includes a preliminary estimate based on the quantities determined during phase I. If material quantity estimates are not available and will not be available within a reasonable time frame, then the estimating procedure described above could be used. Major items such as bridges or interchanges should be listed separately and clearly identified by their location in the estimate. On rehabilitation projects, it may be necessary to break down costs for certain items separately, especially if they may later be eliminated from the scope. The phase I estimate should also identify construction, right-of-way, utility adjustments, and engineering fees separately to facilitate funding for these items.

Phase II Cost Estimate

Preliminary plan reviews occur during the early stages of phase II and a revised cost estimate is developed to ensure that the project funding is still reasonable and appropriate. In this phase, the plans and major quantities are essentially complete. Therefore, the estimate can be prepared using the methodologies discussed earlier (per unit prices). If the project scope changes, or if there has been a significant delay in the project since it was originally designed and estimated, a new construction cost estimate should be prepared. Near the end of phase II, a final estimate is prepared.

- ◆ **Final Estimate.** A cost estimate is prepared based on the final plans. This may be an update of an earlier cost estimate or, for a project without a phase I report, this will be the first detailed project estimate.

- ◆ **Engineer's Estimate.** This estimate is the official and final project cost estimate. The engineer's estimate provides the basis for evaluating the contractor's bids for construction and will allow the municipality to determine if the low bid price is fair and reasonable for the work involved.

Road Project Financing Options

Various funding sources are available for municipal roadway improvements. A project could use a combination of federal, state, and local funds or private contributions. An inherent constraint that exists with transportation funding from state and federal sources where motor fuel taxes are the primary funding source is that such motor fuel taxes are stated in terms of a flat tax per gallon (e.g., the federal rate is 18.4 cents per gallon[4]). This provides additional revenue to result only from higher consumption, in contrast to many other ad valorem taxes, such as sales or property taxes, which allow revenue to grow with inflation. The following is a list of potential sources for local, state, federal, and private funding.

Federal Funds

- ◆ FHWA – Surface Transportation Program funds;
- ◆ FHWA – Highway Bridge Repair and Replacement Program;
- ◆ FHWA – Congestion mitigation and air quality funds;
- ◆ FHWA – Enhancement funds for roads that enhance the transportation system, such as facilities for cyclists and pedestrians, landscaping and beautification, and historic preservation;
- ◆ FTA – Section 5309 New Start/Bus and Bus Facilities Programs;

◆ USDA – Green Streets Program;

◆ FHWA – Intelligent Transportation Systems funding (available to states who may apply on behalf of municipalities); and

◆ Congressional earmarks (funding ultimately comes from one of the above programs).

State Funds

◆ State road funds – motor fuel tax funds;

◆ State economic development funds;

◆ State roads improvement funds;

◆ State Department of Natural Resources – fund for bicycle path development;

◆ State DOT grants for traffic safety; and

◆ State EPA grants for environmental improvement.

Local Funds

◆ Enterprise fund – funds from revenues from a number of local services;

◆ General obligation and revenue bonds;

◆ Tax increment financing;

◆ Dedicated portion of property taxes, vehicles taxes, decal fees, license fees and/or general fund allocation; and

◆ Road impact or cash proffer fees.

Special Assessment Funds

Certain projects require levying a special assessment on property owners to match government funds for improvements. The 50/50 Sidewalk Program and the New Alley Construction Programs are examples of special assessment projects.

Developer-Built roads

Private developers also commonly pay for and build roads. Upon completion, the road improvement is turned over to the public sector for maintenance and ownership. The developer is responsible for bonding the project. The bond is normally kept by the public sector for a period of twelve to eighteen months and used to repair any defect in the road and utility lines.

Roadway Maintenance

Maintenance of roadways is generally the responsibility of both state and local government and includes not only road maintenance, but also grass cutting and litter removal. Maintenance on the roadway itself can be categorized into three areas: routine maintenance, preventive maintenance, and major maintenance. All three maintenance categories may be performed with state or local staff or by contract. *The Federal-Aid Procedure for Local Highway Improvement Manual* requires that the local agency be responsible for

Developer-Maintained Roads

For developer-built roads, an innovative roadway maintenance method includes the option of requiring the developer to offer a "long-term highway warranty, maintenance, and preservation." This concept motivates the contractor to build highways for the best overall lifecycle costs. By having the developer maintain the road for a specified number of years, the developer is encouraged to build in a level of quality that supports long-term results, not short-term profits.

maintaining any project constructed with federal-aid funds. The manual defines maintenance as "performing normal maintenance operations for the preservation of the entire project, including the roadway surface, shoulders, roadsides, structures, and such traffic control devices as are necessary for its safe and efficient utilization." Most roadway maintenance is not effective if applied to pavement that has been allowed to severely deteriorate. Proper maintenance of roadways can potentially save costs in the long run and prevent replacement projects.

Conclusion

To correctly evaluate, cost, and design a roadway project, all issues and components related to the project need to be identified and investigated including need assessment, private stakeholders' participation, project phases, funding sources, environmental impact, right-of- way acquisition, project timeline, value engineering, cost methodologies, and maintenance of the roadway elements. Carefully evaluating each of these areas is necessary for the success of the project's planning and implementation. If these issues are not addressed in a timely manner, the project could be at risk for being postponed or even cancelled.

130th Street and Torrence Avenue Realignment Project

The 130th Street and Torrence Avenue realignment and grade separation project in Chicago, Illinois, included the realignment of Torrence Avenue, 130th Street, and Brainard Avenue creating the grade separation; construction of six new bridges (two railroad steel girder bridges, one railroad 390-feet truss bridge, one mixed-use bridge, one highway bridge, and one pedestrian bridge); underground water and sewer lines; underground detention chamber; storm water pumps and pump station; 8,000 lineal feet of retaining walls, pavements, lighting, and traffic signals; and landscaping. The project used a contingency of only 10 percent in the phase I engineering design stage. Due to this low contingency and price fluctuations, changes in project elements during the design phase, and a limited number of contractors submitting qualified bids for such a large project, the total project cost ended up more than double the original phase I estimate.

It is recommended that for a standard project the contingency in the estimate cost should be 10 percent to 15 percent. However, the contingency should be at least 30 percent for a project such as this one that has substantial underground work and multiple structures. The 30 percent contingency would cover price escalation, unexpected phase II occurrences, and increases in cost due to further coordination with other agencies.

Source: Project Development Report, 130th Street, Brainard Avenue, and Torrence Avenue Intersection Improvement and Elimination of at-grade Crossing with the Norfolk Southern. Prepared for Chicago Department of Transportation by Alfred Benesch Company. IDOT Project No. P-88-043-99, CDOT P.N. B-9-369.

Notes

1. The American Association of State Highway and Transportation Officials, *A Policy on Geometric Design of Highways and Streets* (Washington, D.C.: American Association of State Highway and Transportation Officials, 2001) and American Association of State Highway and Transportation Officials, *A Policy on Geometric Design of Highways and Arterial Streets* (Washington, D.C.: American Association of State Highway and Transportation Officials, 1973).

2. *Federal-Aid Procedures for Local Highways Improvement*, Rev. 5-90, Illinois Department of Transportation, Bureau of Local Roads and Streets.

3. Illinois Department of Transportation, *Land Acquisition Manual* (December 2000).

4. Federal Highway Department, *Federal Highway User Fees* (http://www.fhwa.dot.gov).

|11|

Water and Wastewater Systems

By Marcia Maurer

Throughout the history of the United States, local governments have been providing water and wastewater services. Government control allows operation as a natural monopoly and thus enables greater efficiencies in building and maintaining infrastructure necessary to deliver safe, reliable access to water and successfully remove and treat wastewater and sewage. With the development of new technologies for filtration, distribution, and treatment, current systems are much more advanced today than ever before. Finance officers must understand the entire process to properly finance and budget for water and wastewater infrastructure projects.

Government Roles in Water and Wastewater Systems

Like many services provided by government in the United States, responsibility for delivering water and wastewater services, regulating the service, and providing financing is divided among the federal, state, and local governments. Understanding this division of responsibility is important to developing a successful capital plan and budget.

Local Governments

Local governments with water or wastewater systems typically provide services directly to the end customer. Often set up as enterprise funds with dedicated revenue sources, local government water and wastewater departments or agencies provide services, collect user fees, and function with relative independence from other general-purpose government departments.

Special Districts

Because water and wastewater systems are capital intensive and because both rely heavily on user charges as a primary funding source, special districts commonly provide these services. There are 3,405 single-function water districts, 2,004 single-function sewer districts, and 1,446 combined water and sewer districts across the United States.[1] Special districts that provide only water or wastewater services will operate in cooperation with either a local general-purpose government jurisdiction or another special district.

State Governments

The role of state government in water and wastewater service can best be described as a regulator. State natural resource departments are often responsible for enforcing environmental regulation and administration related to the permitting processes. In addition, state governments often administer clean water fund loan programs that provide subsidized interest rates for projects that meet certain criteria. Because of their role as a regulator and a potential funding source, local governments may want to involve the appropriate state agency as a stakeholder in the capital planning process.

Federal Government

The federal government functions as a policy maker and funding source for both water and wastewater programs. The Clean Water Act gave the Environmental Protection Agency (EPA) broad discretion to create regulatory policies that must be enforced by the states. The federal government also makes annual appropriations to the Clean Water Fund that may be used by state and local governments as administered by the states. Local governments preparing capital plans for water or wastewater facilities should be familiar with the requirements of the Clean Water Act and any other applicable legislation.

| Water Systems |

Recognizing the importance of a safe and reliable source of water, governments have controlled all aspects of the delivery of potable water to its residents from resource extraction to filtration, storage, and distribution. Water systems vary dramatically in size. Larger systems, such as the Metropolitan Water District of Southern California,[2] process over 1.7 billion gallons per day and supply water to more than 18 million people, while the smaller systems may only process water from a single well with a capacity of less than 1,000 gallons per day and serve a small town. Each system, regardless of size, will need to include four vital steps: extracting water from its source, filtration, storage, and distribution.

Source Development

Water comes from surface sources (rivers and lakes) and groundwater wells. The choice to use groundwater or surface water depends on the location of the community and the nearest water source. In general, communities will tend to use surface water first if it is readily available and then use groundwater. Using surface water requires the construction of infrastructure including intake structures for the diversion of water, water treatment plants, and water distribution systems for delivery to the customer.

In many areas, rights to surface water have been in place for many years and in some places for over a century. Even so, those rights are increasingly challenged by competing demands including water quality, wildlife habitat, farming, and even distant domestic water needs. For example, lack of access to water in Southern California forces the Los Angeles basin to transport and use water from Northern California. Especially in the Southwest United States, access to water is limited and many cities must secure water rights before continuing with additional developments.

When trying to obtain permits to withdraw water, state and federal authorities will determine the necessity of the request to the potential and long-term needs of the greater area, especially those downstream of rivers. One manner in which to mitigate the impact of the request is to request withdrawal during heavier periods of river flow, such as during or after storms, into a holding facility, reservoir, or quarry site. Water is then stored until needed.

Groundwater requires little or no treatment unless the source has been contaminated. Common sources of groundwater contamination include leakage from underground fuel storage tanks, solvents used in dry cleaning such as trichloroethylene (TCE), and gasoline additives such as methyl tertiary-butyl ether (MTBE). Not all contamination is the result of human activities. The presence of naturally occurring elements in groundwater, such as arsenic, may also require treatment. Federal and state regulations limit the concentration of contaminants allowed in safe drinking water. Water quality regulations continue to change as further studies increase our knowledge of potential health problems caused by long-term exposure to various chemical substances.

Water Filtration and Treatment

The water supply must meet treatment levels mandated by federal, state, and local regulatory agen-

Reclaimed Water

Reclaimed wastewater is an emerging source of non-potable water in many communities that can reduce the strain on water systems during times of drought or supply shortage. Reclaimed wastewater is highly treated effluent from the wastewater treatment system that it is suitable for a controlled use. Common uses for reclaimed wastewater include irrigation of lawns, parks, and highway medians and industrial applications, such as the use in cooling towers for power generation.

cies. Treatment normally includes chlorination and, in some parts of the country, fluoridation. Potassium permanganate is added to water when iron or manganese levels high are to reduce iron discoloration or staining. Other treatment processes control local contaminants, such as arsenic, lead, nitrates, and radon. Water treatment plants should be located near water surface or groundwater sources for convenience. If the end users of such potable water are not expected to be adjacent to the water sources, then treatment facilities may be located away from the source and near the end users. The rationale behind this strategy is two-fold: 1) mitigate contaminants from entering potable water lines by not having potable water travel great distances and 2) control growth by not having potable water available to areas that are targeted to be preserved or protected.

Water Storage

Water storage is traditionally done with above and below ground tanks and with surface storage. Safeguarding and preserving groundwater supplies for use in "dry" years is becoming an expected best practice in many parts of the country. Above-ground water storage tanks can range in size, but typically have a capacity between one and five million gallons. The pump serving the storage tank can pump water into the tank twenty-four hours a day and during peak demand the water levels in the tank may decrease only to be replenished during low demand hours.

Surface storage is also an option for some communities. Large reservoirs or below-ground tanks offer alternatives to above ground tanks. When reservoirs are used, they are often developed as part of a park project providing recreational opportunities. Additionally, jurisdictions near mining sites are capable of storing millions, if not billions of gallons of water in abandoned mining shafts lined with granite or other dense rocks. Other communities are able to pump water back into the ground to recharge underground aquifers and storage for later use.

Water Distribution

Potable water distribution systems include pump and piping networks that deliver water to customers throughout the jurisdiction's service area. The location of water lines is usually planned in an orderly manner to best position the lines with customer needs while mitigating impacts during water line construction and subsequent maintenance. Many water lines are co-located as part of road networks, with the goal of aligning future road projects with water line construction and/or rehab. For lines that are located on private property, easement acquisitions are usually required in order to enable the line to be constructed on the property and then to be maintained. The cost for easement acquisition costs, and possibly easement maintenance that enable utility workers access to water lines, should be factored into any project cost.

Wastewater Systems

Similar to water systems, wastewater systems are essential to preventing disease and safeguarding citizen health and safety. The majority of wastewater systems provide a separate system for sewage collection and for stormwater discharge, but older communities may still be using a combined sewer system. The primary disadvantage with a combined sewer system is that during heavy rainfalls, large volumes of stormwater enter sewer pipes and overload the treatment plant, forcing it to bypass some stages in the treatment process, which results in the discharge of untreated sewage. Most combined sewer systems have gone through large rehabilitation projects to separate the sewer from stormwater infrastructure. Most systems now have components for wastewater collection, conveyance, treatment, and disposal and separate systems for stormwater collection, conveyance, and drainage.

Wastewater Collection and Conveyance

Collection and conveyance systems comprise the network of smaller pipes that are constructed throughout neighborhoods, commercial and office developments, and industrial properties that connect local pumping stations (also called lift stations) and the larger pipes that carry wastewater to treatment facilities. Local considerations dictate maintenance responsibilities for each component, but normally private owners maintain piping systems on their own private property and local public agencies maintain and operate pipe networks and pumping facilities.

Many wastewater lines are constructed to use gravity as the primary manner in which such sewage flows, with lines constructed along naturally declining topography (e.g., creeks, streams, etc.). While this is efficient for sewage flow, infiltration may present problems. Infiltration occurs when water or stormwater seeps into the wastewater line. The infiltration amount is then treated along with the sewage, causing an increased quantity of wastewater to be treated at the treatment plant. The

Septic Tanks

Many homeowners use a septic tank system instead of being connected to the public sewer. This occurs when there is no sewage pipe near their home or the pipe was constructed after their home was built. When a septic system fails it is often very costly for the property owner to obtain public sewer service, even when there are sewer facilities nearby. Many jurisdictions are now encouraging homeowners to convert from septic tanks, as leaching from the tanks can infiltrate local groundwater systems. A cooperative approach between the local health department and sewer utility may prove most effective in identifying homeowners with septic tanks and which septic tanks have had problems. In some areas, low-cost loan programs have been used to help homeowners offset the cost of installing pipe and connecting to the local sewer system.

better a jurisdiction can limit the infiltration contaminants into its sewer system, the better it can mitigate the cost of treating excess quantities of wastewater.

Wastewater Conveyance

As with water distribution systems, the wastewater pump's external structures such as concrete housing can last fifty years or more while the pumps themselves may last twenty-five to thirty years. Piping usually has a useful life of one hundred years or more.

Wastewater Treatment

Wastewater treatment plants receive wastewater and treat it by removing impurities to a level prescribed in a discharge permit issued by the state in which the facility is located. Discharge requirements vary widely depending on whether the discharge is to a local pond, field, river, or to the ocean. Wastewater systems discharging into a river or pond may be required to meet higher standards than systems that discharge directly to the ocean because of the potential for discharge to infiltrate water sources downstream or contaminate groundwater.

The main types of treatment are primary, secondary, and tertiary (advanced). Primary treatment will remove a substantial amount of suspended matter from the wastewater and discharge the remaining liquid. Secondary treatment will add a biological process after the primary treatment to remove at least 85 percent of the suspended solids. Tertiary treatment removes nutrients such as phosphorus and nitrogen and even more suspended solids. The cost of wastewater treatment plants will vary with the amount of wastewater treated and the type of treatment used.

Generally, wastewater treatment plants are located adjacent to their discharge point. However, they may also be strategically placed in areas to control growth by not enabling development to occur in certain areas. In these cases, the wastewater treatment plant is located on the perimeter of the planned developed area and then lines carry the effluent to the discharge point. Growth control measures are stronger under this scenario, as most lines from treatment plant to discharge point are downhill and rely upon gravity. This makes it even more difficult and expensive for development to occur between the plant and the discharge point as sewage would need to be pumped uphill.

Wastewater Disposal

Disposal facilities include piping necessary to deliver treated wastewater to a local pond, river, ocean, or other appropriate disposal point, such as fields and ponds where treated "solids" are stored for indefinite periods until fully disinfected. In addition to traditional processes, emerging disposal technologies are enabling agencies to recycle, or reclaim, treated water and return it to prescribed uses in the community or water stream. Solids remaining from the treatment process, sometimes referred to as "sludge," can be further processed into fertilizers and other useful components. Such advanced reclamation processes are expensive and do not have a market value great enough to recover costs, but environmental benefits may be great enough to justify the project.

Stormwater Drainage

Stormwater drainage systems are similar to wastewater systems except there is little or no treatment of stormwater. Prior to the creation of the EPA, wastewater and stormwater were traditionally collected and transported together in combined systems. While this required only one set of pipes, it led to terrible odors in dry weather when there was no stormwater to flush the system of sewage. Another disadvantage with a combined sewer system is that during heavy rainfalls, large volumes of stormwater will enter sewer system and increase the quantity needed to be carried and eventually treated by the system. If the system is overloaded, combined systems also face the risk of having to bypass part of the treatment process or face a potential sewage back up.

Many large older cities such as San Francisco, California, still have portions of combined systems under their streets. Current best practice, and in many cases a practice that is legally required, is to have separate systems for stormwater and wastewater. The stormwater pipe system tends to follow the natural path of stormwater within a given area to the nearest creek or other waterway. While pipes are used in developed areas, many other areas have a series of creeks or channels to direct the stormwater to the nearest waterway.

Since stormwater goes directly from the drainage system into the drainage basin, river, lake, or ocean untreated, it is important that contaminants are prevented from entering the stormwater drainage system. Common contaminants that should be prevented from entering stormwater drainage systems include automobile products, fertilizers, pesticides, household cleaners, and yard waste. Some communities are now using filtration methods to treat the stormwater before it gets into the stormwater pipes. For example, the use of grassy swales to collect runoff from parking lots will filter out most pollutants while letting the stormwater flow past.

Needs Assessment: Planning for Water and Wastewater Systems

The needs assessment and planning process should be a team effort combining the knowledge and skills of planners, engineers, operational staff, and finance officers. Given the competing demands of regulatory agencies, development needs, and customer service, a significant amount of time and energy must be devoted to planning for water and wastewater systems.

Demand Forecast

For many water and wastewater systems, the planning process begins with demand forecasting. Demand forecasting requires planners to forecast the peak demand for water and wastewater and will determine the size and location for water and wastewater infrastructure. To develop a comprehensive plan that will allow the finance office to accurately cost and plan for necessary capital improvements, the jurisdiction needs to consider many factors.

Growth

Planning for water and wastewater services requires governments to plan for future developments that will be part of the water and wastewater systems. Industrial developments will have different demands than commercial or residential developments. Even within each type of development, demand will vary. For example, multi-family apartment buildings demand more water than single-family homes.

Location

The specific location of water and wastewater demand services is important. Depending on the concentration of demand, the jurisdiction may need to install pipes capable of a larger capacity. Additionally, elevation differences may require additional pump stations. The jurisdiction should also consider the location of anticipated demand long into the future to effectively plan the location of infrastructure. Many economic development prospects require utility capacity to be in place before moving forward with a complete site analysis. Therefore, advance funding should provide required infrastructure and/or incentives to factor a developer's needs into capital plans.

Construction Trends

Construction trends and changes to existing developments have an impact on water demand. Jurisdictions should consider water-saving devices such as low-flush toilets and water-saving washing machines. Also, the installation of lawn irrigation systems could considerably increase water demand, but have less of an effect on wastewater needs.

Peak Usage

The system must be able to accommodate peak demand for services. It is necessary to locate appropriately sized water tanks and holding facilities to accommodate surges in water demand, such as during the workday when many industrial customers are using water.

Development Timeline

The timing of developments is also important to ensure there is enough revenue to support the costs of additional infrastructure. Planning for water and wastewater infrastructure is also a multi-year process that must start early enough to have the infrastructure in place when it is needed.

Technology Improvements

Technology improvements will have an impact on the facility's design as well as on the project's cost. Options such as the use of membranes rather than standard filtration units should be factored into the planning process. New technologies such as supervisory control and data acquisition (SCADA) systems are also changing how projects are planned and constructed.

Fire Suppression Standards

Local commercial codes will usually require a certain fire suppression system to be part of any project; therefore, demand forecasts for such water would also need to include peak demands that may be needed under critical conditions (e.g., fire). In addition, the location of hydrants and the fire suppression standards needed to serve the community also would be factored into demand forecasts. For example, the Insurance Services Office (ISO), an organization that sets requirements that are used to evaluate property and liability risk, requires that a water system provide a minimum of 250 gallons per minute for two hours in addition to the community's maximum daily rate of consumption to achieve its lowest ranking.[3] Exhibit 11.1 provides more information on needed fire flow for residential areas. In evaluating the system, the ISO also looks at the capacity of supply, capacity of water distribution, and the distribution of water hydrants, among other factors. For systems that exceed the minimum requirement, the ISO evaluates the needed fire flow by the type of construction, type of occupancy, exposure, and distance to other buildings.[4]

Exhibit 11.1 Needed Fire Flow

Distance between Residential Dwellings	Needed Fire Flow (gallons per minute)
More than 100 feet	500
31 to 100 feet	750
11 to 30 feet	1,000
10 feet or less	1,500

Source: Insurance Services Office Mitigation Online, "Water-Supply Evaluations" (http://www.isomitigation.com/ppc).

Additional Regulations

State regulatory agencies may place additional requirements on water and wastewater systems. It is important to fully understand all applicable regulations while planning any project.

Master Plans

Using the information obtained from components of the needs analysis, the jurisdiction should be able to develop a master plan. This master plan includes information on what facilities need to be constructed, their appropriate location, and a cost estimate. These cost estimates tend to be very general and are normally based on past experience or comparable projects in similar jurisdictions. In addition to structural improvements, the master plan will also include non-structural improvements such as offset programs, source pollution controls,[5] waste minimization programs or flow minimization incentive, or informational programs to encourage water conservation.

The master plan is the planner's best estimate as to what new facilities need to be constructed or what improvements should occur to existing facilities. It is important to determine if the proposed solution to the problem is the best solution. One way of evaluating this is to prepare a business case evaluation (BCE) for each project. A BCE helps management determine if the proposed solution is the best use of the agency's resources and how well the proposed project answers the following questions:

◆ Does this alternative meet all service-level requirements?

◆ Does this alternative provide the lowest lifecycle cost?

◆ What are the potential risks with this alternative?

◆ What are the environmental impacts associated with this alternative?

◆ Are there any other community impacts that will occur if the project is completed?

The master plan should cover at least five years and preferably identify potential issues as far as twenty years in the future. In some cases, it is useful to develop a master plan that anticipates the eventual build out of the entire system to ensure that proper sizing considerations and easement acquisition policies are in place to accomplish long-term objectives. Regardless of the planning horizon, master plans for water and sewer infrastructure should be reviewed annually to account for any new or proposed developments that could have an impact on service demand. An annual review also allows for the master plan to be updated with any changes in scheduling or cost.

Water and Wastewater Quality Standards

To ensure public health and safety, many standards exist to regulate water and wastewater quality. The federal government, through the federal Safe Drinking Water Act and the Federal Water Pollution Control Act, sets standards on contaminant levels in drinking water and controls wastewater discharge. In addition, states and local health departments may also set quality standards.

Drinking Water Standards

The Safe Drinking Water Act, approved in 1974, is the main federal law that protects the quality of Americans' drinking water. The EPA administers the act by setting standards for drinking water quality and provides oversight to the state and local governments responsible for implementing the standards. The EPA currently sets concentration limits, or a maximum contaminant level, for approximately 90 contaminants found in drinking water.[6] Based on current scientific studies, water that meets standards for contaminants is safe for human consumption. As scientific knowledge changes, standards are updated.

Clean Water Act

The Federal Water Pollution Control Act Amendments of 1972, better known as the "Clean Water Act," was created to restore and maintain the chemical, physical, and biological integrity of the nation's water systems including rivers, streams, lakes, wetlands, and estuaries. The act established the National Pollutant Discharge Elimination System (NPDES) for all point sources of pollution. In 1987, the Clean Water Act was amended to include non-point source pollution.

NPDES permits are required for combined sewer systems, separated sewer systems, and stormwater pollution. Each of these systems can contribute to water quality problems in the nation's waters in the form of combined sewer overflows and sanitary sewer overflows. The Clean Water Act requires jurisdictions to monitor the number of combined sewer overflows and sanitary sewer overflows and can levy fines against the jurisdiction for repeated violations.

Each state is responsible for implementing the Clean Water Act. Through the state NPDES permit process, each treatment plant is given a standard to which it must adhere for its treated wastewater. These standards are subject to negotiation but can become contentious as the EPA puts more emphasis on enforcement. The specific standards for a local government will depend primarily on the statewide standards and site-specific conditions.

Project Management Issues for Water and Wastewater Projects

The primary difference between water and wastewater construction and other general construction projects is the potential for large environmental impacts. Any number of environmental issues can delay the project and greatly increase costs. To effectively manage water and wastewater construction projects and control potential setbacks, precautions must be taken for potential environmental problems and the construction schedule may need to account for environmental issues. Listed below are a few of the environmental issues faced with these water and wastewater infrastructure projects.

Spills

One major concern with the construction of wastewater projects is the possibility of a sewage spill. This is especially critical if the spill reaches the receiving waters of an area. Even if the spill is accidental, such as if the contractor hits a sewer line while digging, the jurisdiction may be required to pay a fine to the local regulatory board or state environmental protection enforcement agency.

Contamination

One major challenge for the construction of water infrastructure, especially water piping, is the need to keep the pipes disinfected with tight joints so there is no intrusion of other substances. Small leaks will allow contaminants such as dirt, wastewater, and recycled water into the water lines.

Ground Saturation

If the water table is near the surface and groundwater has saturated the project site, the contractor may be required to dewater the project area. Dewatering is the process of removing excess water from the construction area and can greatly increase costs, especially depending on where the excess water is discharged.

Environmentally Protected Areas/Species

Some construction projects can only be active at certain times during the year due to endangered species present in the area. For example, the Sacramento Regional County Sanitation District was limited in construction of its Lower Northwest Interceptor Project due to the breeding periods of giant garter snakes and elderberry longhorn beetles. While these issues were anticipated and scheduled for, they added cost and time to the project. Another issue that is less likely to be anticipated is the presence of archeological items found while digging for sewer and water pipes. Native American remains and fossils are just two of the items that can indefinitely delay construction and increase costs while archeologists examine the finds and re-locate the remains to a safer area.

Timing

In some sections of the country, ground freeze can limit construction season and only allow work to be completed when the ground is thawed or add costs necessary to heat the ground. Construction work can also be delayed during certain times of the day. For example, water and wastewater infrastructure located under roads may create many inconveniences if work is done during rush hour. Additionally, work done near schools may be required to be completed on weekends or during the summer to lessen the impact on students.

Security

Enhanced focus on the safety and security of water and sewer systems nationally may result in additional scope items being added to projects. For example, projects may require fencing around pump stations and treatment facilities or redundancy of lines to mitigate the potential impact from breaks.

Developer-Built Lines

Private developers often construct water and wastewater lines for new residential or commercial developments. For those lines built by a developer, the infrastructure must conform to government standards. In addition, appropriate supporting documentation, such as all construction plans, must be made available to the jurisdiction, as developers traditionally donate such infrastructure back to the jurisdiction upon completion of project

Multi-Jurisdiction Agreements

Not all jurisdictions provide water and wastewater services for their residents. Services can be purchased from or provided to neighboring jurisdictions. In this case, the capital plan should include assumptions of what would be needed to recover the cost of over-sizing infrastructure for external users. Depending on the contractual term, some contracts that guarantee access to another jurisdiction's capacity may be required to report the guarantee as a capital item and capital asset in the financial statements.

Financing Water and Wastewater Systems

The American Water Works Association (AWWA) estimates that $250 billion will be needed in the next thirty years for drinking water infrastructure needs. The National Association of Clean Water Agencies in a separate estimate states that an annual capital investment need of $17.6 billion will be required throughout the United States. Other estimates place the cost of necessary upgrades due to growing populations and new water quality standards to be between $300 billion and $1 trillion over the next twenty years.[7] Due to the long useful lives of water and sewer infrastructure, long-term revenue bonds backed by revenue from service fees is a common strategy that spreads the costs over an extended time period. User charges fund the majority of projects, but grant funding and general fund contributions are also used with water and wastewater projects.[8]

Bond rating agencies will give more credit to less speculative revenue streams, such as monthly service charges that have already been approved by the jurisdiction. Connection fee revenues are more speculative, depending on local construction activity that may not occur. Such revenue streams may be discounted by rating agencies when bond coverage levels are determined. In general, rating agencies consider water and sewer revenue bonds as an extremely creditworthy debt sector since they provide highly essential services with an enduring natural monopoly.

Enterprise Funds

When local government provides water and wastewater services it can establish an enterprise fund, rather than operate the water and wastewater services as a general fund obligation. An enterprise fund is a segregated accounting fund, within the jurisdiction's budget, that enables the water and wastewater services (utility) to operate like a business. Revenues and expenditures associated with the utility are accounted for independently. Often, annual profit and loss statements for the utility are developed as part of a comprehensive financial planning and oversight program.

Depending on local practice and state law, the creation of an enterprise fund may provide more flexibility in purchasing, contracting, debt issuance, and revenue generation than general-purpose governments. An important benefit of enterprise accounting is that user charges can be more easily compared to those of other similar agencies, which can be especially important for bond rating determination.

User Charges

User charges finance operation and maintenance costs for water and wastewater systems and one-time connection fees[9] that recover the costs of connecting a new customer to an existing system as well as contribute to the capital costs of providing conveyance and treatment capacity. Connection fee calculations require estimation of capital costs over some future period. Many larger communities determine those costs through the development of the master plan that envisions system growth, regulatory changes, and long-term replacement priorities. If debt is used as a financing resource, then the annual debt service on existing and anticipated future debt issues normally is included in the calculation of a connection fee.

Generally, jurisdictions should have a policy that defines connection fees and their intended uses that are separate from user fees. For many governments, these fees are both sensitive to market pressures (i.e., how do they compare to neighboring jurisdictions) and customer pressures (e.g., does the existing customer pay for some portion of capital as part of a monthly user fee bill vs. a new homeowner making a lump-sum upon connecting to system). As part of the capital budget, it is critical to align such funding sources to capital projects and ensure that existing and ongoing revenue sources are available for long-term capital improvement programs and/or as funding source for debt service.

To determine appropriate service charges, residential, commercial, and industrial customers are separated and costs are assigned to each sector in accordance with engineering study findings. For wastewater systems, volume and strength are the principal service charge determinants, and for water systems, volume is the primary determinant. Some agencies also include a demand component to a service charge that reflects peak capacity. Demand charges are typically charged to commercial and industrial customers. They are normally not used for residential customers who are assessed a unit charge per time period.

Fees are also used according to the size of pipe; the larger the size of the pipe, the higher the fee. Exhibit 11.2 illustrates meter sizes that range from a typical single-family residence (5/8-inch meter size) to a large industrial customer (3-inch meter size). The size of the meter is in direct proportion to the number of gallons that can be supplied to each customer. For example, a 5/8-inch meter can supply twenty gallons per minute. To determine the proper connection fee based on the supply capacity, a 5/8-inch meter is given an equivalent residence unit (ERU) factor of 1. A commercial customer, whose water supply need is 300 gallons per minute or fifteen times that of a residential customer, would be given an ERU of 15. Fees then could be based on ERU.

Exhibit 11.2 Equivalent Meter Factors

Meter Size (inches)	Max Flow (gallons per minute)	Equivalent Residence Unit
5/8	20	1
1	50	2.5
1 ½	100	5
2	160	8
3	300	15

Grant Funding

While user fees provide the majority of financing for water and wastewater infrastructure projects, jurisdictions should not overlook the possibility of obtaining grants and/or loans for capital project financing. Since the passage of the Federal Water Pollution Control Act of 1956, the federal government has provided grants for construction of water and wastewater infrastructure. Later amendments in 1981 and 1987 reduced and phased out the grant program, but replaced it with aid to states through the EPA to capitalize state revolving loan funds.[10]

State revolving funds offer loans that can be a significant source of financing for water and wastewater projects. Such funds are normally controlled by regulatory agencies and are offered on a project-priority basis. Waiting lists for funding are common. Revolving funds are replenished through repayments and loan terms are typically shorter than with various types of public debt issues, but may have lower interest rates. Repayment of the loan does not need to be from project revenues, but can come from property owner/developer fees, dedicated taxes, stormwater management fees, or donations.

Along with the EPA, eight other federal agencies provide infrastructure funding, grants, and loans directly to local governments or states that then disburse the funding to local governments. The Department of Agriculture's (USDA) Rural Assistance Program provides loans, grants, and loan guarantees for drinking water, sewers, and storm drainage facilities in rural areas with populations under 10,000.[11] The Department of Housing and Urban Development (HUD) makes its community block grants available to entitled communities for water and wastewater infrastructure.[12] The Department of Commerce's Economic Development Administration (EDA) provides assistance to help support the construction or rehabilitation of essential public infrastructure in distressed communities.[13] In 2002, the EPA, USDA, HUD, and EDA provided $8.53 billion for water and wastewater infrastructure. Specific funding by program is shown in Exhibit 11.3. Other funding is provided by the Appalachian Regional Commission, Federal Emergency Management Agency, Department of the Interior, the Small Business Administration, and the U.S. Army Corps of Engineers.

Exhibit 11.3 Federal Grant Funding

Agency	Program	Annual Amount (FY 2002)
EPA	Drinking water state revolving funds	$ 1.3 billion
EPA	Clean water state revolving funds	$ 4.4 billion
USDA	Rural Assistance Program	$ 2.1 billion
HUD	Community Development Block Grants	$488 million
Dept. of Commerce	Economic Development Administration	$250 million

Source: U.S. Environmental Protection Agency, *Handbook on Coordinating Funding for Water and Wastewater Infrastructure* (Washington, D.C.: U.S. Environmental Protection Agency, October 2003).

Infrastructure Maintenance and Management

Asset management can be defined for water and wastewater systems as a means of managing infrastructure to deliver service levels that customers desire at an acceptable level of risk, while minimizing the cost of owning and operating the asset. Local governments are moving towards asset management principles to deal with a variety of challenges including aging infrastructure, regulatory pressures, doing "more with less," keeping rates reasonable, providing better information for the city council or governing board, and sustaining infrastructure.

Using a risk assessment tool to evaluate the city's sewer and drainage systems, Seattle Public Utilities was able to calculate monetary consequences of pipe failure based on the model attributes. The city found that rather than videotaping all of the pipes once every thirty years, it could switch to videotaping only the high-risk pipes once every five years. This allows the city to operate within the budget allocated to videotaping, but reduce additional risk. The following is a list of potential benefits from asset management programs.

◆ It lowers the total life-cycle cost for the agency. The EPA estimates that life cycle cost savings of up to 20 percent are possible by implementing asset management practices with water and wastewater infrastructure.

◆ It provides the governing board with better information on which to make decisions. The board can make trade offs between acceptable levels of risk and costs since the customers have provided information through service levels of what they want versus what they are willing to pay.

◆ It may help maintain bond ratings for the agency, which would lower future debt issuance costs. The EPA is considering requiring asset management programs for all federal grants and loans.

As a result of asset management programs, long-term capital plans should include rehab and replacement funding to recognize that as systems age, including treatment facilities and holding storage tanks, pumping stations, and other equipment, re-investment will help ensure that water and sewer services are being provided at targeted goals and standards. While certain rehab and replacement programs may be project specific, some jurisdictions allocate a generic use of funding to meet anticipated needs. Sometimes such allocations are based upon a formula (e.g., equal to depreciation expense) and if funding is not utilized in one year it is accumulated in a reserve account to be used in subsequent years.

Conclusion

Providing water and wastewater service is one of the most important local government services. Planning for water and wastewater infrastructure is often a lengthy process. Due to the location of most infrastructure, it is often difficult to replace, so careful consideration should be given to the potential for community growth and anticipated demand levels. The finance officer should play a key role in the planning of additional water and wastewater capital projects to properly develop the financing plan.

The Lower Northwest Interceptor Project

The Lower Northwest Interceptor (LNWI) project, constructed by the Sacramento Regional County Sanitation District (SRCSD), is a nineteen-mile pipeline connecting the northern portion of the City of Sacramento, California, with the treatment plant in the City of Elk Grove, California. The LNWI includes ten major projects: two pump stations, five pipeline segments, and three major tunnels, two of which pass under the Sacramento River. The project was necessary to provide reliable sewer service to an area in the northern portion of Sacramento County undergoing explosive growth.

When the project was originally planned, the estimated cost was $240 million. Later, the route of the project was changed to avoid going directly through the City of Sacramento. Environmental impact mitigation and scheduling issues pushed the total project cost to almost $600 million, and the finance office was responsible for finding additional funds.

SRCSD did not have enough reserve funding in the bank, so the only solution was to issue additional bonds to cover the new project cost. The projected rates and fees were updated to cover the additional costs using a phased approach that gradually increased connection fees over a three-year period. Modeling showed that the phased approach to increased connection fees would impact total revenue, as the amount of growth within the district more than offset the loss of fees. The board of directors agreed to additional rate and fee increases to pay for the debt service on the bonds.

Notes

1. Information was taken from the U.S. Census Bureau's 2002 Census of Governments (http://www.census.gov).

2. Information was taken from Metropolitan Water District of Southern California Web site (http://www.mwdh2o.com).

3. Insurance Services Office Mitigation Online, "Water-Supply Evaluations" (http://www.isomitigation.com/ppc).

4. Insurance Services Office, "Guide for Determination of Needed Fire Flow" (http://www.isomitigation.com/ppc).

5. An example of a source pollution control would be strategies aimed at reducing a toxic element such as mercury at the source rather than when it enters the treatment plant.

6. More information on EPA maximum contaminant levels can be found on the EPA Web site (http://www.epa.gov).

7. U.S. General Accountability Office, *Water Infrastructure: Information on Federal and State Financial Assistance* (Washington, D.C.: U.S. General Accountability Office, November 2001).

8. U.S. Environmental Protection Agency, *Handbook on Coordinating Funding for Water and Wastewater Infrastructure* (Washington, D.C.: U.S. Environmental Protection Agency, October 2003).

9. One-time connection fees include hookup fees, capacity fees, or impact fees.

10. U.S. General Accountability Office, *Water Infrastructure*, November 2001.

11. Information was taken from the U.S. Department of Agriculture "Water and Environmental Homepage" (http://www.usda.gov/rus/water/index.htm).

12. Information was taken from the U.S. Department of Housing and Urban Development Web site, (www.hud.gov).

13. Information was taken from the U.S. Department of Commerce Web site, "Investment Programs" (http://www.eda.gov/AboutEDA/Programs.xml).

12

Administrative Facilities

By Joseph P. Casey

While many of the facilities described in this book pertain to specific local government services such as fire/EMS stations, jails, or libraries, jurisdictions also provide many services in general administrative offices. Administrative facilities are usually designed to best accommodate the administrative, clerical, technical, and managerial personnel related to the department or division, but also contain areas for customer service where primary "counter" or "window" services are provided. Over the years, administrative facilities have assumed many shapes and sizes depending on the services provided and the jurisdiction's function.

In older jurisdictions, local city halls were often situated prominently in the center of the community as part of the town square or in a location from which residential areas and businesses grew. Some newer facilities resemble an office park where government services are provided from a complex or campus-style arrangement of buildings that offer a "one-stop shopping" experience. Other decentralized centers divide the administrative functions among many smaller facilities located closer to citizens to better achieve common customer service objectives, such as paying a water bill or obtaining a permit.

As governments continue to focus on how best to provide service to their customers while also housing their workforce in a productive atmosphere, better-designed facilities accommodate constituents and workflow more effectively. However, each community has its unique needs and customer service demands that may require different facility designs. Jurisdictions should assess all needs and services in choosing the manner in which to provide facility space. This chapter highlights certain types of administrative facilities to illustrate the core concepts by which administrative facility space can be better planned.

Needs Assessment: Planning for Administrative Facilities

A needs assessment for administrative facilities should include both a programming analysis and a space analysis to help determine which specific features to include, the layout necessary, and the amount of space needed. The analysis should consider the jurisdiction's present and future needs. Using a space needs model and determining the best position and location of functions or departments can be a complex undertaking, and external professional consultants may be required, especially if the jurisdiction has never done it before. Items to include in the analysis are:

- Individual spaces, their quantity, and approximate sizes;
- Space standards for position types and special functions;
- Space needs model;
- Summary of space needs by function;
- Estimating total building space;
- Primary location of departments;
- Parking needs by user type (council members, staff, visitors);
- Special equipment requirements;
- Technical requirements; and
- Security features.

Determine Required Workspace

Using current employee counts and the expected number of future employees, the jurisdiction should estimate the required workspace through the use of models developed to illustrate the number of employees by classification within each department. Generally, employee workspaces can be classified by manager, station, customer service, field workers, and other.

Managers

Managers generally require an office with walls and a door to conduct small meetings, perform supervisory duties, or deal with sensitive issues in privacy.

Station Positions

For station positions, a standard workstation or cubicle provides an independent workspace for employees who do not require privacy to do their jobs.

Customer Service Positions

Customer service employees include those stationed at the front counter, receptionist/administrative assistants, and/or customer service agents. Workspace is generally similar to that of the station position classification, but also includes counter space and a lobby or waiting area to better serve the public. In cases where money is exchanged, special security and counter separations may be required. Note that while the title used here is customer service, it should not be confused with call takers who may be referred to as customer service agents. Call takers may not have face-to-face interaction with customers and do not need additional waiting area and front counter space.

Field Positions

Employees with field positions, such as building inspectors, do not generally require traditional office space since their responsibilities often take them on the road. In many cases, a government vehicle will be required, although some office space is needed in the administrative facility for processing paperwork and responding to citizen inquiries. If all field workers start and end their day at the same time and at the same place, more space is required than if shifts are staggered, allowing more than one employee to share the same space or report to decentralized locations. For example, if all police officers were to meet at one central office, more space would be required than if officers reported to multiple precincts throughout the jurisdiction at staggered shift start times.

Other Positions

This classification covers individuals who usually do not require a dedicated workspace, such as elected officials or citizen committees that use public meeting areas, or part-time employees that generally can take advantage of vacant work stations.

Exhibit 12.1 shows the number of employees in Hanover County, Virginia, for each classification by department and the area available for each department.[1] Remember that space-planning models should also project the space required for future years.

Exhibit 12.1 Position Classification for Hanover County, Virginia

Building	Department	Positions 2005						Area
		Mgr	Station	Cust	Field	Other	Total	Sq ft
Bldg 1	Building inspections	3	5	5	10		23	3,264
Bldg 1	City administrator/ board	5	3	1			9	4,643
Bldg 1	City attorney	6	3				9	3,144

Building	Department	Positions 2005						Area
		Mgr	Station	Cust	Field	Other	Total	Sq ft
Bldg 1	Planning	4	17	3	5	14	43	4,894
Bldg 1	Public utilities	10	11	2	4		27	6,131
Bldg 1	Public works	4	6	2			12	2,210
Bldg 2	Public works	1	2		4		7	1,739
Bldg 2	Assessor	3	8	1			12	3,273
Bldg 3	Facilities management	2		1	5	1	9	1,415
Bldg 4	Finance	5	8	1			14	3,615
Bldg 4	Internal audit	1	2				3	1,440
Bldg 5	Revenue commissioner	4	7	7			18	5,003
Bldg 5	GIS	1	3				4	827
Bldg 5	Human resources	3	6	1			10	1,898
Bldg 5	Information technology	8	22	1			31	9,329
Bldg 5	Purchasing	2	3	2			7	1,897
Bldg 5	Registrar	1	1	1		3	6	602
Bldg 5	Treasurer	5	3	10		10	28	4,117

Source: Hanover County, Virginia

Space Standards for Position Types and Special Functions

A key assumption in planning for administrative facilities is the area required for each position. A reasonable starting point is the amount of space currently being used, although it is also beneficial to compare current space usage estimates with space planning consultants or industry guides. When evaluating the amount of required space, it is helpful to have current job descriptions for all positions and to note any working environment conditions that require additional space. Exhibit 12.2 includes estimates of required space by employee position classification used for planning in Hanover County, Virginia.

Exhibit 12.2 Space Allocations per Position Type

Position	Approximate Square Foot Allocation
Department head private office	180 – 250
Supervisor private office	150 – 200
Staff private office	120 – 180
Staff work station (cubicle)	50 – 80
Customer service workstation	50 – 80
Field personnel workstation	30 – 50

- If an employee requires more than 80 square feet, then it may be more practical to provide them with a private office rather than a workstation.
- Common areas and lobbies are not accounted for in customer service workstations' square feet allotments, therefore an additional space needs to be provided depending on the use or purpose.

Source: Hanover County, Virginia

Space Needs Model

A space needs model will estimate the required square footage for a new facility using projections of future employee numbers. If the amount of space provided to each employee classification is known, a jurisdiction can simply multiply the projected employee counts in each classification to develop an overall estimate of needed space. Jurisdictions can check to determine if the estimate is reasonable by multiplying current employee numbers by the per-employee estimate and comparing it to current space available.

Using general per-employee assumptions does not account for unique requirements for some services or departments. Jurisdictions should pay careful attention to each department's unique space requirements that would not be included in per-employee workspace assumptions. The following are examples of features that may warrant adjustments to the estimate:

Shifts

Departments that have more than one shift can utilize the same workspace for different employees at different times of the day. This most likely occurs in public safety positions and other 24-hour service functions.

Meeting Rooms

Jurisdictions should account for conference rooms and other meeting areas that would be used for normal operations.

Special Meeting Rooms

Special meeting rooms for elected officials, community meeting rooms, or court rooms should be sized to accommodate all projected long-term demands. Space for public access and audience seating should also be planned.

Non-Administrative Functions

Departments that perform non-office or general administrative facility-related work may need to be separated from standard space needs models and have estimates that more closely relate to services that are provided. For example, building inspectors may need additional space to analyze large construction drawings. Additionally, maintenance and construction-related services such as roads, water/sewer, fleet, and maintenance departments should have space for equipment or other workstations that fit their needs.

Courts

Space needs for court facilities are more closely estimated by projecting activity levels rather than employee counts. The number of needed courtrooms can be estimated using caseload thresholds for judges and the anticipated number of cases. Courts also need space for security and clerical functions that would also depend on activity levels.

Summary of Space Needs by Function

Many jurisdictions segment facility space needs into four categories: general government, courts, human services, and public safety. Grouping services allows customers to have easy access. Therefore, in the process of determining how to best utilize space and determine a jurisdiction's needs, it may be practical to subtotal departments and their respective needs into one of these four categories. For example, Hanover County, Virginia, was able to group services and forecast the required space twenty years into the future for each functional group, as shown in Exhibit 12.3.

In 2006, a staff of 910 occupied 208,519 square feet of building space. Using the position classification and space needs analysis discussed earlier in the chapter, as well as anticipated future staffing levels based on the county's growth patterns, Hanover County estimated that in 2027 its space needs would reach approximately 350,000 square feet.

The additional 141,892 square feet would need to be created by building additional facilities, expanding the current facility, or increasing the efficiency factor of existing space.

Exhibit 12.3 Projected Square Feet Need for Workforce and Workforce-Related Services

	Employees	Space Needs	Space per Employee (Sq. Ft.)	Employees	Space per Employee (Standard)	Space Required (Sq. Ft.)	Additional Space Needs (Sq. Ft.)
	2006			**2027**			
Courts	100	38,844	388	160	555	88,800	49,956
General government	286	73,839	258	450	272	122,400	48,561
Human services	210	54,874	261	278	262	72,836	17,962
Public safety	314	40,962	269	531	125	66,375	25,413
Total	**910**	**208,519**	**229**	**1,419**	**247**	**350,411**	**141,892**

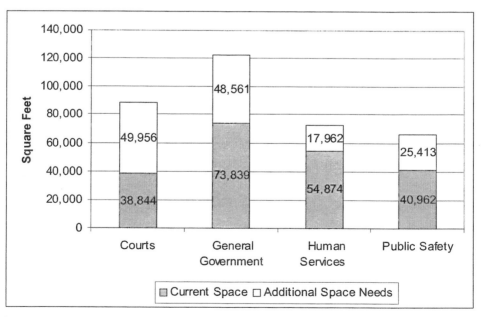

Source: Hanover County, Virginia

Estimating Total Building Space

Space needs calculated by estimating workspace requirements for each employee do not account for areas such as restrooms, hallways, or housing for utilities. Using a conversion factor or efficiency factor, total building area needs can be estimated. Efficiency factors indicate what percent of the building is used by employees for work and usually ranges from 0.6 to 0.8. To calculate overall space needs, divide the space needs estimate by the efficiency factor. For example, with an efficiency factor of 0.7, 10,000 square feet of space needs would indicate the entire facility should contain 14,285 square feet. Efficiency factors can be estimated by looking at current building designs.

Location of Departments

Public Art

Many administrative facilities use lobby and entrance areas to display public art, awards, or items of historical significance. Often local volunteer groups partner with the jurisdiction and arrange rotating exhibits of local art or history. The administrative center then takes on the role of visitor center and museum. Some governments have enacted policies that mandate a portion of construction costs for public buildings go to public art.

With these "percent for art" policies, jurisdictions will allocate a percentage (often 1 percent) of either the project or construction costs to provide and fund public art displays. Some notable jurisdictions that have implemented such policies include Allegheny County, Pennsylvania; Atlanta, Georgia; Charlotte, North Carolina; King County, Washington; Oklahoma City, Oklahoma; Phoenix, Arizona; and Portland, Oregon. Many more jurisdictions of all sizes also have similar policies in place.

Before beginning to plan for, design, and construct a new facility, it may be beneficial to re-evaluate how government facilities are organized and determine if more or less centralization will allow the jurisdiction to operate more effectively. Some questions to ask include: Is it advantageous to locate administrative departments and the police department at the same facility? What about public works and administration, or administration and community development? Locating all departments together has the potential to save on overhead building costs, but each department may operate more effectively in a different type of building. All options have advantages and disadvantages and each should be carefully considered. What is best for one jurisdiction may not be the best for another.

To determine the proper place for departments within one facility, jurisdictions should develop an adjacency diagram. Adjacency diagrams display a conceptual arrangement of space that reflects the facility's functional needs. The alignment of departments and related business functions with workflow diagrams can be effective in making sure the departments and points of citizen contact are located properly. In addition, floor plan analysis can be conducted to determine the proper size, shape, and location of furniture and equipment within a department.

Exhibit 12.4 illustrates how space on one floor of the facility is assigned. Illustrations of this type can help identify space constraints and opportunities for re-allocation. The image also displays areas used as workspace versus common areas and can be used to calculate efficiency factors.

Exhibit 12.4 Example Adjacency Diagram

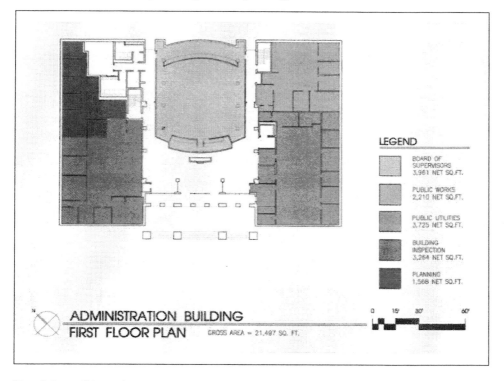

Parking Needs

Administrative facilities will require adequate parking for staff, government vehicles such as police cars stored at the site, and any visitors. The facility will also need parking for council meetings and community events. It is important to evaluate the timing of parking needs. For example, parking requirements for council meetings and staff probably will not overlap, as most staff work during regular business hours and most council meetings are conducted in the evening. If the facility serves as a primary point of contact for residents, parking studies may be necessary to determine the proper number of spaces. In many urban areas where parking may be limited, it is important for the jurisdiction to provide some parking, possibly in a parking garage, to allow easy access for citizens, businesses, and other visitors.

Technical Features

The manner in which employees work and citizens access services has also changed significantly in recent years through increased use of Web-based products, as well as heightened ability to communicate through e-mail, cell phones, and mobile devices. Field personnel are able to perform more and more of their work offsite and transmit data back to the administrative office from the field. Many administrative personnel may also be able to perform more of their work at home through remote access to systems.

Information technology can provide opportunities for government to be more efficient and effective in meeting customer service demands and technological infrastructure should be considered along with any new facility. More information on technology investments is available in chapter 13.

Security Features

For security and safety measures, buildings or specific areas of the building may be designed with limited access points. Security cameras and automated door-locking systems are also common. In addition, some jurisdictions have installed magnometers and other screening devices at entrances; others require all visitors to enter through one entrance and obtain a visitor pass. The location of the facility itself can be buffered from close proximity to the parking lot or roads.

Planning for Disasters

Planning for natural disasters is an increasingly important factor in designing new administrative facilities. Proper planning for back-up generators and emergency offsite access to technology applications should be a high priority and enable the jurisdiction to function at all times. Understanding the facility's dependence on particular electrical transmission, cable, and telephone communication lines will allow the jurisdiction to strategically place back-ups. If a disaster occurs, it is vital to maintain the ability to communicate and function.

Developing Cost Estimates

Rough cost estimates can be calculated by applying cost-per-square-foot assumptions to required space needs. Professional consultants or cost estimating tools can provide an approximate cost-per-square-foot estimate. Exhibit 12.5 shows a cost estimation worksheet used by Hanover County, Virginia, to build a new facility and renovate an existing facility. Site improvements and other project cost factors have been estimated to be 15 percent and 30 percent of total construction costs. Of course, these costs will be different for each jurisdiction. Professional engineers or architects should review all project cost assumptions and cost estimates.

Exhibit 12.5 Projected Facility Space Needs and Capital Cost

(All area in square feet)	Courts	General	Human Services	Public Safety
New Facility				
Current space	37,421	75,254	54,874	29,800
Efficiency factor	0.64	0.74	0.9	0.9
Current gross building area	58,470	101,695	60,971	33,111
Projected space needs	71,625	102,432	63,500	41,200
Projected efficiency factor	0.65	0.75	0.9	0.82
Projected gross building area needs	110,192	136,576	70,556	50,244
Additional space needed	51,722	34,881	9,584	17,133
Capital cost per square foot	$ 250	$ 210	$ 210	$ 250
Total construction cost	$12,930,499	$ 7,325,095	$2,012,733	$4,283,198
Site improvement approximation	$ 1,939,575	$ 1,098,764	$ 301,910	$ 642,480
15% of construction costs				
Other Cost Approximation (Contingency)	$ 4,461,022	$ 2,527,158	$ 694,393	$1,477,703
30% of construction costs				
Total new facility cost	$19,331,096	$10,951,017	$3,009,036	$6,403,381
Renovation				
Square feet of renovation	58,470	35,593	21,340	7,284
Renovation cost per square foot	$ 110	$ 65	$ 65	$ 85
Construction cost	$ 6,431,734	$ 2,313,552	$1,387,093	$ 619,178
Other cost approximation (contingency)	$ 1,929,520	$ 694,066	$ 416,128	$ 185,753
30% of renovation costs				
Total renovation cost	$ 8,361,255	$ 3,007,618	$1,803,221	$ 804,931
Total capital project	$27,692,350	$13,958,635	$4,812,257	$7,208,312

Source: Hanover County, Virginia

Facility Space: Build, Renovate, or Lease

Once the need for facility space has been quantified and an assessment and inventory of existing space has been completed, the jurisdiction must determine how to meet the additional need. In addition to building a new facility, space can be attained by renovating an existing government facility, buying and moving into an existing building, or leasing.

When renovating an existing government facility, jurisdictions should evaluate the level of disruption that may occur to any current employees, customers, and business operations during renovation work. Generally, renovation projects will be staggered to allow sections of the facility to be in use while work is done in other areas. If the disruption is significant, temporary facilities may be required. Temporary facilities generally also would be required if the renovations to the HVAC, electrical, or other wiring would disrupt the entire facility.

It is also common for jurisdictions to move into existing buildings in the community. For example, jurisdictions can easily move into old private sector office space once used for insurance companies, banks, or other firms. Many jurisdictions, school districts especially, often move administrative offices into an old school. By rehabilitating an old building in an economically depressed area, the jurisdiction can also act as an urban renewal catalyst and use its investment in the area to attract more private investment in the neighborhood.

Moving into existing facilities usually involves lower costs and requires less time to complete. On the other hand, renovating existing structures may result in a space that is not ideally suited to meet the jurisdiction's needs. Features such as state-of-the-art technology architecture; energy efficient heating, lighting, and cooling systems; and modern communication capabilities may not be possible.

Leasing facility space gives the jurisdiction more options that could potentially result in cost savings. Jurisdictions are able to enter into two different types of leases. With an operating lease, the jurisdiction and owner of the property agree to a contract that would allow the government to use the facility for a specific time period in exchange for payments. At the end of the lease period, the jurisdiction would then re-evaluate its space needs and potentially renew the lease. Capital leases are similar to operating leases, although payments serve as a pathway towards ownership. Having a government lease space from a private sector owner has many potential benefits. As tax-exempt organizations, governments are unable to take advantage of any tax benefits, such as depreciation tax shields or tax incentives for renovating historic structures, but privately owned buildings leased to the government would generally be eligible for some savings. Often these savings are at least partially passed on to the government lessee in the form of lower payments.

Funding Sources

Traditional funding sources for administrative facilities are general fund cash allocations or general obligation debt financing, although costs for enterprise fund-related departments, such as utilities, may be recovered through revenue-generating activities and interfund charges. One of the biggest challenges in funding administrative facilities is the competition for limited funding with other more high profile projects that the public might view as more important. However, establishing service-level goals and communicating the link between the project and customer service expectations can better secure funding sources.

One option to guarantee that proper funding is available for administrative facilities is to develop a cash funding plan that accumulates funding and allows projects to be funded with cash. Using capital improvement fund planning, funds can be accumulated over years to finance construction or renovations. This is especially important in localities where debt financing may not be readily accepted for administrative facilities, such as those jurisdictions that use bond referenda for debt financing.

Conclusion

Many of the other chapters in this book describe capital projects that are often viewed by the public or elected officials as necessities and generally receive broader support. Administrative facilities are somewhat challenged by the fact that they represent the support services of government, and not those with a direct impact on service delivery such as parks, schools, or fire stations. If administrative facility needs are constantly deferred in lieu of other priorities, the result can be a cramped workforce, loss of employee morale, inefficient business operations, and in the end, a failure to effectively provide basic services for the community or increased costs of services. Therefore, establishment of clear standards for space with reasonable assumptions that allow the jurisdiction to anticipate long-term needs will ensure a proactive approach and a continued delivery of administrative services.

Note

1. All diagrams and figures used for exhibits in this chapter are findings from the 2006 facility space study done in Hanover, Virginia.

|13|

Planning and Evaluating Technology Investments

By Shayne C. Kavanagh and Huy Nguyen

Information technology (IT) has become an increasingly important part of the business of government. Technology enables government to keep up with the increasing demands placed upon it while limiting corresponding increases in personnel costs. Technology investments, though, must be carefully planned and evaluated so that jurisdictions realize maximum value and invest in the technology that is most useful for solving their particular problems.

Technology assets can also become rapidly obsolete. Lifecycles are as short as three years for certain types of investments, such as software or personal computers. As a result, such investments may not warrant inclusion in a capital budget, but are nevertheless an important operating budget consideration. IT has the potential to dramatically impact the day-to-day operations of large segments of the jurisdiction as it becomes a more pervasive feature of government business processes.

This chapter will focus on technology investment decisions from the perspective of two major types of IT investments: infrastructure and business applications. Infrastructure serves as the foundation for technology applications and includes investments such as personal computers (PCs), networks, and servers. Business applications are used to enhance government operations such as financial management systems, utility billing systems, or enterprise resource planning (ERP) systems.

With all technology investments decisions, the role of IT governance is critical. IT governance specifies how decisions involving planning, investment, and prioritization will be made and who will make them. IT governance also establishes the accountability framework needed to encourage desirable behavior in IT usage – namely those behaviors needed to realize value from IT investments.[1] Because IT governance provides structure to the decision-making and accountability processes around IT assets, it has important implications for planning and evaluating technology investments.

What Constitutes a "Capital Project"?

Some IT purchases can be difficult to distinguish as a capital project versus a normal operating expense due to their shorter useful lives and relatively low costs for the individual assets that might be included in a project, such as PCs and lower-end servers. Governments should therefore establish a clear policy for what constitutes an IT capital project. In addition to a dollar threshold for defining a project, there are several other considerations that should enter into a policy. First, entirely new capacity or functionality should generally be considered a capital project, whereas upgrades to existing functionality could be part of a normal replacement schedule that is not part of a capital improvement plan. For example, replacing PCs (even if they are being replaced with more powerful ones) would generally not be considered a capital project, but building new infrastructure for desk-to-desk video conferencing would be considered a capital endeavor. Second, since personnel- related costs are often a major component of an IT project, if not the most important component, decision makers must develop a clear policy on whether these costs contribute to the total project cost. Finally, the government must consider how its policy will relate to its IT governance and purchasing procedures.

> **Personal Computers and the Capital Budget**
>
> Because of the low cost of individual PCs, they are usually not subject to a capital budget. However, their acquisition in support of a project may warrant their inclusion into a capital budget. In addition to supporting capital projects, PC replacement programs should be established and regularly funded. A regular replacement program helps smooth out replacement costs from year to year and ensures that employees have productive equipment. Replacement programs could be funded as part of a capital improvement plan (due the substantial total cost involved) or could be funded as an operating expense since replacements represent an ongoing cost of doing business.

Because IT projects are usually made up of lower-cost component pieces (i.e., multiple pieces of hardware, labor, software, etc.), it might be possible to break the project into separate purchases in order to escape the scrutiny of a capital project evaluation. This risk can be mitigated in two ways. First, a strong governance structure that is characterized by joint decision making and trust between central IT services and user departments will discourage such behavior, because participants will perceive it as disadvantageous to work outside the governance structure and without the assistance of central IT. Second, purchasing controls such as having central IT review and approve technology purchases can help guard against maverick purchasing.

IT Governance and Resource Allocation

IT governance helps the jurisdiction maximize the value of its IT investments by engaging stakeholders from across the organization in the decision-making and accountability processes around IT assets. Given the significant amount of resources spent on IT in many governments and the wide array of operational areas across which this spending occurs, a robust governance structure is important for creating consensus on the broader, strategic business objectives technology investments should fulfill, identifying the criteria for evaluating technology investments, directing spending towards the highest priority areas, evaluating the results of technology spending and providing accountability for those results, and realizing economies of scale and synergies from IT spending across the organization. IT governance is central to effective technology project planning and evaluation. Successful governance does not occur spontaneously; rather it is consciously designed. IT governance structures should be used to answer a number of questions relative to the effective use of technology within the jurisdiction, but this chapter will focus on IT governance's role in project planning, evaluation, and resource allocation in particular. Key design features characteristic of good governance that fulfill these roles include:

- ◆ **Joint Decision Making.** Good IT governance in the public sector is characterized by joint decision making between IT professionals who have insight into the technical issues and business professionals such as end users or a manager who utilize information for decisions.[2]

- ◆ **Involvement of Top Decision Makers.** The involvement of top executives such as the CEO, CIO, and CFO legitimize the governance process. Their involvement is most crucial at the point of funding approval for the highest priority projects.

- ◆ **Standard Evaluation Method.** Good IT governance in the public sector is also characterized by communication.[3] A central element of communication is a shared understanding of the criteria by which projects will be judged.

- ◆ **Evaluation for Technical Considerations.** This ensures the project's conformance with technology standards and/or identification of projects proposed by different business units that exhibit possible synergies. This design feature can be especially valuable in jurisdictions with decentralized IT decision making, where there is greater potential for duplicate spending.

- ◆ **Development of Formal Business Case.** The business case describes the rationale for the project, including anticipated cost and benefits. Critical elements of a business case include:

  - ☐ *Vision and Goals* – How the project aligns with the jurisdiction's strategic direction;

☐ *Critical Business Issues* – How the project will solve day-to-day management and business process problems;

☐ *Costs/Benefits* – How much the project will cost and an estimation of the benefits to be realized;

☐ *Risks* – Identifies inherent project risks in order to develop a plan to mitigate them; and

☐ *Performance Indicators* – Performance measures are used to assess the results of the project against intended goals.

◆ **Partnership with the Finance Office.** The budget office should be closely involved in IT governance so that it is kept apprised of likely spending requests over the planning period.

◆ **IT Strategic Plan.** An IT strategic plan sets forth a multi-year direction for development of IT capabilities, including spending on new IT capital projects. An IT strategic plan starts by identifying the most important business goals of the government and opportunities to use technology to help achieve those goals. Strategies are then developed to take advantage of the opportunities. Typically, some gap will exist between the jurisdiction's current capabilities and the capabilities required by the strategies (e.g., the strategy requires the use of a technology the jurisdiction does not currently possess). This gap suggests prioritization of certain technology investments. IT strategic plans typically span from eighteen months to five years and cover both infrastructure and business application investments.

A Case Study of Oakland County, Michigan

Oakland County's governance structure revolves around leadership groups, which are user committees organized by functional areas. The leadership groups are constituted and headed by representatives from business departments, but also include IT personnel in order to help resolve technical issues that might arise during the groups' deliberations. Oakland County's IT operations are highly centralized, yet the Oakland County model still is able to incorporate a high degree of input from functional departments through the leadership groups.

Oakland County prioritizes and approves projects through a two-year IT master planning process that begins when project sponsors use a "scope and approach" document and a return on investment (ROI) spreadsheet to submit project requests to a leadership group The project scope and approach document provides the basis for all projects to be evaluated and controlled consistently across the county. The project request must identify a project goal, business objective(s), major deliverables, approach, and benefits such as cost savings, cost avoidance, and intangibles. The request also details staffing, facilities, technical needs, and other assumptions. The ROI spreadsheet evaluates the anticipated benefits resulting from a successful project. This analysis is used to ensure all projects comply with the county's six-year payback guideline for IT projects.

The leadership group then reviews proposed projects based on defined evaluation criteria and if approved, the project is considered "authorized for sizing." At this point the leadership group's IT representatives work with the project sponsor to elaborate on the scope and approach in documents and ROI analysis. This step also gives IT the opportunity to officially screen the project for technical feasibility and conformance with the county's technical architecture direction and standards. The leadership group then assigns priority to the project using a consensus-based approach and forwards the project to the IT department for inclusion in the countywide IT master plan.

After the master plan has been formulated, it goes back the leadership groups for review and approval. If a leadership group is not satisfied with the funding allocation its projects have received, it has a few options. It could decide to reprioritize its projects to de-fund one project in favor of another, approach the county board for additional funding, or divest a current technology to free up resources.

In addition to its IT master plan, Oakland County also accounts for longer-range technology needs in its capital improvement plan. While the IT master plan is used primarily to fund new business applications, the capital plan is focused more on upgrades to existing technology. For example, the capital improvement plan includes major upgrades to the county's financial system and major hardware replacement programs. The IT department works with user departments to identify requirements for infrastructure and application upgrades that will be needed over a multi-year period. The IT department then develops cost estimates and works with the department of management and budget to schedule these items into the capital improvement plan.

Note: Oakland County's leadership groups are the approximate equivalent of "communities of interest," a term used in similar models of IT governance.

Technology Infrastructure Projects

Technology infrastructure such as a servers, network devices, and operating system software is the platform through which technology applications are delivered. While infrastructure is largely invisible to the end user, these components are essential to effective service delivery. This means that infrastructure does not occupy as prominent a place in the minds of decision makers outside of the IT department when compared to business applications that have more visible impact on citizen service delivery. A good planning process for technology investment must provide a way for infrastructure needs to be properly evaluated and financed relative to competing resource uses.

Components of Technology Infrastructure

Technology infrastructure includes many cost elements that must be evaluated. First for consideration are initial acquisition and implementation costs (i.e., costs associated with planning, hardware, software, training, and installation).

- ◆ **Planning Costs.** Infrastructure projects, especially larger, more complex ones, might require extensive preparation, including outside assistance, to plan the project and to procure the proper equipment.

- ◆ **Hardware Costs.** This represents the cost of the physical infrastructure itself, such as server hardware, network hardware, and PCs. Due to the increasing power of hardware and decreasing costs, hardware is becoming a less significant cost item.

- ◆ **Software.** This is the cost of licenses for operating software. The most important types of software for infrastructure are typically server operating system software and database software. Software costs can vary significantly.

- ◆ **Training.** Staff may require training to most effectively use new infrastructure. In particular, IT staff may need training on advanced features that have the potential to reduce the overall maintenance effort needed for infrastructure.

- ◆ **Installation.** This represents the personnel time required to install the new infrastructure. Internal staff time needed to set up the infrastructure should be accounted for, as well as consulting support that may be required for infrastructure installation if staff expertise is not available. Alternatively, the jurisdiction may need to hire staff trained in this area.

Needs Assessment

Infrastructure needs can be identified through formal plans and standards, replacement schedules, and other ways of rationally identifying needs for increases in infrastructure capacity. Each of these sources brings a different perspective to technology planning and evaluation, ranging from philosophical guidance to detailed purchasing recommendations.

Architecture Plans

Ideally, infrastructure decisions will be guided by a formal architecture plan, often referred to as an enterprise architecture (EA) plan. An EA plan provides a common, strategic vision for using technology to support the jurisdiction's business processes. An EA plan typically does not describe specific technology purchases the jurisdiction should make. Rather, it provides guidelines and strategies that can help the jurisdiction to:[4]

◆ Base technology decisions on how they would improve agency services as a whole;

◆ Minimize acquisition, support, and replacement costs of technology products and services;

◆ Improve consistency, quality, and timeliness of data that is shared government-wide; and

◆ Ensure reliability of the government's computer business systems and communications networks.

For example, the EA plan used in the City of Phoenix, Arizona, describes a strategy for reviewing the city's infrastructure and replacing it incrementally as the situation dictates based on the use of proven, inexpensive, and adaptable technologies. The city's EA plan goes on to describe seven different "technology architecture domains" (data, server and infrastructure, network and telecommunications, security, end user, management, applications). These domains are then divided into more specific "disciplines" for which the EA plan describes a common vision that promotes common development across the organization. Some examples of concepts articulated in the city's EA plan include:

◆ In the hardware and software support discipline of the end-user domain:

   ☐ "Continue to use standard desktop computer hardware configurations."

   ☐ "Expand enterprise support for an increasing variety of hand-held devices."

◆ In the computer system administration discipline of the platforms and infrastructure domain:

   ☐ "Size and locate servers appropriately."

   ☐ "Consider satisfying requirements with clustered, commodity Intel servers."

Replacement Schedule

A formal replacement or depreciation schedule can provide specific guidance on the infrastructure assets that need to be replaced each year. A replacement schedule assigns a standard depreciation period to different classes of equipment.

Different sources of information can be used to form a composite estimate of asset useful life. Professional trade organizations can provide general guidance on replacement cycles. Manufacturer warranty periods suggest how long the producer of a product expects it to last. Actual experience with how long given assets tend to last should also influence the standard. For example, some users have found that network switches have much longer useful lives than might be expected due to the absence of moving parts.

Replacement schedules help mitigate the problems associated with technology obsolescence. Technology obsolescence can cause unexpected spikes in required spending for replacement and can reduce employee productivity and hurt morale. These problems can be avoided by establishing a useful life for various asset classes and planning for replacement before obsolescence occurs.

Capacity Increases

In addition to replacing current infrastructure, the process for planning and evaluating for technology infrastructure must also address capacity increases to support expanded use of technology. The need for infrastructure capacity increases can be suggested by three main sources. The first source is new business applications. For example, the installation of a new financial management system may require more powerful servers, or a work management system may require PCs or mobile access devices for employees that did not have

> ### The Hype Cycle and Technology Investment
>
> A potential problem of IT asset replacement is over-investment in technology by either investing too early in a technology or by replacing a technology before sufficient value has been realized from the initial investment. Sarasota County, Florida tries to lessen this hazard by remaining cognizant of the technology "hype cycle." The hype cycle concept posits that new technology is the subject of excessive press and vendor marketing when first released and therefore customers have unrealistic expectations for its benefits.
>
> Eventually, the hype is discredited and the market enters a post-hype period of disillusionment with the technology. Then, the technology stabilizes and customers begin to realize benefit, albeit less than the original hype promised. By keeping the hype cycle in mind, Sarasota County avoids investing in new technologies at the peak of the hype cycle and looks to invest after the market has settled into more realistic expectations.
>
> *Note:* The Gartner Group originated the hype cycle concept. See www.gartner.com.

them previously. The planning process and business case for new business applications should always consider associated infrastructure needs. A desire to provide fundamental functionality improvements can also drive infrastructure capacity increases. Examples might include a more functional communication system or upgrading from copper wiring to fiber optics. In these instances, a case must be made for the additional spending, and this case must compete with other potential uses of technology dollars. Performance monitoring of infrastructure can also suggest capacity increase needs. If response time and processing speed metrics are not keeping up with targets, a capacity increase may be warranted.

Technology Standards

While an EA plan provides strategic guidance for infrastructure development, technology standards can provide more specific tactical guidance. Technology standards define the specific types of technologies that the jurisdiction will consider for purchase and perhaps even the vendors it will purchase from. Technology standards are a vital component of IT governance and project planning and evaluation as they proscribe the specific technologies that can be considered and can greatly improve the service quality and reduce infrastructure cost.[5] Below are some specific ways in which standardization can achieve these benefits:

◆ Standardization allows IT staff to concentrate their skill sets in a particular technology. This reduces training costs and allows for deeper support.

◆ Large-scale purchasing of standard technology (e.g., one type of PC) allows negotiation of better pricing through bulk purchasing or preferred provider contracts.

◆ Some technologies may be a particularly appropriate fit for the jurisdiction due to considerations such as functionality of the platform or convenience to operate.

For example, the City of Evanston, Illinois, has standardized on Dell desktops because it has a preferred provider agreement with Dell, on Unix operating systems because the city's IT staff skill sets are concentrated on Unix, and on Microsoft Office productivity software due to overall convenience and its ubiquity.

Technology standards should be developed and administered through the jurisdiction's technology governance structure so that the interests of organizational subunits will be accounted for. Otherwise, standards may come to be seen as an impediment to innovation rather than a benefit for organization-wide IT management. Fairfax County, Virginia, exemplifies an inclusive approach to standards development and administration. There are two key committees involved in IT standards at Fairfax. The first is the strategic architecture committee, which is made up of representatives from key county agencies who meet about four times a year to work with the IT department on technology standards. The other group is the architectural review board (ARB), a group of senior IT professionals from within the IT department. The ARB reviews proposed projects in the concept stages to discuss the technical approach and business objectives. When the concept relies on new products or non-standard configurations, the ARB may direct the project to use standard technologies or may grant a waiver from the standards, if the business benefits are compelling enough. The ARB could also recommend that the new technology replace the existing standard or be added to the list of supported standards. The Fairfax approach provides flexibility to modify or abrogate the standards if there is a consensus that a suitable business reason exists to do so. Also, the standard-setting process represents the business needs of stakeholder agencies via input provided by the strategic architecture committee while leaving the more detailed administration of standards to the more technically oriented ARB.

Funding for IT Infrastructure

Funding for infrastructure can come from a variety of sources. For example, the governments interviewed for this chapter realized funding for infrastructure from sources as diverse as the general fund, internal service funds, grants, and capital funds. While there is no "correct" answer as to where funds for infrastructure should originate, the Government Finance Officers Association's (GFOA) research has identified key funding issues that should be evaluated when planning for technology infrastructure.

Using IT Charge-Backs

Charge-backs are the practice of allocating IT costs out to users based on usage statistics (e.g., number of users, number of PCs, person-hours of service provided, etc.). Charge-backs can include both labor costs and an allowance for infrastructure. Specifically for infrastructure, charge-backs are potentially useful for making the cost of infrastructure more visible to users through its inclusion in a periodic statement of charges. This can help facilitate discussion about the nature and cost of IT. Charge-backs can also serve to limit infrastructure use by associating a cost with use. This provides a more accurate picture of demand and thus helps avoid over-investment in infrastructure.

Funding Replacement Schedules

The jurisdiction, preferably using its IT governance process, should determine how an IT asset replacement schedule will be funded. Because the useful life of some IT assets is so much shorter than other types of assets, the impacts of an unfunded replacement program can be felt much more quickly than for other liabilities. If such useful lives do not meet the threshold of capital asset, then such replacements should be part of the operating budget.

Several methods are available for funding replacement schedules. Many of the agencies GFOA conducted research with for this chapter allocated a portion of their charge-back rate to fund replacement schedules. Another option is a revolving fund where IT, as an internal service, makes use of charge-backs based on the previous year's cost of providing service, but the decreasing cost of computing and other efficiencies are then used to realize a margin that is re-invested into infrastructure. Finally, an annual allocation can simply be made from general revenue into a replacement fund.

Outsourcing

Technology infrastructure is a highly commoditized activity that differs little from organization to organization. Also, infrastructure is becoming increasing reliable, stable, and interoperable. These considerations mean that infrastructure will become more and more amenable to outsourcing solutions. Some common examples of outsourced infrastructure include disaster recovery centers (e.g., "hot"sites[6]), server hosting, and infrastructure maintenance. Outsourcing is useful for providing more visible and predictable infrastructure costs and may even help reduce costs. Depending on the agreement structure, outsourcing can also be used to make IT infrastructure a variable cost, rather than a fixed cost where charges depend on level of use. Much like IT service charge-backs, variable use charges introduce a market mechanism into use that can guard against over-investment. When such infrastructure is outsourced, then such costs may be categorized as an operating cost rather than a capital cost.

Portfolio Management in Oakland County, Michigan

A distinguishing characteristic of Oakland County's governance structure is that leadership groups have a prominent role in managing the ongoing success of the IT project portfolio located in the group's purview. An interesting governance mechanism that impacts ongoing management and initial resource allocation is an IT service hours allocation pool. Each group is assigned a defined pool of person-hours from the IT department from which all IT services are drawn. This pool is divided into activities such as maintenance of existing applications, enhancements/new development, and customer support. Each group is then responsible for managing its own pool of hours and must be aware of how new projects might impact it. For example, if a new technology will require a large ongoing maintenance commitment from central IT, the group will have to consider what older technologies in its portfolio may be able to be decommissioned in order to make room for the new technology. This approach causes the county to give greater consideration to the total ongoing costs of new technologies and provides greater incentive to divest of older, less productive technologies when new ones are added, rather than simply layering the new on top of the old.

Operating Impacts

After initial implementation, the ongoing support costs of infrastructure must be considered. These support costs often have important implications for the operating budget.

◆ **Vendor Maintenance and Support Programs.** Many types of infrastructure have vendor-provided maintenance and support programs available to address problems encountered during use of the technology. Recently, infrastructure has become more reliable, including self-monitoring and even self-repair capabilities. Therefore, with many types of infrastructure, maintenance comes bundled with the initial purchase price in the form of an extended warranty (e.g., three years). Maintenance costs can vary significantly depending on the type of infrastructure in question. Generally hardware maintenance costs are between 5 percent and 10 percent of the original hardware cost. Maintenance on infrastructure software can be much higher (18 percent to 25 percent), but this price may include upgrades.

◆ **Upgrades.** Hardware is often upgraded in a piecemeal fashion to increase processing power or storage space, for example. The cost of these upgrades varies with the type of upgrade, but should be less than the original purchase. For software, vendors often offer access to upgrades through their maintenance programs or upgrades can be purchase separately in the absence of such a program. Separately purchased upgrades generally cost the same as the original purchase.

◆ **Training.** Just as IT staff requires training during the initial installation, they need ongoing training on upgrades and possibly on more advanced features that were not addressed during the initial installation.

IT Business Application Projects

Business applications are the most visible aspect of government investment into technology as they have the most direct impact on the performance of public services and are, increasingly, becoming a primary point of interaction with government for constituents though e-government applications. The cost components associated with business applications differ when purchasing a commercially available system from an outside vendor compared to when developing a custom application, and practitioners should be aware of these differences when planning project costs.

Commercial Off-the-Shelf Software Projects

Commercial off-the-shelf (COTS) software projects have three primary cost components: acquisition, implementation, and post-implementation support. Acquisition begins with the development of a business case for the application. In many cases, these costs will be internal but in other cases external assistance may be required in order to properly estimate the cost, benefits, and other details associated with a technology with which neither internal IT resources or business staff have much familiarity. Acquisition costs also include the cost of developing bid documents and performing a bid evaluation. As with business case development, external assistance may be required for more complex applications.

The most visible costs of implementation are usually the software and consulting/training services. Software costs consist of the purchase cost of user licenses for the application(s) or the rental fee if access is being leased. Vendors can base software costs on a variety of metrics including user head counts, transaction processing volume, and jurisdiction size. Different types of applications tend to gravitate towards certain industry standard means of licensing, which market research during business case development can help reveal.

Implementation consulting and training on the software is an important cost component. For some more complex applications (especially when implemented in complex environments), implementation and training costs can run multiple times the amount of the software licenses. Even for less complex applications, these types of cost are, by their nature, often much harder to estimate accurately than software costs. While discussions with vendors can be helpful for proper estimating, it is also important to speak with other jurisdictions that have implemented the technology in order to determine their experiences with the proper level of consulting/training support needed to successfully implement.

There also may be hardware acquisition costs besides supporting infrastructure. For example, a financial system may include the need for cash receipting drawers or a utility billing system might require devices to automate meter reading. For some types of projects these hardware costs can be a significant investment.

The final implementation cost to consider is internal costs. Internal staff time to participate in the implementation of the software ensures that the technology is implemented to best satisfy the government's business requirements. Through participation on the project, staff becomes competent in the technology's use so that it can be operated independently of consultant support after initial implementation. Internal costs might also include facility costs. Facilities may need to be redesigned in order to make best use of technology. Larger projects might also require temporary, but dedicated space for the project team during initial implementation so that the team can best concentrate on its task.

Custom Software Development

A custom software development project has four basic steps:

◆ **Design.** Detailed user requirements are gathered and a system is designed and perhaps prototyped;

◆ **Build.** The system is built out based on an approved design;

◆ **Test.** The resulting product is tested for performance and conformance to user specifications; and

◆ **Maintain.** The application is maintained over its life cycle.

An estimate for custom development should budget expenditures for all of these activities, considering both the role of internal staff as well as contracted developers. Unfortunately, custom development can be more difficult to estimate than COTS applications. If internal resources are being used, the government's developers can provide an estimate based on prior experience. In many instances, however, outside contractors will be engaged. In this case, other methods include:

- ◆ Gather less formal cost estimates through mechanisms like a request for information (RFI).
- ◆ Get data on comparable projects from similar governments. This can be difficult as custom projects are, by definition, often not very comparable.
- ◆ Make a conservative best-estimate and plan to phase the project into discrete sections, doing as much as the proposals and budget allow for, saving the remainder for the future.

No matter the estimation method used, custom software development projects require strong risk mitigation techniques due to the large number of unknown factors in play. Therefore, practitioners should also strongly consider the use of outside procurement advisory consultants and legal counsel specializing in IT in order to draft a detailed contract and scope of work.

Needs Assessment

Evaluating the need for business applications occurs primarily through a business case. Business application needs can also be influenced by technical standards set through the governance process. The most common type of influence is when standards for infrastructure influence available choices for a business application. For example, if the jurisdiction has standardized on a particular type of relational database management system, a business application that runs on a different relational database management system would face a higher hurdle for approval. Standards may also govern the business applications themselves. For example, a jurisdiction may have set a standard for a particular type of report writer in order to gain economies of scale in license purchasing, user training, and system administration. Another example of a standardization occurs when a jurisdiction commits to an enterprise software package, such as an ERP system, and has a policy to leverage functionality within the system before looking to other products.

Project Management

A business application implementation of any complexity is typically accounted for as a project. Project accounting allows all the costs associated with the implementation to be accounted for as a unified whole, which enables better monitoring against budget and better accountability for promised results. In fact, many larger governments have established a project management office (PMO) that specializes in the discipline of running projects. The PMO is often intimately involved in the IT governance process. Even smaller jurisdictions are participating in this trend – while not establishing a full PMO, staff are trained in specialized project management skills through organizations such as the Project Management Institute.[7]

Taking a project-based approach to technology implementations will require a definition for what constitutes a project versus a more routine operational change. Since the business case is central to technology project evaluation and planning, it plays a central role in this determination. As part of Sarasota County's business case process, requesters are required to complete a sizing and complexity form. The form poses a series of eighteen multiple-choice questions and the answers lead to a project size score. Among the topics covered include:

◆ The estimated number of maximum users;

◆ The required support schedule (i.e., 24/7 or normal business hours only, etc.);

◆ The level of integration with other systems; and

◆ The extent to which new hardware will be required.

A business case that does not have a high enough size score is not considered a project and does not continue through the rest of Sarasota's business case evaluation and prioritization process. Rather, the request is considered more appropriate to the day-to-day services provided by the county's help desk, application support, and operations groups and is sent to the help desk for routing to the appropriate party.

Funding Applications

Business applications are primarily funded from general fund cash contributions for projects supporting general purpose governmental units and user fees for business-type fund projects, with lease financing plans sometimes offered by vendors. While grant opportunities to fund applications may also exist, such prospects may relate only to a certain type of governmental service. When planning for business applications funding, several key issues should be considered.

Outsourcing Applications

Different aspects of a business application can often be outsourced, ranging from technical maintenance to application hosting to outsourcing an entire business process and its associated supporting technology. Outsourcing has the potential to reduce or at least control the cost of operating an application and can spread the cost of the application more evenly over its lifecycle (i.e., reduce the upfront investment). As with infrastructure outsourcing, some outsourcing arrangements can even transform application investments from a fixed cost to a variable cost as the outsourced application is paid for based on the volume of use.

Funding Infrastructure for New Applications

New business applications often require additional infrastructure above what the jurisdiction already has in place. When developing long-term technology plans, an estimated cost for additional infrastructure should be included and that infrastructure (e.g., servers, network infrastructure, etc.) would typically be made part of the normal infrastructure replacement and funding schedule after the capital project is completed.

It is sometimes difficult, however, to determine when new infrastructure needs are most appropriately attributable to a new business application versus a normal expansion of infrastructure capacity. Professional judgment is required to allocate costs accurately between the project budget and the standard infrastructure replacement program. For example, if a project requires new PCs and the new PCs are within what would

Moore's Law and IT Budgets

Moore's Law predicts that processing power of computer chips will double every eighteen months. The resulting increasing power and decreasing costs of infrastructure along with the advent of Web-based applications that minimize the strain on desktop PCs have meant that infrastructure is becoming a less important cost of new business application projects.

normally be provided by the standard PC replacement program, then the PC costs might not be allocated to the project. However, if the PCs required are much more powerful than those that would normally be provided, then the PCs would likely be allocated to the project.

Gain-Sharing Potential

Gain sharing is the practice of compensating a private vendor through a percentage of gains realized through new technology.[7] For example, new revenue collection technology might be purchased through a gain-sharing agreement where the vendor is compensated through a share of new revenues resulting from a more effective collection of delinquent bills or more effective enforcement. Another example of gain-sharing is fraud reduction, where new technology can be used to better assess eligibility for programs and thereby reduce fraudulent use of government services.

User Fees

User fees apply a surcharge to those who receive a unique benefit from the use of government technology. For example, attorneys who choose real-time, secure access to sensitive client information held in state systems might pay an additional fee to offset the cost of authenticating them as authorized users. In contrast, attorneys using conventional channels need not pay for online authentication, but would incur the costs of copying and couriers and would experience longer periods of time to acquire the needed information.[8]

When applying user fees, jurisdictions need to be mindful of fees acting as a disincentive to use technology-enabled channels. Channels such as the Web or automated phone response can offer significant efficiencies over walk-in or conventional mail. Nevertheless, if constituents are discouraged from using those channels by a convenience charge then government will forego potential cost savings.

Can the Application be Self-Funded?

Some applications have the potential to be self-funded by the vendor. In these cases, government authorizes a vendor to operate an application on its behalf and the vendor is paid via transaction fees generated through the application. For example, the State of North Carolina implemented its e-procurement solution through a self-funded model where the system vendor was paid via a small per-transaction fee charged to sellers. Self-funding can also apply to multi-purpose citizen service portals where the combination of fee-based services and economies of scale across multiple participating jurisdictions allows for a larger portfolio of services to be provided via a self-funded approach.

If self-funded approaches are not possible, general fund contributions or cash financing along with debt and grant funding are also common. Just as more traditional capital projects are funded by debt financing, so too can technology investments. However, an important departure from tradition is that technology application investments are made in intangible software rather than tangible physical assets. The loans should preferably be repaid through hard-dollar savings achieved from implementation of the technology, rather than through general tax allocations.[9]

Grant Funding

Grant funding is a particularly viable option when the application in question is innovative and/or is consistent with the desired policy outcomes of a granting agency.[10] The viability of grant funding is limited by the availability of appropriate grants and the grantee's ability to maintain the system after the initial grant runs out.

Operating Impacts

After a technology enters production it must be supported and maintained. Most vendors offer an ongoing maintenance and support program that provides assistance with problems encountered and access to upgrades. Software upgrades are essential for avoiding or at least delaying product obsolescence. The magnitude of these charges can vary considerably from application to application. If the application is outsourced, for instance, a substantial ongoing access fee is likely. Also, larger, ongoing support costs may be necessary for applications, such as property tax administration systems, that have significant potential requirements for the vendor to adjust the program to comply with local laws.

Support and maintenance also usually require a significant effort by internal staff unless the application is outsourced. Therefore, any application cost estimate should consider the staff effort to be devoted to basic system maintenance. Other customers who have implemented a system are the best source information on maintenance requirements. In addition to the basic "care and feeding" of an application, ongoing cost estimates should consider an allowance for system optimization. Often, the initial system implementation will not realize all of the potential benefits of new technology due to time/resource constraints or simply due to the limited human capacity to absorb change. Optimization activities should at least account for periodic refresher training on the baseline technology and might go so far as to account for the introduction of new technology features or process/job redesign to better take advantage of technological capabilities.

Conclusion

Planning and evaluating IT projects presents special challenges that are distinct from other types of assets. The nature of the investment is often intangible relative to other infrastructure investments and its benefit can only be maximized in concert with changes to employee behavior and business processes designed to take advantage of new technological capabilities. As a result, it is important to bring stakeholders from across the organization into a process for joint decision making that encourages desirable behaviors in the use of IT. Development of an IT governance structure is a conscious means to address these challenges. Successful IT governance exhibits a number of design features, and perhaps the feature with most direct salience to project planning and evaluation is the business case. The business case serves as the locus for planning because that is where a project's exponents describe the business rationale for the project, its goals, costs and benefits, estimated timeline, and project risks. The business case also serves as the basis for project evaluation as it allows decision makers to weigh different IT investment opportunities against available resources.

Successful planning and evaluation of IT projects as well as effective management of IT assets through IT oversight is key for realizing value from funds invested in technology and for transforming government jurisdictions into twenty-first century organizations.

Notes

1. Peter Weill and Jeanne W. Ross, *IT Governance: How Top Performers Manage IT Decision Rights for Superior Results* (Boston, Massachusetts: Harvard Business School Press, 2004).

2. Ibid.

3. Ibid.

4. This chapter uses the City of Phoenix's enterprise architecture plan as the main example of EA planning. The potential benefits cited here are adapted from the city's plan.

5. Jerome A. Schulz, *Information Technology in Local Government: A Practical Guide for Managers* (Washington, D.C.: International City/County Management Association, 2001).

6. A vendor provides an offsite location with redundant technology for use in an emergency.

7. More information on the Project Management Institute is available on its Web site, http://www.pmi.org.

8. Examples of gain sharing are taken from Paul W. Taylor, "Pay IT Forward: Doing the Public's Business with Digital Technologies while Reducing Pressure on the General Fund" (Center for Digital Government, 2003).

9. Example of user fee taken from Taylor, "Pay IT Forward," 2003.

10. Taylor, "Pay IT Forward," 2003.

11. Ibid.

|14|

Solid Waste Facilities

By C. Brooke Beal

Solid waste management is becoming a more challenging problem for local governments. Rising costs, liability concerns, increased environmental regulations, and technology advancements have contributed to the need for local governments to reevaluate how solid waste is managed. Also, with the private sector playing a larger role, local governments need to thoroughly evaluate the many types of facilities that can manage waste to ensure that the facility selected can efficiently and effectively address community needs.

Local governments have historically provided solid waste collection services. A 1902 survey of municipalities indicated that 79 percent of cities provided waste collection services from houses. Most municipalities deposited waste in landfills, but alternative waste disposal technologies were also used. The first waste incinerator and recycling center began in New York over 100 years ago.[1] Today, landfills, recycling centers, and waste-to-energy generation facilities are the primary means of solid waste disposal.

| Solid Waste Facilities |

Citizens and businesses expect the jurisdiction to handle solid waste as effectively and efficiently as possible. In total, 54 percent of municipal waste ends up in a landfill, 32 percent is recycled, and 14 percent is burned in an incinerator.[2] Additionally, other facilities, such as transfer stations and drop-off centers, are used to collect or process waste.

Landfills

Landfills have traditionally been the most common method of waste disposal. Many communities once had a local landfill that was commonly referred to as the "dump." In contrast, today's active landfills are complex facilities that are designed to meet stringent environmental regulations. While many communities had their own small landfill, the trend now is toward large regional landfills that manage thousands of tons of waste per day. This trend has evolved as landfill regulations have strengthened and the cost to develop and operate landfills has increased, making the business decision to retain smaller landfills less practical from a compliance and cost perspective. A large regional facility is better positioned to absorb these increased costs.

Landfills are heavily regulated and have the potential to create environmental problems. Leachate, a by-product of landfills, is often subject to the strongest regulations. Many landfills have leachate collection systems to mitigate contaminants from infiltrating groundwater supplies, rivers, or lakes.

Recycling Facilities

Recycling facilities or material recovery facilities (MRF) are facilities where recycled material is separated, processed, and transported to recycling processing facilities. In addition to traditional recyclable materials such as glass, aluminum, and paper, other materials separated from the solid waste stream include paint, oil, appliances, computers, scrap metal, and other materials that could have resale value or present problems in landfills. In some instances, transfer stations and recycling facilities can be incorporated into the same facility. These facilities are called "dirty MRFs" because recycled material arrives commingled with solid waste and is then sorted mechanically and by hand to recover any recyclable material.

Waste-to-Energy Facilities

Waste-to-energy (WTE) facilities burn solid waste to generate electricity and reduce the quantity of landfill waste. In densely populated areas, WTE facilities have replaced landfills due to the lack of available vacant land. While many WTE facilities have been developed, their large capital and ongoing capital improvement requirements have hindered wide acceptance.

Transfer Stations

Transfer stations are facilities that temporarily receive solid waste before final disposal. They generally combine the waste from two to three traditional collection vehicles into large transfer trailers to transport solid waste to distant landfills more cost effectively. Solid waste transfer facilities are the most common type of facility developed today, largely because they require less capital, reduce long-term liability, can be developed quickly, and can adapt to changes in the solid waste market place. These facilities tend to be in urban areas where landfills have closed and vacant land for landfill development is scarce.

Transfer stations have bridged the gap between developing a landfill or WTE facility. Transfer stations are prevalent in urban areas and also in rural areas that generate small amounts of waste. Per day, transfer stations can handle as much as thousands of tons and can be a cost-effective alternative to capital-intensive landfills and waste-to-energy facilities. As part of their efficiency, transfer stations often utilize compactors that compress the waste into a more dense material that enable greater amounts of such waste to then be hauled. Utilizing a transfer station can reduce the operating costs of transporting solid waste. The waste from multiple collection trucks can be combined into a truck with a larger capacity for travel to the disposal site.

Drop-Off Centers/Convenience Centers

Drop-off and convenience centers generally allow residents and businesses to drop off waste and recyclables. Material is then aggregated into larger containers, such as a roll-off container, and then transported to a disposal facility or material recovery facility. Many convenience centers may also have compactors and trailers that can be directly hauled to disposal rather than an additional haul to the transfer station, affording some of the same benefits as the transfer stations.

Needs Assessment

Before selecting the type of facility to develop, a comprehensive needs assessment should be conducted to ensure that the most optimal facility is selected. A needs assessment consists of three areas:

◆ Type of waste processed;

◆ Amount of waste to be processed; and

◆ Market analysis of available facilities.

Type of Waste

Many communities develop systems to handle solid waste destined for a landfill or waste-to-energy facility. However, with the proliferation of environmental laws requiring separate management of certain wastes, a program that allows for flexible solid waste management facilities is essential.

For example, in the 1990s many states banned green waste (landscaping), white goods (appliances), tires, and other recyclable materials from landfills. Existing solid waste facilities either had to be modified or new facilities retrofitted to process segregated wastes in compliance with the new regulations. Governments must analyze all types of waste that will need to be managed to ensure that the most optimal and adaptable facility is developed.

Amount of Waste

Estimating both the total quantities of waste to be processed and the actual quantities of each waste type is vital to ensure adequate facility sizing and waste-processing capacity. In addition, gauging the amount of waste to be processed each day is also important to ensure that the waste can be processed on peak days. Seasonal waste variations also must be considered. Twenty-year waste projections should be developed, factoring in population growth, economic development, and employment projections. In 2005, households and businesses produced 245 million tons of waste, which equates to 4.5 pounds of waste per person per day.[3] Business and industrial waste will vary based upon the business type, with some businesses generating mostly paper waste while others produce varied by-products. Therefore, models of existing businesses and their waste streams and anticipated future businesses can help determine how best to serve such customers in the future. The amount of recyclable content can also have a large impact on the amount of waste generated. Exhibit 14.1 shows recycling rates for common recyclable materials.

Exhibit 14.1 Recycling Rates for Selected Materials

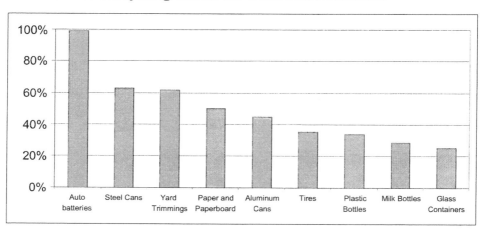

Source: U.S. Environmental Protection Agency, "Municipal Solid Waste" (http://www.epa.gov/garbage/facts.htm).

Market Analysis

A market analysis evaluates the current solid waste management facilities in the intended service area. Each facility's evaluation will include the current amount and types of wastes processed, processing capacity, remaining life of the facility (landfill only), current service area, restrictions on waste acceptance, and facility cost and/or tipping fee.

Once the amount and types of waste to be managed are determined, the optimal solid waste management facility can be selected. There is not a one-size-fits-all facility recommendation, as local needs, distance to landfills, transportation network, zoning, and other factors can impact facility selection.

The optimal facility selection depends on a wide variety of factors, with many decision inputs gleaned from the needs assessment, including:

◆ Amount of waste and types of waste processed;

◆ Recycling method and status of program;

◆ Available vacant or developable land; and

◆ Other useable solid waste facilities.

As determined from the needs assessment, the amount and types of waste to be managed have the greatest impact on facility development. If a community needs to manage only its solid waste destined for disposal, the landfill or WTE facility could be sufficient. If the needs assessment identifies a wide range of material, such as solid waste, recyclable material, and landscape waste, then a transfer station would allow numerous materials to be processed and transported to different facilities most efficiently and cost effectively.

The status of the community's recycling program can also impact the type of facility developed. If the community has a traditional curbside recycling program and a locally available MRF to process the material, there is less need for a dirty MRF, or a transfer station that could recover recyclable material.

Conversely, a dirty MRF can provide a community with a low-cost method to recover recyclable material from the waste stream instead of providing a separate, sorted curbside recycling collection. The downside to this type of recycling is that the material quality might not be as clean as recyclable materials collected separately from solid waste, and the mechanical process to separate the material is costly to develop and maintain.

Market for Recycled Materials

Markets for recyclable material fluctuate similar to markets for other commodities, but some recyclable materials, such as newspaper, have actually had a negative value at times. This disparity in recyclable material values has made it difficult to plan for the cost effectiveness of a martial recycling facility. In addition, some recyclable materials may be processed for purposes unknown to most customers (e.g., crushed glass being used as landfill liners and filters).

Today, the markets for recyclable material have matured and the wide fluctuations in the market for recyclable materials are not as common. More importantly, the emergence of commodity hedges as an instrument in managing the risk has decreased the impact from wide price fluctuations.

Project Planning

Planning for a solid waste facility or landfill is a complex task that involves finding a suitable site, obtaining necessary permits, and estimating the costs of both equipment and operation. During site selection, the jurisdiction will need to consider the facility's impact on surrounding areas, transportation, and accessibility for waste-hauling trucks.

Site Suitability Analysis

When reviewing the available land for developing a solid waste facility, a site suitability analysis needs to be performed. The site suitability study is a two-phase process that analyzes the land available for development, screens for incompatible uses and regulatory requirements, and then evaluates each site for optimal development and operational capabilities.

Phase I of the analysis reviews the jurisdiction's available property after applying the regulatory standards that exclude many sites. While regulatory requirements vary by state, the common location standards that should be avoided are:

- ◆ Wetlands and floodplains;
- ◆ Endangered and protected flora and fauna habitats;
- ◆ Historical, archeological, or culturally significant areas;
- ◆ Proximity to airports, schools, or parks; and
- ◆ Proximity to residential areas and institutional facilities.

Once a list of acceptable sites has been identified in light of applicable regulatory location standards, phase II of the analysis can proceed. Phase II evaluates and ranks each site for its developmental capabilities and operational efficiency. Several criteria detailed below are applied in phase II.

Minimal Site Size and Layout

The site size of each solid waste facility varies with the amount of waste processed, type of facility, waste-processing technology, and for a transfer station, the distance to the landfill. In addition, the site's layout is important because although a long, narrow site may meet the size requirement, it might not provide the optimal layout. Site layout can ensure efficient facility operations by having enough onsite parking for queuing collection vehicles and an internal roadway network, thus reducing the impact on surrounding roadways. To mitigate impact on the community, solid waste facilities should be located in an area that provides separation from sensitive adjoining land uses such as residences, schools, and recreational areas. Buffers can mitigate negative affects of incompatible uses. Natural or constructed buffers can take many forms, including open spaces, fences, sound walls, trees, berms, and landscaping.

Transportation Analysis

A complete transportation analysis should be completed for each potential site. This analysis includes access to major transportation routes, local roadway condition and layout, network traffic capacity, and potential for rail or barge access. Solid waste facilities traditionally have large traffic surges in the late morning and in the late afternoon. These traffic surges usually do not interfere with local, traditional traffic patterns but need to be assessed depending on the surrounding land uses.

Location of Solid Waste Facilities

Locating solid waste facilities near the center of waste generation reduces transportation costs. While this is not always workable, the next-best option is to select a site convenient for the existing collection routes or easily modified collection routes. Officials in growing communities who understand future land development patterns can better position such facilities by keeping in mind the long life cycles in question: while the location's initial distance may not be the most ideal, over time the community will grow, making it much more convenient. Jurisdictions should also keep in mind that solid waste facilities require electricity to operate equipment and lighting; water for facility cleaning, restrooms, and drinking; and sanitary sewer systems for wastewater disposal.

Landfill Closure Liability

Local governments that are contemplating entering the landfill disposal arena must fully assess the financial impact for the long-term management of the landfill into the post-closure period after waste acceptance has ceased.

To ensure that the facility will be managed during the post-closure period, federal regulations require that all owners and operators of municipal solid waste landfills demonstrate financial wherewithal, or financial assurance, to safely close the site and perform post-closure care activities. Activities would also include corrective actions that might be necessary due to the presence of contaminants into the surrounding environment.

Closure and post-closure cost estimates are prepared before beginning operations and must be adjusted annually during the facility's operating life. Corrective-action cost estimates are also prepared when contaminants are first detected. These cost estimates are adjusted for inflation and it is also assumed that a third-party will perform the required actions. Most states have adopted specific regulations pertaining to financial assurance, but generally some type of trust fund, insurance, or financial test can illustrate compliance.

Ability for Expansion

Sites should be reviewed relative to the potential for future increases in the quantity of waste the facility handles, or added processing capabilities necessary for recycling and diversion. It is often less expensive to expand an existing transfer station than to develop a new site due to the ability to use existing operations staff, utility connections, traffic control systems, office space, buildings, and other existing amenities. However, permitting for such facilities may be capped at a certain capacity, and unless such higher capacities are initially permitted, future regulations may mitigate the ability to increase permitted capacity. Therefore, it may be a responsible business decision to get a higher capacity permitted initially, even if it is not needed for many years.

Permitting

Solid waste facilities are required to go through extensive local and state approval processes. While approval processes vary from state to state, the purpose of the process is to limit negative environmental impacts caused by the facility. In addition, in 1970 the Environmental Protection Agency (EPA) developed nationwide standards for landfills.[4]

Location standards mentioned earlier are usually part of the approval process. A complete and thorough site selection analysis will ensure that the facility site will withstand the regulatory approval process.

Project Costs

Capital costs of solid waste facilities range from over $100 million for a waste-to-energy facility to several hundred thousands of dollars for a low-tech transfer station.

For example, a transfer station's capital costs can range greatly due to the size of the facility and the waste-processing technology selected. A transfer station's capital costs depend on three main factors: the size of the facility, waste-processing technology used, and location mitigation factors.

Size

Size of the facility obviously affects the capital cost, but a facility can be oversized, thus artificially increasing the capital costs. Conversely, a transfer station needs to be large enough to process peak waste volumes and allow for volume increases over the service life of the facility.

Waste-Processing Technology

Waste-processing technology employed at transfer stations can be as simple as collection vehicles dumping waste directly into a transfer container, or more complex with waste mechanically sorted and compressed into transfer trailers. The technology employed depends on the volume of waste processed, size of available land, and distance to landfills.

When large volumes of waste are processed, transfer stations can employ more capital-intensive waste-processing technology to reduce the volume of waste by compacting waste into transfer trailers more densely than a direct-dump operation. By increasing the compaction and waste density in the transfer trailers, more waste can be transferred per trailer, thus reducing transportation costs to distant landfills.

To determine if more capital-intensive waste processing will be beneficial, the jurisdiction should conduct an analysis comparing potential transportation savings against the increased capital and operation costs of employing a more sophisticated waste-processing system.

Location Mitigation Factors

In addition to waste processing, other equipment can influence operations costs. How the waste will be transported to a landfill impacts the overall operational cost of processing waste. There are three main types of transfer trailers utilized in the solid waste industry: walking floor/ejection, tippers, and non-ejection.

Walking-floor trailers have a mechanical floor that unloads the solid waste. Tipping trailers have a hydraulic lift to dump the waste. Non-ejection trailers require a separate tipper that lifts the trailers to empty the waste. Each system has benefits. Walking-floor trailers allow waste to be delivered to any landfill but add weight to the trailer, thus reducing the amount of solid waste per trailer and increasing transportation cost per ton. Tipping trailers allow greater amounts of solid waste per trailer, thus reducing transportation costs, but can only be utilized at landfills with tipping machines.

One other area that can affect solid waste facility operating costs is a host benefit fee that usually consists of a payment to local governments for the right to operate in the jurisdiction. Host benefit fees are generally based on the amount of waste processed. Even some governmental facilities pay this fee to offset the cost of regulation and services provided. Host benefit fees can range from cents per ton to several dollars per ton. These fees can add substantial costs to solid waste facility operations. To fully analyze facility competitiveness, the host benefit fee amount should be determined before development begins and factored into all financial projections.

Equipment

Much of the heavy equipment for a landfill and solid waste collection process is often at costs that warrant inclusion in the capital budget. Therefore, a capital asset listing of such equipment and its useful life needs to be reviewed to ensure that it is replaced in a timely manner. Often equipment companies will lease landfill equipment to the jurisdiction. Before purchasing, jurisdictions should evaluate any rental options that exist. Common waste-processing and landfill equipment includes wheeled and track loaders, trash compactors, articulated trucks, and trash grinders and balers.

Project Financing

While solid waste facilities can be financed like most capital projects, either through user fees, general obligation bonds, or revenue bonds, there are some operational issues that can affect the type of financing used.

Flow Control

Many solid waste facilities were financed on the concept that local governments could mandate that all waste generated within the jurisdiction be delivered to a determined solid waste facility. This concept, known as flow control, has been traditionally used to finance facilities without regard for competition in the marketplace. Flow control ensured that local solid waste facilities received adequate volumes of solid waste and corresponding revenues to guarantee the bonds issued to develop the facilities. In 1994, this unilateral regulatory flow control was deemed unconstitutional by the United States Supreme Court (*C&A Carbone, Inc. v. Town of Clarkstown, NY*).

Since this ruling, governments have created modified flow-control measures, implementing systems that guarantee waste deliveries without violating the *Carbone* case ruling. Many of these modified flow-control measures have withstood legal challenges to provide local governments with a tool to issue revenue bonds instead of general obligation bonds for solid waste facility development.

Private Sector Participation

The use of a private sector firm to operate the facility may also impact the type of financing required. If a local government develops the facility and operates the facility, tax-exempt bonds can be used. If the private sector will operate a government-owned facility, a private benefit test needs to be conducted. Should the private benefit prove substantial as defined by the Internal Revenue Service, then private activity bonds or taxable bonds may need to be utilized.

User Fees

User fees are generally comprised of two sources: 1) tipping fees for those transporting waste to government and 2) pick-up fees for the government service of picking up waste at customers' locations (curbside pick-up). In setting such fees, the jurisdiction needs to determine what business model logic should be in place to recover costs for operations and capital. For fee revenues below operating and capital costs that are not recovered from other revenue sources previously noted, general fund contributions are the local funding for such budgets. There are also other considerations in setting such fees, as high tipping fees may encourage customers to haul waste to another location. This may be a strategy where waste capacity is limited at the facility (e.g., landfill nearing capacity), but it may also mean waste transport vehicles are driving further to dispose of such waste. For those governments that operate transfer stations where contracted hauling to ultimate disposal site exists, fee recovery models may need to account for the targeted margin between tipping fees received and contracted hauling services.

Operating Solid Waste Facilities

Solid waste facilities require unique equipment to operate that should be included in capital budgets when planning for a facility. Jurisdictions also need to consider the potential for private sector involvement. Many private sector firms offer waste management services and can provide services more efficiently than the public sector.

Equipment Used in Hauling and Landfill Operation

When planning for equipment in solid waste-hauling operations, the first factor to consider is the degree of automation that will be utilized. This is important because it will affect which type of curbside collection methods (cart versus cans and bags) will be used and the collection system's productivity. Generally, the productivity of fully automated collection is less than a non-automated collection. However, increasing automation will increase worker safety and limit the number of worker compensation claims and injuries.

On the landfill operations, heavy machinery is required for both the construction of new cells at the landfill and the facility's general operations. Landfills are ever-evolving facilities with constant construction and closure operations. Different landfill equipment requirements need to be evaluated based on the type of waste received. For example, if the majority of waste will be delivered from transfer stations, a tipper may unload the transfer, allowing for more efficient waste transfer by reducing the weight of the transfer trailers (eliminating the walking floor auto-unloading component).

Public vs. Private Operation

The role of the public and private sectors can vary in a solid waste system. For example, governments traditionally collected solid waste and disposed of it in government-owned landfills. As privatization has become more prevalent, governments issue an exclusive franchise or license to operate a total solid waste system. This system can include collection and delivery directly to a landfill or waste-to-energy facility, or there can be an intermediate step of delivery to a transfer station for waste processing to recover recyclable material or to reduce transportation costs.

Privatization can mean different things for different jurisdictions. Typical privatization arrangements include government contracts with a private firm to perform service curbside pick-up services and/or operate a private disposal facility. Some governments may enable residents and businesses to enter into their own arrangements for curbside pick-up or through drop-off convenience centers. The jurisdiction can often act as a conduit, giving access to private firms providing such services and/or through participation in a regional authority that may also perform waste and/or recyclable services. Neighborhoods can also act as their own agents through homeowner associations and select one curbside pick-up firm, eliminating a situation where different firms come on different days. There is no one ideal approach; rather, jurisdictions should review their options through community input, business models, and legal authority to provide the best service at the most efficient cost.

Jurisdictions most often look to privatization for two main reasons: lower costs and risk management. When a government privatizes its solid waste disposal system, it remains accountable to its residents for environmentally sound and cost effective disposal of the waste. When the system is privatized, governments remain accountable because they become the purchaser of solid waste services on behalf of their residents.

Privatization can also provide lower overall solid waste collection and disposal costs. Lowering costs can be accomplished through taking advantage of open market economics and competitive pressures that can exist in the marketplace. Private sector companies can take advantage of economies of scale offered by spreading development and environmental compliance costs across a larger base, as is possible with large, regional solid waste facilities. Conversely, local governments usually do not have this flexibility.

Privatization provides risk management by contractually shifting the responsibility for liability and environmental compliance to the private sector. Private sector contracts often release local governments from liabilities that can occur under Subtitle D of the Resource Conservation and Recovery Act, including landfill post-closure costs and financial assurance, requiring local governments to account for future costs and financial exposure in their annual financial statements.

According to a recent study by the environmental consulting firm R.W. Beck, more than 27,000 organizations operate in the solid waste industry to provide services including collection of recycling and solid waste, and operation of landfills, transfer stations, material recovery facilities, landscape waste compost facilities, and waste-to-energy facilities.[5] The study also reports $40 billion in revenues in 2000, of which 76 percent were generated by private sector firms. The public sector generated only 24 percent of the revenue but managed over 47 percent of solid waste facilities.

Public sector facilities tend to be smaller and serve single jurisdictions, compared to the private sector's large regional facilities.[6] As the public sector's small facilities reach capacity or require large capital expenditures to maintain environmental regulation compliance, privatization is one strategy for governments to ensure that solid waste management is provided to residents cost effectively.

R. W. Beck also reviewed ongoing privatization trends in the solid waste industry and identified the following:[7]

◆ More than 50 percent of the surveyed communities are at least partially serviced by private waste haulers;

◆ The number of communities using private haulers grew by about 2 percent annually;

◆ The annual growth rate in private hauler use is likely to increase to 3 or 4 percent; and

◆ As of the year 2000, private haulers serviced 67 to 70 percent of communities, at least in part.

The increasing privatization of the solid waste services is in part related to the more stringent environmental regulations that have been placed on the disposal of solid waste. With the reauthorization of the Resource Conservation and Recovery Act in 1984, landfills were required to incorporate numerous costly design and operating standards. Due to these more costly requirements, many smaller government-owned landfills could not incorporate these requirements cost effectively and were closed or sold to private operators, who could increase the quantity of waste processed to offset the costs.

With the increasing trend of privatizing solid waste systems, local government officials need to consider if expanding or developing a government owned-or-operated facility can compete with private sector facilities. Local governments also need to evaluate regional solid waste management solutions.

Conclusion

When a government develops a solid waste facility, special care must be applied to how the facility will be financed. With flow-control options reduced, governments need to ensure that both the site selected and the waste processing technology chosen provide for an economically competitive facility. This can only be determined through a thorough analysis of many factors, including community need, transportation options, siting regulations, financing options, and many other considerations as outlined in this chapter. In addition, governments need to ensure that the vital public service of environmentally sound solid waste management will be administered either by the private sector or public sector.

Notes

1. Information was taken from the U.S. Environmental Protection Agency's Web site (http://www.epa.gov).

2. U.S. Environmental Protection Agency, "Municipal Solid Waste USA 2005 Facts and Figures" (http://www.epa.gov).

3. U.S. Environmental Protection Agency, "Municipal Solid Waste" (http:// www.epa. gov/garbage/facts.htm).

4. U.S. Environmental Protection Agency (http://www.epa.gov).

5. R.W. Beck, Orlando, Florida and Chartwell Information Publishers, San Diego, California (April 2001). Published by Environmental Research and Education Foundation.

6. Geoffrey F. Segal and Adrian T. Moore, *Privatizing Landfills: Market Solutions for Solid-Waste Disposal* (May 2000), a whitepaper from the Reason Foundation (http:// www.reason.org).

7. Jonathan Burgiel, *Trends in Privatization and Managed Competition: National Survey Results* (Seattle, Washington: R. W. Beck, 1998).

|15|

Schools

By John H. Tuohy

While public schools exist throughout the United States and every child has the right to a free and appropriate education, the governmental structures that provide education differ significantly from jurisdiction to jurisdiction. The means of funding public education vary widely among the states, and may even differ within individual states. While many states have elected school boards with taxing powers, this is by no means true everywhere. Some school boards are fiscally dependent on the city or county and school boards appointed by the jurisdiction's governing body. School districts often are not all inclusive as there may be separate districts representing each level of education from primary through secondary. The universal feature of education funding is that every state provides some amount of money in addition to what is levied at the local level.

For purposes of this chapter, the generic term "school district" is used to describe any public sector entity providing kindergarten through twelfth-grade education. Counties, municipalities, school districts, and other governmental jurisdictions providing public educational services can all evaluate capital projects using the information supplied in this chapter.

| Description of School Facilities |

There are over 93,000 school buildings in the United States, over 40 percent of which were built before 1970.[1] The average school was built with an anticipated useful life of thirty years, making the replacement and renovation of school facilities a matter of major importance in most communities' capital planning process.

Capital projects for schools are not, however, necessarily limited to actual schools. School districts require administrative and support facilities such as bus garages and may have unique types of facilities such as theaters, nature centers, or planetariums. In general, though, educational facilities break down into elementary schools, middle schools, and high schools. There may also be special purpose schools for vocational education, special education, or for students in alternative programs. These special-purpose schools would be needed either because of the demand for unique facilities, such as industrial equipment for vocational education, or as required by law, in the case of very low student/teacher ratios for students with profound disabilities. The diverse requirements of each facility will drive the capital planning process.

Elementary Schools

A typical elementary school educates students from kindergarten through fifth or sixth grade. Students spend most of their days in one classroom. Additional space is required for offices, special education classes, a cafeteria, an auditorium,[2] a gymnasium, a library, and usually there is also space for the fine arts. Some schools may also need to accommodate pre-schools and before- and after-school care. Space outside the facility generally contains playgrounds and perhaps playing fields. The sizes of elementary schools can vary significantly based upon community standards, including student-teacher ratios, but generally have capacities ranging from 300 to 1,000 students. Therefore, the land needed for an elementary school would also depend upon its size, but a typical school occupies approximately fifteen acres. In the case where schools experience overcrowding or redistricting, school sites may need additional land to accommodate modular trailers while waiting for new school sites.

Middle Schools

A middle school (junior high) usually educates students from sixth or seventh grade through eighth or ninth grade. Although middle schools serve fewer grades than elementary schools, they require larger facilities for several reasons: they often serve students from multiple elementary schools within the district, students often move from room to room for classes, and curricula often include a greater specialization of classes, thus requiring greater specialization of classroom space. Many middle schools field sports teams, which require gymnasiums, an outdoor track, baseball fields, and other facilities. The sizes of these schools also vary based upon community standards, but generally have capacities ranging from 500 to 2,000 students.

High Schools

A high school educates students from either ninth or tenth grade through twelfth grade. The specialization of classroom space is even greater than that of the middle school. High schools have full-sized gymnasiums and auditoriums, and may have science labs, auto repair bays, art studios, welding or woodworking shops, facilities to accommodate vocational education, or other ancillary activities. Parking lots must be sized to accommodate not only staff and visitors, but also students. Sports fields are both more numerous and more developed to include bleachers, dugouts, concession stands, and lights. High schools vary considerably in the size of their student bodies, with larger schools usually having many more additional facilities. A typical high school could have as few as 500 students and as many as 5,000. One high school will often serve one middle school and in some cases such schools are co-located on the same property to realize crossover economies of scale such as shared athletic fields, combined bus drop-off zones and parking spaces.

Alternative Schools

Alternative schools may be built for students with disciplinary problems or special educational needs. Class sizes are typically much smaller than in regular schools and require far more classrooms than in standard schools with similarly sized student bodies. Some of this demand for classroom space may be reduced by having students attend mainstream schools for part of the day. It is not uncommon for alternative schools to be co-located with other school facilities.

Other Alternatives for Dealing with Growth

The list and description of facilities outlined in this section is by no means exhaustive. There may be elementary schools with as few as two grades or unified schools built to accommodate the entire school spectrum from pre-K through twelfth grade.

This chapter assumes that temporary measures to address school needs have either been tried and found insufficient or have been considered and rejected. School systems may seek to accommodate short-term demand for facilities by leasing space or installing trailers or other temporary buildings. Redistricting may be used to shift students from crowded facilities to those with excess capacity, if such facilities exist in the system.

Temporary Facilities

Trailers, often used as temporary solutions to overcrowding, are unpopular with parents if they are used for classrooms, especially if they remain in place for several years.[3] They sometimes are often perceived as inferior to bricks and mortar as a learning environment. The reality is that there are no known findings indicating that students who attend classes in a trailer score lower on tests than those in a traditional school building. The use of trailers should not be reactive, but rather part of a larger strategic plan of ensuring that schools operate at peak performance with proper alignment of new school capacity and redistricting. Also, these temporary classrooms are not intended for extended service and may themselves become significant maintenance problems over time. Nevertheless, temporary classrooms are frequently employed either to accommodate short-term overcrowding or because no other option is available in the near term while longer-term solutions are sought.

Redistricting

Changing boundary lines for school districts can be used to solve space problems if some schools in the district are over capacity and others are under capacity. Redistricting should be undertaken with specific goals in mind, in addition to optimizing the number of students per school. Redistricting should not divide up neighborhoods, should follow natural dividers such as major roads, and should minimize the possibility of a child being redistricted from one school to another more than once during his or her elementary years. Further consideration should be given to the system of "feeder schools" whereby many elementary schools feed into several middle schools that then feed into one high school. Redistricting should not be taken lightly as it is disruptive for both parents and students. Redistricting can also be influenced by the school district's need or desire to "balance" a school's student population with respect to socioeconomic and/or targeted composition.

Needs Assessment for Planning School Facilities

School projects tend to be both very costly and have very high visibility with the public, requiring a needs assessment that can withstand in-depth scrutiny. At the highest level, the local government's comprehensive plan and land use plans may be used to illustrate the total need for school facilities at build-out. Long-range capital planning should align with these plans. The basis for any needs analysis for school construction is a projection of student enrollment and current and future programmatic requirements. Producing projections is a staff-intensive process, however, school districts frequently engage outside consultants.

Enrollment forecasts for a total system are important to ensure that needs are addressed at a macro-level capacity. Unless redistricting is the preferred option for handling available capacity in one part of an area verses overcapacity in another, such enrollment projections should also be done at the micro level, school by school and by grade by grade, where practical. There are four common methods for producing such projections: forecasting from total population, forecasting from similar districts, forecasting with cohort survival ratios, and forecasting with geo-referenced data.

Forecasting from Total Population

This method assumes that there is an observable ratio between total population and school enrollments and that that ratio will continue into the future. Forecasting under this method has the advantage of being quite simple and can use readily available data, typically from the U.S. Census Bureau. Census data for age groups is not generally consistent with enrollment age groupings though, and census tracts are not necessarily congruent with school attendance areas. This introduces the possibility of error because additional calculations and assumptions are required above and beyond those for the total population. If it appears that the community's future land use plans target a different demographic than is generally represented today, the correlations between population and enrollment would need to account for such possible changing demographic trends.

Forecasting from Similar Districts

The analogy method of projecting student populations assumes that a school district's student population will have growth characteristics similar to another school district whose past growth characteristics have already been observed. This method is best used in suburban settings where there are discernible rings of growth from the center of the population density. Forecasting by analogy is an easy method of projecting student population if data is readily available from neighboring school districts. With minimal mathematical manipulation, the growth rate can be determined and applied. However, the accuracy of the results may be less than desired if the assumption that the school district will grow at a rate similar to another school district proves incorrect. A district must be careful in making such assumptions and should only do so after a thorough analysis of the two school districts and the unequivocal conclusion that comparable growth will occur. Frequent monitoring is necessary to detect differences in growth patterns. When the slightest change in growth patterns occurs, the accuracy of the forecast should be questioned. This method of projection should be used only as a check or back-up for another type of student enrollment projection method.

Forecasting with Cohort Survival Ratios

The cohort survival ratio[4] method uses birth-rate statistics and migration factors to determine future enrollment and assumes the historical survival rate of the members of a designated cohort or group such as a kindergarten class which is tracked through graduation. This can be used as the basis for predicting the size of similar cohorts (other kindergarten classes) as they progress through the system. This is a common methodology and has the advantage of being simple to calculate using readily available data. The disadvantage is that error can be introduced if the community experiences a sudden and significant change affecting population such as an annexation, construction of a large housing development, or the loss of a major employer. It is also a difficult method to use in a rapidly growing community where data used can quickly become outdated.

Forecasting with Geo-Referenced Data

The geo-referenced data method, sometimes referred to as the land saturation method, is based on the assumption that eventually all land in a given geographical area will be used for some purpose, most likely consistent with current zoning. Data are obtained either through the U.S. Census or a special census that can be used to estimate population and enrollment figures from each type of anticipated development. A family composition index that describes the average family that lives in each dwelling or development is developed. The index also indicates a breakdown within the family unit of the percentage of adults and dependents by age group in a household. These percentages can then be applied to the number of anticipated housing units to forecast the demand for additional capacity for each age group that will be generated. Two major advantages associated with this method are 1) the nature of the increase in student enrollments and the direction of growth can be predicted with a high degree of accuracy and 2) the timing of the growth can be anticipated based on estimates of completion of housing developments and on actual completions. The major disadvantages are that the software systems necessary to support this method tend to be costly and the databases necessary to generate good projections require constant maintenance.

Other Considerations with Enrollment Forecasts

Dual Use Facilities

In addition to the instructional uses for a school building, the facility may be used for other purposes such as administrative functions, recreation usage, community theater productions, or other activities. Dual use is a particularly attractive option when one of the uses may not enjoy sufficient support on its own, such as administrative offices or school facilities in developed urban areas where land is expensive. In evaluating dual use possibilities, it is critical to ensure that any proposed secondary use will not compromise the primary use of the facility.

One example of dual use is to locate the community's public library within a school. Advantages to such an arrangement would include reduced costs due to shared infrastructure, increased availability, and a larger book collection. Disadvantages would include additional security concerns due to large numbers of individuals having access to the school building, especially when children are present, and concerns over the appropriateness of some library materials deemed appropriate for a public library, but not a school library.

Another dual use example is the ability and increased interest in using the school building in disaster preparedness plans. Many schools are now being designed for use as shelters. To a degree, this represents a return to earlier times when schools frequently were designed as air raid or fallout shelters.

In projecting school enrollment, special care should be taken in determining the portion of the student body that will be considered special education students. Smaller class sizes (often as low as five per class) and unique qualifications required for teachers and other para-professional staff can impact facility sizing. Costs of special education services have increased more rapidly than general educational costs recently. This is partially due to additional state and federal mandates and better methods of identifying students with special needs, resulting in the identification of more special needs students.

Regardless of the projection methods employed, it is important to consider the difference between school age population and enrollment. A portion of school age children will attend private schools or will be home schooled. In some areas, home-schooled students can opt in to specialized classes and extracurricular activities, and must be considered in enrollment forecasts. There may also be arrangements allowing the school system to accept students from outside the district through an agreement with another district on a tuition basis or even as a benefit extended to the local government employees.

Planning for School Facilities

School boards usually need a high degree of public support for any capital project because of referendum requirements for issuing debt and/or because the capital project directly affects the tax rate. To gain public support, boards often create committees to review the requirements of the system and make recommendations. The make-up of these committees varies, however, it is suggested that members of the community who possess appropriate qualifications be included along with elected officials and staff. Engineering and architectural consultants should also be included as a resource capable of contributing valuable information, not as a voting body. More information on involving citizens in committees can be found in chapter 2. Regardless of the committee's make-up, it will need certain basic information to carry out its responsibilities:

- ◆ Ten-year student population projections by grade level and geographic distribution;
- ◆ Instructional requirements, especially if the facility will house vocational programs, special education classes, or other unique programs;
- ◆ Resources available for the project, including both financial and physical resources such as land and building space; and
- ◆ Mandates and constraints, usually imposed at the state level, such as minimum acreage requirements or maximum floor area ratios, or formulas for determining requirements to build new rather than rebuild/rehabilitate.

New Construction vs. Expansion of Existing School

After determining that anticipated enrollment will exceed current capacity, the district must decide if the additional capacity needs should be met by constructing a new facility or by rehabilitating and expanding an existing facility or facilities.

Some states require a formula-based decision process to determine if school divisions should build new buildings or rehabilitate/expand existing buildings. An example of one formula is outlined in Exhibit 15.1.

Exhibit 15.1 Castaldi Formula

The Castaldi Formula is a nationally utilized standard developed in the 1980s by Dr. Basil Castaldi.

$$\frac{Ce + Ch + Cs}{(Lm)(Ia)} > \frac{R}{Lr}$$

Ce = Total cost of educational improvements
Ch = Total cost for improvements in healthfulness (physical, aesthetic, and psychological)
Cs = Total cost for improvements in safety
Lm = Estimated useful life of the modernized school
Ia = Estimated index of educational adequacy (0-1)
R = Cost of replacement of school considered for modernization
Lr = Estimated life of new building

The index of educational adequacy is a somewhat subjective number based on an estimate of how adequate the rehabilitated structure will be expressed as a percent. If the formula on the left yields a number higher than the formula on the right, then rehabilitation/expansion may be undertaken; otherwise an entirely new structure is required. The converse is generally not the case; school systems are never prohibited from building new.

The strict use of formulas in the build vs. renew decision has been criticized as being too simplistic. Some states have attempted to add additional criteria, such as estimates of life cycle costs that include transportation costs. However, even if it is not required, applying a formula may be useful during the discussion on whether or not to build a new school or expand and renovate an existing school. Other factors that have bearing on build/renew decision making include traffic issues, environmental considerations, plans for future expansion needs, and adjoining neighborhood feedback.

Rehabilitation

One concept introduced in planning for rehabilitation and expansion of existing structures is reclaimed capacity. School buildings may have "hidden" usable space that may be found and can be reprogrammed, redesigned, and reconfigured to help meet changing educational needs. Examples of ways space can be reclaimed include converting an old auditorium to a new media center, changing a wood shop into a special education suite, and making offices out of old storage areas. Furthermore, some of the over-designed spaces can be identified and redistributed to other program uses, and large classrooms can be subdivided to meet other needs. Many times the special needs programs do not require a full-size classroom but are placed in one due to lack of smaller spaces. The reclaimed space will add to the total capacity update of the school.

Planning for a New School

The planning process should be assumed to take a minimum of eighteen months and may take significantly longer if there are challenges in obtaining an appropriate site or necessary zoning approvals. This section will focus on specific issues unique to schools that occur during the planning process.

The first step is to select the project site. It is absolutely necessary to determine the site before undertaking the project's engineering and architectural phases. Each piece of property has unique aspects that can profoundly affect the project's design and price. Even if a facility is being renovated, additional land may be necessary. Some states impose formula-based requirements for the minimum amount of land necessary for a school. In one state, laws require the site for an elementary school be at least ten acres plus one acre per 100 students in design capacity.[5] This formula is generally provided by statute or regulation and varies from state to state. The intent is to ensure sufficient space is allowed for buildings, parking, playgrounds, and athletic fields. Where practical, school sites should be larger than the state requirement to allow for growth and potential changes to requirements. Waivers or exemptions may be necessary where land acquisition is impractical or cost prohibitive, especially in urban areas.

Since land acquisition can be difficult and potentially contentious, it is best to acquire it well in advance of need. Clearly, this is a function of the school district's confidence that the land will be needed at that particular site. Purchasing land that is never used can be as politically embarrassing as being caught short and having to rush a land purchase.

A school will draw students from a designated geographic attendance area. As a general rule, the site selected should be convenient to the entire area. In considering property for a facility, the following should be taken into consideration:

- The convenience of the location for both school activities and any other non-school activities if the facility is considered for dual use;
- Traffic patterns and safe access, such as separating the bus loop from the pick-up/drop-off area for parents driving children to school or designated access for emergency vehicles;
- Access to municipal services such as water, sewer, and refuse pick up;
- Sufficient usable acreage for all anticipated programs, taking into account the existence of land taken up by wetlands, flood plains, archeological sites, and unsuitable topographic features;

◆ Cost estimates for site development construction;

◆ Impact of noise, both by the school on the surrounding area and by the surrounding area on the school;

◆ Environmental and safety threats, such as flooding or industrial hazards;

◆ Space to accommodate growth in numbers of students or in additional programs;

◆ Impact of field lighting on the surrounding neighborhood, especially if lighting impact is governed by local ordinance; and

◆ Aesthetic appeal.

For various reasons, a landowner may offer to donate site for a school or a site may be donated as part of a subdivision development. In other areas, large developments may be required to proffer land for a school site. The fact that the property is free does not eliminate the necessity to take all the items outlined above into consideration. Free land may carry costs not immediately apparent, such as difficult site work or environmental clean up.

Zoning

It is highly unusual for a site selected for a school building to be appropriately zoned for that use. In creating a timeline for the project, sufficient time must be built in for any required permitting and zoning issues. New construction and large renovation projects generally require significant variances or zoning changes. Completing this process can be expensive and time-consuming, especially if environmental or traffic studies are necessary. Although the community as a whole may be supportive, the immediate neighbors of a proposed school facility are often less enthusiastic. Resolving the political issues may be the most difficult element of locating a facility.

Permits

Permitting is generally a mechanical process that continues throughout the project. The local officials' procedures and workload will affect the amount of time that should be included in the construction timeline. The building official should be engaged early enough in the planning process to allow for a reasonable estimate.

Design

Although prior experience in designing schools is useful, it may not be necessary if a firm can demonstrate a thorough knowledge of the mandated elements of school design as they apply to the project. There are a number of architects that specialize in school design. These firms may have several "stock" school designs that they pull off the shelf and modify to meet a site's requirements. Although

Size of School

Proponents of small schools cite benefits from the closer and more personal environment and its positive impact on both learning and discipline. Teachers have fewer students and can therefore get to know them better and can provide more individualized attention. Proponents of larger schools point out the economies of scale that free up scarce education dollars. In addition, larger numbers of students bring the critical mass that makes it practical to offer certain educational opportunities, such as specialized foreign languages or advanced math and science classes.

There is no consensus among educators and academics regarding optimum school size. Even the definitions of "large school" and "small school" vary. Although smaller schools are often popular among teachers and parents, the cost of building and operating numerous small schools rather than a few large ones may not be sustainable.

Many published documents have been produced over the years debating this issue. Organizations such as the Small Schools Project or the Small Schools Workshop at the College of Education at the University of South Florida advocate for building smaller schools or for school divisions to attain a middle ground by co-locating multiple smaller schools on one campus.

School boards often attempt to adopt a size standard, regardless of where they stand on the small/large continuum, if only to provide balance among schools in terms of such things as class choices, standardized curricula, and competition among sports teams.

Note: The Small Schools Project is part of the Coalition of Essential Schools Northwest. More information on the Coalition of Essential Schools Northwest can be found on its Web site, http://www.cesnorthwest. org/

such designs may not satisfy the community's aesthetic desires, there can be significant cost savings in selecting this approach.

School Development Standards

The construction of educational facilities is highly regulated by the department of education within each state. For example, many states publish minimum acreage requirements for a school site, depending on the nature of the school and the student capacity. Design details such as hallway and door widths, ceiling heights, number and type of classrooms, offices for counselors, cafeteria size, and many other requirements are laid out in other state regulations and federal requirements, such as the Americans with Disabilities Act. Though there are many common elements among the states, there is no general set of rules that can be applied for capital planning. A familiarity with the specific requirements and the waiver process, if meeting the requirement is impossible, is necessary early in the process.

To determine the project scope, planners consider the number of students, any policies on school and class size, and any options for alternative or additional uses of the facility. In planning for the facility, both design capacity and program capacity must be considered. Design capacity refers to the maximum number of students a school can accommodate. State or local standards may have set requirements for the maximum number of students per classroom, a minimum classroom size, or minimum square footage per student. Some example standards are shown in Exhibit 15.2. The design capacity is also reflected in the sizing needed for common areas of the school, such as a gymnasium or cafeteria.

Program capacity, or functional capacity, is the number of students that can be accommodated given the mix of instructional programs in the school. A classroom that could hold thirty students may be used for a special education class that cannot exceed fifteen per state law, or school division may set a maximum student/teacher ratio of 25:1. Thus, design capacity may provide a theoretical maximum number of students, but program capacity represents the actual number of students the building can serve. Many times a school's first need for additional space, such as trailers, is because it does not have any program capacity left. However, if design capacity still exists, then such trailers may not impact the school as much as a school with no design capacity left. An example of an immediate constraint when no design capacity exists is when students have lunch very early or late in the school day because the cafeteria cannot serve all students during traditional lunch hours.

Exhibit 15.2 Sample School Development Standards

Development Standard	Example Standard
Maximum number of students per classroom	25-30*
Minimum classroom size	960 square feet**
Minimum square footage per student	150 sq ft for elementary school***
	180 sq ft for high school****

* From "Educational Specifications for Elementary Schools," Seattle Public Schools.
** From "School Design Guide," Los Angeles Unified School District.
*** From "School Planning Manual," Commonwealth of Virginia Department of Education.
**** Ibid.

Special Education Needs

The effect that special education needs have on school design cannot be overstated. Although state law may allow up to 15 students per special education classroom, many special education classes have as few as five students due to the nature of the students' disabilities. Some additional rooms may also be needed for specialized functions such as audiology labs. Providing special services will increase the number of rooms and total space needed.

Capacity Measures

Capacity measures, once adopted, form a critical element in developing the capital improvement program. For example, the adopted policy goal might be that no individual school will be over design capacity by 10 percent for three consecutive years without providing relief either through the addition of new capacity and/or redistricting and without increasing the student/teacher ratio This may mean that the need for trailers during those three years is explicitly considered acceptable. A program capacity exceeding 120 percent for a three-year period could be another means of accomplishing the same end. It may be possible to use both for internal planning, but since explaining the differences between the two types of ratios can be confusing for the average citizen, it is best to adopt one or the other as policy. Policy goals should always be implemented with practical considerations in mind and should enable the district to make sound decisions without being "held hostage" by poorly constructed policies.

Financing Options for Schools

The method of financing school projects varies considerably from state to state. Each state has a unique history and collection of laws that determine the possible funding sources that can be used. In this chapter, options are discussed broadly, acknowledging that the details will vary from state to state and that some options may not be available. General obligation bonds are the most generic funding source and are usually available for most school projects. Many states assume some of the responsibility for school capital funding, but their responsibility is often limited to funding the minimum facility requirements. For example, the state would fund the minimum square footage per student and any additional costs would be the responsibility of the local school district. Additionally, some states have grant programs for school capital funds. Often these grants are needs based, with preference going to the school districts with the least ability to pay for the projects with locally derived resources. The ability to pay generally is determined by a formula, and can be based on assessed property values in the district. Other sources of funds common used by school districts include pooled lending programs, federal grants, or impact fees.

Pooled Lending Programs

Some states sponsor pooled lending programs specifically for school construction. In this type of program, the state issues debt for the project and the individual entities borrow funds from the state. In addition to economies of scale, these programs can be especially helpful in cases where the state's bond rating is significantly better than the bond rating for the school district.

Federal Programs

Some federal programs are available to assist with certain specific aspects of school construction, such as Qualified Zone Academy Bonds or the Credit Enhancement for Charter School Facilities Program. The details of these programs change from year to year, thus requiring research on a case-by-case basis before anticipating the use of this financing source.

Impact Fees

Some states may allow the school district to collect impact fees from new developments to help mitigate the costs of providing school facilities for rapidly growing areas. Fees are generally charged to every new residential development and collected at the time permits are issued or the final plat is approved. Exceptions may exist for low-income or temporary housing. In lieu of impact fees, some developers may proffer land for a new school.

| Conclusion |

Building, renovating, and maintaining the capital assets for education are among local governments' most expensive undertakings. Although education generally enjoys widespread public support, meeting the needs of public education can be a difficult and sometimes frustrating enterprise. Elected and appointed officials find themselves attempting to accommodate many requirements and desires, but should use caution in not attempting to accommodate them all. School projects should remain focused on providing suitable space for children to learn. Overall, education is a highly regulated enterprise with numerous mandates passed down to local government from higher levels. Planning and executing school capital projects involves large numbers of people, money, and investments of time. Invested wisely, the community can realize significant dividends.

Case Study from Fauquier County, Virginia

Fauquier County, a rapidly growing outer suburb of Washington, D.C., anticipated the need for a new elementary school using a combination of cohort survival ratio projections and a geo-referenced ratio projection based on the county's comprehensive plan. The school board was able to delay the construction of the new school for two years through a redistricting plan and the use of mobile classrooms. After the approval of an 800-unit housing development, expected to generate 350 more elementary school students than included in the "normal" growth rate, the county decided it was time to construct a new school.

The farmer who sold the property to the developer for the housing development donated 20 acres of land for the construction of the school. The transfer of title was handled in an expedited manner in order to match the donation with the landowner's profit from the sale of the other property. Since the property had been used exclusively for farming for the past two hundred years, a minimum environmental assessment was considered sufficient (this would not normally be advisable if there is uncertainty regarding previous usages of the property).

The school design was a standard one provided by the architects with minor modifications to fit it to the site. The county engaged a value-engineering (VE) firm to review the design before bidding the construction contract, resulting in estimated cost savings of $700,000 on a project of approximately $14 million. In addition, the VE firm suggested modifications that increased certain construction costs in order to realize life cycle savings, such as HVAC systems and flooring materials. The VE exercise also had the additional benefit of reducing change orders during the construction period simply because the plans had been reviewed one extra time, resulting in additional savings of contingency funds.

The school was cash funded using funds derived from a budgetary "windfall" resulting from a change from an annual to a semi-annual collection of real estate taxes.

Notes

1. Deb Moore, "Maybe It's Time We Rethink How We Construct School Buildings," *School Planning and Management* (August 2004).

2. The cafeteria and auditorium are often combined into a "cafetorium."

3. Other terms for trailers include modular classrooms, temporary classrooms, or educational cottages.

4. Other terms used for this method are age, class, grade retention, or grade progression ratio; percentage of survival; percentage of retention; grade persistence; survival-ratio method; and retention ratio method.

5. This example comes from the Commonwealth of Virginia Department of Education, School Planning Manual.

|16|

Public Libraries

By Sue Cutsogeorge and Bradley G. Black

Libraries in the twenty-first century are much more than a place to store books and periodicals. With the advent of the electronic information age, libraries now provide a crucial link for citizens of all backgrounds, abilities, and income levels to access information throughout the world. Technology is also making the library more user friendly for patrons and more efficient for staff. For example, there are systems that will automatically take books from a book drop, check them in, sort them, and place them on the appropriate cart for re-shelving. To take advantage of the latest technology, library buildings must be adaptable to meet ever-changing community needs. Prudent planning for a library facility requires making decisions that ensure that the facility is adequate to serve a community's needs for a long time.

| Description of Library Facilities |

Library systems can take different physical forms. Some communities have one central library facility, while others have a central library that serves both as a library and a central processing facility, along with a series of branches located throughout the community. A library system can also be made up of a series of branches, without a central main facility. Some communities have even linked their public library facility with school libraries or senior centers or built branch libraries in shopping centers. Public libraries provide citizens with a place to gather and it is even common for newer libraries to include coffee shops. Additionally, libraries often host reading groups and seminars on topics of interest, and house meeting rooms where community groups can assemble to conduct their business.

Each library should establish a service program detailing all the activities to be conducted in the proposed building. The program will help establish what public spaces should be designed and the relative size of the different kinds of public spaces within the library. The public spaces often reflect the community's unique characteristics and could include historical artifacts, items of community pride, or public art. In the end, a library still must function and allow library staff the necessary space to re-shelve books, find information, and assist patrons.

The major components of a library include space for the collection, seating space for patrons, computers for public use, meeting rooms, technology infrastructure, administrative areas, and miscellaneous space, all of which is designed to meet the library's service program.

Space for the Collection

A library collection can contain different types of materials including books; periodicals; non-print materials such as CDs, DVDs, and books on tape; and digital resources. Each type of material requires a different space arrangement and may require special equipment to use. Most collections require shelving, but each may have different requirements.

Seating Space for Patrons

Scattered throughout a library should be areas for patrons to sit while using the collection. Usage varies by patron: one person might browse through a magazine, another might access reference materials, or a small student group might collaborate on a homework assignment. Areas with lounge-type seating, as well as tables for individual and group use, will provide patrons with choices in how they use the collection.

Computers and Technology for Public Use

Technology continues to change rapidly, so designing a facility to accommodate computers and technology can be challenging. As more and more information has become available either online or through some form of electronic media, the public has embraced the need for access to computer technology in libraries. Providing computer stations to allow public access to the Web or the electronic collection is now the norm, and computer stations require increased floor space, as well as proximity to power and data outlets.

Design features could include work stations for individual access to computer terminals, areas for patrons to plug in their own computers, and wireless Internet access. Computer access spaces may or may not provide seating, and might include areas for books and other working materials, or they may be designed solely for computer access. It may also be beneficial to design separate computer areas for adults, teen, and youth. In addition to the computers set up for public use, some libraries include a computer learning lab.

Meeting Rooms

Libraries are commonly used as a gathering place, and community meeting rooms are often included in a facility's design. The rooms could be used for a variety of different purposes, and the community should consider the specific types of activities that might be conducted in them Some possibilities are a large lecture hall, a children's story-telling room with a heated floor, multi-purpose rooms, meeting rooms, small group study rooms, or rooms set up for distance learning. Consideration should also be given to the technology needs for lecture halls and meeting rooms, such as sound-proofing rooms so that activities do not disturb patrons in other areas of the library.

When the City of Eugene, Oregon, designed its new main library, a large multi-purpose room was included in the design. The room can be divided into two separate spaces, or used as one large space. It includes the technology necessary to broadcast meetings on public television, as well as other high-tech meeting needs.

Technology Infrastructure

Rising labor costs and liability concerns have spawned the development of book conveying and sorting systems as well as patron self check-out systems. All are designed to improve the level of service delivered to the customer while reducing the overall labor effort and costs. Book conveying and sorting systems have significantly reduced the number of staff and amount of time required to process returned collections items and to manage patron accounts. A conveying and sorting system can virtually eliminate the traditional backlog of items waiting to be processed while maintaining real-time records of patron activity. However, the introduction of this type of new technology may reduce the need for traditional library staff and increase the need for more highly trained technical staff to maintain the computer and mechanical-electrical systems.

Administrative Areas

Staff areas include service points to the public, as well as back-room spaces for processing materials and performing general administrative functions. The move to a new facility provides an opportunity for staff to reconsider their work processes and the relationships of staff to each other and to the patrons. Typical staff areas include reference, circulation, technical services, acquisition, cataloging and processing, and administrative offices. The staff will also require a break area or a lunch room. Libraries may also need space to house bookmobiles or delivery vans that transfer materials from one library within the system to another. Covered loading docks and space for organizing the bookmobile collection, as well as delivery boxes or bags and staff workstations for these functions would also be necessary.

Miscellaneous Space

The design will need to include other types of space, including miscellaneous patron-related spaces, as well as building and administrative areas. The miscellaneous patron-related areas can include hallways, stairwells, elevators, restrooms, photocopy machines, and so on. Facility parking needs should also be considered.

Alternate Governance Models

Alternate governance models or partnerships can provide additional opportunities for funding a library construction project or for operating the library. Some examples of alternative governance models include special library districts, regional sharing of services, public/private partnerships, and partnerships with other libraries.

Library Districts. Special-purpose districts can be created in some areas to serve a larger regional base than the boundaries of a city, which enables capital and operating costs to be spread over a wider range of taxpayers. Library districts may be able to establish their own property tax levy authority, which can then be used to finance construction projects.

Regional or Shared Services. Reciprocal agreements with neighboring localities could provide for sharing collections and facilities. The Oregon Library Association's Vision 2010 includes a goal to create a system where libraries in the state would "sweep away regional, jurisdictional, and procedural boundaries so every Oregonian has a library card that works at any publicly supported library."

Public/Private Partnerships. Public/private partnership can include privatization of services, direct investment of public funds in a private enterprise, joint development of projects, and other approaches to providing ongoing services or funding of capital costs.

Partnerships with Other Library Facilities. Partnerships between municipalities and public school libraries or senior centers are becoming more common. Some municipalities are also partnering with a local university or community college. For example, in 2003 the City of Jose, California, opened a $177 million library facility that was jointly funded, built, and managed by the city and San Jose State University. The benefit from this kind of partnership may not be additional construction funding, but rather a reduced cost for building and/or operating the joint facility. When considering a co-location option, it is important to carefully consider whether the joint interests are compatible.

Sources:

*Oregon Library Association, Vision 2010 (http://www.olaweb.org/v2010/).

**San Jose Public Libraries, "Timeline of the New Dr. Martin Luther King Jr. Library Project" (http://www.sjlibrary.org/about/history/timeline.htm).

Needs Assessment: Evaluating the Need for Library Facilities

Performing a needs assessment will show how well current facilities are meeting the needs of the library patrons and staff, and expose areas for potential improvement. Needs assessments are also vital in determining the project's budget and scope. Generally, jurisdictions will use outside consultants and incorporate opinions of library staff, government staff, community groups, citizens, and other stakeholders such as library volunteers. The following information should be considered in any needs assessment.

Economic and Demographic Trends

It is helpful to look at the make-up of the population the library serves. The assessment would also review projections for how the community is expected to change over time. These demographic factors can impact the way in which the library may better serve the community now and in the future. Some examples of potential factors to examine include:

◆ The percentage of the population that is over 65 and under 18;

◆ Socio-economic data;

◆ The proportion of non-native English-speaking citizens in the community; and

◆ The number of people living near the proposed library location.

Library Usage Data

One way to determine how well the current facility and services are meeting the community's needs is to review useful performance data. These statistics should be looked at over multiple years, and compared to other similar libraries or state association standards. The way in which the current facility is used can provide some information about what is needed in a new facility. Some performance measures the library should consider are:

◆ Books in circulation;

◆ Library holdings;

◆ Hours of operation;

◆ Full-time employees;

◆ Meeting room occupancy rates;

◆ Listing of the most frequently requested and used services;

◆ Computer use rate;

◆ Number of reference questions or patron inquiries answered;

◆ Listing of the services not used; and

◆ Portion of the library not accessible to people with disabilities.

Location of the New Facility

Designing a library that is accessible to the public is essential. This includes locating the facility near patrons and providing the appropriate accessibility features. A geographic information system analysis of the service area could provide data on how much of the population would be served from various location options. A goal of this type of analysis might be to have library services available within a certain distance from library patrons' homes. Citizen surveys, focus groups, and studies of similar libraries and cities can be used to gather the following types of information to determine the correct features for accessing the facility:

◆ The type (surface or structure) and number of parking spaces that will be required;

◆ The anticipated demand for parking at different times during the day;

◆ Location and number of bike parking spaces;

◆ Access to public transportation;

◆ Pedestrian connections from neighborhoods, schools, etc.; and

◆ Area surrounding the library

Technology

A technology assessment is one of the most important tasks in the early stages of developing a library project. In recent years, the types of technology available for library purposes have increased significantly. One example is an automatic book sorting and conveying system, which can reduce the need for additional staff, but also increases the complexity of work, requiring more skilled employees. A technology assessment should include an analysis of the potential benefits from technology as well as the skills on staff that would be necessary to operate and maintain the technology. In making a decision on technology options, the jurisdiction determines if it is more appropriate to purchase tried-and-true technology solutions or be part of the "leading edge."

Safety and Security

Safety of staff, patrons, and the library collection itself should also be considered. The jurisdiction's public safety staff can usually provide input that will help in identifying design responses to improve safety. Depending on the identified needs and risks, a new facility may include safety features such as access control systems, closed circuit television to monitor areas inside and outside the facility, and panic buttons.

Security of library materials must also be considered during the design process. Several options are available to protect library materials from unauthorized removal from the facility, including embedded magnetic strips and electronic chips for radio frequency identification (RFID). If a new security system is selected, some library processes may have to be adjusted. It is important to note that while it is possible to convert to a new security system at the same time as building a new facility, both projects require careful planning and significant amounts of time. In addition, paying for a security system conversion may require a different funding source than other capital items, since the RFID chips will probably not qualify as capital expenditures.

Accessibility

Requirements of the Americans with Disabilities Act (ADA) can present unique challenges for libraries. Both the height and spacing of stacks can be an issue. To strictly comply with ADA requirements for those in wheelchairs, stacks can not exceed about 54 inches in height. If all stacks in a library were of this height, the floor space required would double. As an alternate ADA compliance measure, the library can establish administrative measures to assist the disabled. In the case of stacks, 84-inch-tall stacks can be used as long as the library provides a staff person to assist those in wheelchairs with access to the upper shelves.

ADA accommodations may also need to be considered for the technology libraries provide to allow public access to the Web or electronic media. For those with sight impairment, larger monitors with large-scale fonts may be required. For those with no sight abilities, brail or audio equipment should be considered. Technology supporting the disabled continues to improve and offer more and more opportunities to allow greater accessibility of library materials.

Design for Future Flexibility

Because no one knows exactly what the future will bring in terms of demand for services, media types, and technology systems, it is important to build flexibility into the design of a new library. The design team should have a good idea of the

Book Replacement

During the development of the architectural space program and subsequent design, library professionals need to identify and address the question of collection management and replacement. What the collection looks like and how it will change over time are issues that the library staff must address from the beginning of the project. It is vital that staff identify its vision of collection management in both the short and long term. Examples of collection management strategies include moving away from VHS tapes in favor of DVDs, increasing the number of large-print materials available for the aging population, or adding to the collection of foreign language titles to address changes in the community's demographics.

growth horizon to be used for determining the facility's size. A new library should include sufficient room to accommodate the community's projected needs for a defined time period.

There are several approaches to building in future capacity for collections when designing stack layouts. Empty shelf space at the opening of a new facility directly translates into more expansion capacity long term. One approach is to fill all shelves to a predetermined capacity (i.e., 60 percent or top/bottom shelves empty), using the remaining space to accommodate future acquisitions.

The Eugene Public Library made long-term flexibility a design requirement. An entire floor containing approximately 32,000 square feet was constructed as future expansion space to accommodate anticipated growth beyond the first ten years of operation. During the ten-year interim period, the space is being used for other city functions, thereby saving on rental costs that would have been incurred.

Library Standards

Some state library associations recommend standards that can help to determine parameters for a new library. For example, the Oregon Library Association recommends a review of space needs at least every ten years, and provides for minimum space requirements. Some of the Oregon Library Association standards are set out in Exhibit 16.1.[1]

Exhibit 16.1 Oregon Library Association Standards

Space Requirements	
Population Served	**Minimum space requirements**
0 - 3,999	3,050 square feet
4,000-49,999	3,050 square feet for the first 4,000 population and 0.76 square feet per capita in excess of 4,000 population
50,000+	38,750 square feet for the first 50,000 and 0.61 square feet per capita in excess of 50,000 population

Hours of Operation Standards			
Population Served	**Threshold**	**Adequate**	**Excellent**
0 - 4,999	20	35	50
5,000 - 9,999	30	45	60
10,000 - 24,999	40	55	70
25,000 +	50	60	75

Collection Standards			
Population Served	**Threshold**	**Adequate**	**Excellent**
0 - 49,999	Book collection of 5,000 books or 2 books per capita, whichever is greater	Book collection of 10,000 books or 3 books per capita, whichever is greater	Book collection of 20,000 books or 4 books per capita, whichever is greater
50,000+	Book collection of 2 books per capita	Book collection of 150,000 books or 2.5 books per capita, whichever is greater	Book collection of 200,000 books or 3 books per capita, whichever is greater

The State of Virginia's library standard for service is 0.6 square feet per person in the library district. For example, a jurisdiction with a population of 100,000 people would need 60,000 square feet of library space.[2] Many other states have similar requirements or guidelines.

Some states also have resources available that can help with determining the appropriate size for various portions of a new library facility. For example, the State of Wisconsin Department of Public Instruction[3] and the State of Connecticut[4] have both published a space needs guide that includes information on how to determine the size of a new facility.

While standards can provide one method for determining a new library's size and program requirements, it is important that a jurisdiction review all other relevant factors described in this chapter and not adopt state standards without consideration of individual community preferences.

Citizen Volunteers

For an important community project like construction of a new library, there may be strong interest by citizens in participating. The City of Eugene, Oregon, took advantage of this by asking volunteers to convert the collection from the old magnetic strips to the new radio frequency identification chip system. This conversion took over a year to complete. Additionally, citizens in Ashland, Virginia, used a community-wide "book brigade" to move the 30,000 volume collection across the street and over the railroad tracks to the new Richard S. Gillis, Jr. Library. While these citizen volunteer programs are popular with the public, jurisdictions should carefully consider the implications for insurance liability and union contracts before developing such a program.

Source: Information was taken from the Pamunkey Regional Library Web site, "Richard S. Gillis, Jr./Ashland Branch Library," Pamunkey Regional Library (http://www.pamunkeylibrary.org).

Project Management: Coordinating Moving Day

The complexity of moving a collection to a new facility is directly related to the size of the collection and distance. It is not a task that should be put off until the last minute. Two significant steps need to be taken to ensure a successful move: 1) assign one person primary work responsibility to be in charge of all move activities and 2) institute an effective preplanning process. In a public setting, that process should begin six to nine months before the anticipated move, particularly if a request for proposals for such services is necessary. In addition, the costs for moving into a new facility should be included in the overall budget for a new library project.

Moving day is also a great opportunity to "clean-up" the collection. Instead of building space into the facility to house many low-use items, the collection could instead be reduced in size. This will also allow more space for items that receive a greater degree of patron interest.

Financing for Libraries

General obligation bonds are a common funding source for most library projects. One advantage of long-term bonds is that they spread the cost of a facility over time while the library is in use, forcing future taxpayers that use the facility to support the project as well. Other potential funding sources for library construction projects exist, many of which vary from state to state. Brief descriptions of some of the funding sources that could be applicable to library projects are set out below:

Private Donations and Grants

Library foundations and other citizen organizations created to support library services are often used to help with fundraising for capital construction projects. Private foundations also have funding programs. For example, the Gates Foundation through its U.S. Library Program provides funds for libraries to get and stay connected to the Internet.[5] In San Diego, public donations for a new library construction project are expected to account for about $85 million out of a budget of $185 million.[6] In addition, several states, such as California,[7] Florida,[8] Massachusetts,[9] New York,[10] and Texas,[11] have grant programs for library construction projects. Often, these programs may require a matching component from the local government.

In-Kind Donations

In-kind donations from local businesses can be a successful way of reducing costs, but can also create challenges. Often, the specific materials or equipment offered for donation may not be what best suits the project. Rejection of unacceptable donations can present a significant political problem and can possibly result in a loss of citizen support for the project. If accepting in-kind donations, it is important to guarantee that the donation arrives when promised and that the donation is the exact product that was expected. Failure of a donor to come through on a promise can cause schedule delays, redesign fees, and other issues resulting in higher costs, rather than savings. In general, the best in-kind donations are stand-alone items, such as a refrigerator for a staff lounge, carpet for an entire room, or a world globe for the children's area. In-kind donations that usually do not work well are partial donations of an item, such as half of the doors in the facility; critical path materials, such as concrete, reinforcing steel, casework, or roofing; or specialty items, such as hardware, light fixtures, lockers, custom woodwork, signage or elevators.

Dedicated Taxes

Some states allow a municipality to levy a temporary property tax to fund costs of public construction projects, while others have used increases in income taxes, sales taxes, or other taxes. Generally, the tax revenue will be used to repay bonds issued for construction. A voter referendum is usually required to use dedicated taxes to fund projects, so it is important to begin planning efforts far in advance.

Urban Renewal/Tax Increment Funds

The construction of a library, when part of overall economic development strategies, can be used to reinvigorate a neighborhood. The library itself will not generate tax revenue, but it may encourage investment from taxpaying property owners. The City of Eugene, Oregon, received urban renewal funds for approximately 70 percent of the cost of its new library. After the library's opening, the area saw a greater level of private developer interest.

Financing Plans from Recent Projects

Bozeman, Montana. A 53,000-square-foot library opened in 2005. The project cost about $17 million, with funding coming from a bond measure, library foundation donations, sale of the old library building, and other funding sources, such as Gallatin County, tax increment funds, a Northwestern Energy grant, federal funds, and park land reimbursement.

Champaign, Illinois. This $30 million project was funded with additions to the local sales tax and the local telecommunications tax, as well as from an estimated $3 million of private donations. The 122,000-square-foot facility is scheduled to open in fall 2007.

Coeur D'Alene, Idaho. The total cost of the new library is $7.2 million. A bond issue will provide $3 million toward construction costs. The remainder will come from sources such as grants, the sale of the current library, and donations.

Eugene, Oregon. The new main library had a $36.2 million total budget, which included new technology for book moving and sorting systems, as well as an extra floor representing future expansion space. Funding came from $25.4 million in tax increment funds, $5 million from private donations, $1.9 million from a temporary property tax levy, $1.3 million from the sale of surplus property, $1.6 million in interest earnings on cash balances, $0.4 million from reallocating the library budget for one year, and $0.6 million in other miscellaneous sources. The 126,000-square-foot facility opened in December 2002.

Minneapolis, Minnesota. The new central library building was paid for through $110 million in voter-approved bonds, supplemented with $15 million in private funding contributed by more than 200 individuals, foundations, and businesses, and parking bonds that helped pay for parking ramp costs. The 353,000-square-foot building opened in May 2006, and included 140,000 square feet of underground parking.

Morgan Hill, California. A 28,000-square-foot new library facility is currently under construction and was expected to open in summer 2007. The $19 million project is entirely funded by the Morgan Hill Redevelopment Agency.

North Richland Hills, Texas. The budget for the new library is $10.2 million, with the grand opening scheduled for 2008. It will be financed through the issuance of debt obligations repaid from tax increment revenues. The library design includes 49,000 square feet of finished space and 10,000 square feet of shell space for future expansion.

San Diego, California. The $185 million project is expected to be paid from a $20 million state library grant, $80 million of redevelopment funds, and the balance from private donations. The 366,000-square-foot facility is scheduled to open in 2009.

Santa Maria, California. The total project cost for the new 60,000-square-foot library is nearly $33 million, which includes a parking structure. Funding is to come from a grant of $16 million, impact fees, community development block grant funds, and city funds. The Friends of the Library is also raising funds to help pay for the project. Construction began in May 2006.

Sources:
- Bozeman, Montana (http://www.bozemanlibrary.org/).
- Champaign, Illinois (http://www.champaign.org/).
- Coeur D'Alene, Idaho (http://www.newcdalibrary.com).
- Minneapolis, Minnesota, "Central Library Media Tool Kit" (http://www.mpls.lib.mn.us).
- Morgan Hill, California (http://www.morgan-hill.ca.gov).
- North Richland Hills, Texas (http://www.nrhtx.com).
- San Diego, California, "Library Building Projects Frequently Asked Questions" (http://www.sandiego.gov/public-library/).

Operating Issues

A new library facility will most likely result in higher operating costs due to increased facility size, added technology, and heightened community interest. For example, the year before the City of Eugene, Oregon, opened its new main library in 2002, there were 611,000 total visits; the year after the opening, there were 981,000 visits.[12] An increase in usage of this magnitude will mean that operating hours and corresponding staff costs may increase. Insurance requirements will also change for a new, larger building. Additionally, any new technology investments will create the need for maintenance staff with a higher degree of technical skill and training.

Operating Issues with New Library Technology

Operating issues related to the introduction of new or expanded technology must be planned well in advance of opening a new facility. New technologies often carry with them the need for more specialized maintenance, tighter environmental conditions, spare parts, and need for ongoing specialized staff training. When the technology program is prepared, it should identify these ongoing costs so that they are properly planned for in the operating budget.

Technology Replacement

The jurisdiction should develop routine maintenance schedules and a replacement plan for large equipment and technology investments such as book moving systems. Proper planning will also allow for the introduction of new technology. Some new library projects may lack funding for book moving or sorting equipment initially, but should plan for future implementation of these technologies.

Conclusion

Building a twenty-first century library requires much more than designing and constructing a facility to store books. Advanced technology and the community's needs and expectations must be considered and analyzed against the costs of the new features. It is extremely important to solicit and receive quality citizen participation and ensure that it is used in creating or deciding on the final design and services the library will offer. Libraries are one of the most utilized public facilities and care should be taken that the new facility can serve the community with a sense of pride, showcasing art, history, or new sustainable energy-efficient designs for many years to come.

Library Project in the City of Eugene, Oregon

Planning for and managing the new $36 million public library project in the City of Eugene, Oregon, took nearly five years of work. During the process, two difficult situations arose that could have threatened the project.

Once the city received the go-ahead from the city council to proceed, it immediately encountered underground petroleum contamination on the chosen site. Contamination required environmental remediation measures that took over one year to complete. Clean-up work began immediately upon discovery of the problem and occurred concurrently with the development of the facility design and construction drawings. Although remediation measures cost approximately $1.5 million, the early identification and clean-up meant that there was no delay in the construction project.

The city also had problems with its new state-of-the-art book moving and sorting technology designed to improve the processing time for returned items. The technology was in the final testing stage and lacked adequate documentation of installation and maintenance requirements. The lack of information significantly increased the amount of time required both by the project manager and the design consultants, and resulted in additional costs and minor delays.

Notes

1. Oregon Library Association, "Standards for Public Libraries" (2000) (http://www. olaweb.org/pld/standards_all.html).
2. Virginia State Library and Archives, "Planning for Library Excellence" (1988).
3. Anders C. Dahlgren, "Public Library Space Needs: A Planning Outline" (Wisconsin Department of Public Instruction). Available at http://dpi.wi.gov/pld/plspace.html.
4. Information was taken from "Focus on Space Planning for Libraries" (http://www. webjunction.org/).
5. Gates Foundation, "U.S. Libraries Program" (http://www.gatesfoundation.org).
6. San Diego Public Library, "New Library Building Projects Frequently Asked Questions" (http://www.sandiego.gov/public-library).
7. California State Library, Library Services and Technology Act (http://www.library.ca. gov/html/grants.cfm).
8. State Library and Archives of Florida, "Grant Programs" (http://dlis.dos.state.fl.us/ bld/grants/index.htm).
9. Massachusetts Board of Library Commissioners, "Grants and Related Programs" (http://mblc.state.ma.us/grants/index.php).
10. New York State Library, Division of Library Development, "Library Services and Technology Act Program in New York State" (http://www.nysl.nysed.gov/libdev/ lsta/).
11. Texas State Library Archives Commission, "Funding for Libraries" (http://www.tsl. state.tx.us/ld/funding/).
12. City of Eugene, Oregon, "Library, Recreation and Cultural Services Annual Report for 2005" (http://www.eugene-or.gov).

| 17 |

Parks and Recreation Facilities

By Donald W. Penfield, Jr.

The role of the public sector in providing parks and recreation services has evolved over time as the needs and desires of citizens have changed. Many sports programs and opportunities for recreation were initially provided by the private sector, but are now often offered by local governments. Typical recreational opportunities provided by local governments include a wide variety of sports programs, educational programs, community centers, historic preservation programs, the preservation of natural areas and open space, and the construction of trails, multipurpose athletic fields, and neighborhood parks.

With the many positive health and social benefits that parks and park facilities provide for the community, the impetus to construct parks and park facilities deserves serious consideration by governmental officials. In order to ensure that such projects will be successful, a jurisdiction must realistically evaluate the need for the proposed recreational facility, devise a good plan for the desired physical elements, and develop an achievable budget program that is both feasible and sustainable. This chapter will provide insight and direction into the various components of developing a capital program for parks and recreation facilities.

| Potential Park Projects |

Parks are as varied as the communities in which they are found. A small neighborhood pocket park may be built on only a few acres and have minimal playground equipment and picnic structures to serve adjacent residents. On the other hand, a park could encompass hundreds of acres and offer many different recreational opportunities for residents living throughout an entire region. Typical facilities include athletic fields, biking trails, fenced in off-leash dog areas, skate parks, aquatic centers, historical preservation areas, and wildlife refuges. Athletic fields can serve baseball, softball, football, soccer, lacrosse, and other sports. Many times, these fields can be designed to overlap and different activities can be scheduled at different times. This type of facility can increase the effectiveness of a limited land area. Aquatic parks can provide leisure swimming, diving, competition, exercise, and shallow play pools with spray features for younger patrons. Park facilities do not always need to provide activities, however. Large areas of land can be used to host events or be set aside to preserve open space or environmentally sensitive or historically important land.

Community Event Venues

Large parcels of land may be used to accommodate sizeable community events. Providing a venue for community fairs, festivals, car shows, and other major events may offer a recreational and cultural benefit to the community as well as a revenue stream for the jurisdiction if it is able to charge event organizers or attendees for admission or parking.

Preservation of Historic/Environmentally Sensitive Land

Throughout the country, many parks have been created with the specific intent of preserving environmentally sensitive areas or historic places for the enjoyment of residents. Such parks may include historic structures, riparian habitats, significant geologic features, arboretums, and other areas similarly worthy of special protection and attention. These areas can also provide a unique and educational opportunity for visitors.

Parks projects may also be able to accomplish environmental goals of preserving green space or protecting environmentally sensitive areas while accomplishing other recreational goals. For example, athletic fields can be located on areas that also serve as a flood control detention facility and nature trails can be placed through environmentally sensitive land, protecting it from other development. When possible, park projects should be evaluated for other benefits not tied to recreational activities.

Needs Assessment: Planning for Parks

The needs assessment for any jurisdiction will identify current demands and recommend the appropriate type, number, location, size, and amenities of potential park projects. To determine the type of facilities that will provide the greatest benefit, interaction with the public is essential. Understanding recreational trends is also important and if such expertise does not exist on staff, external professionals with knowledge of national and regional trends should be consulted.

This section will summarize several important considerations for government officials when planning for park and recreational facilities.

Planning Consultants

When evaluating a community's recreational needs, the jurisdiction may want to consider the services of a consultant with specific experience in park planning. When entering into a contract for consulting services, the government should consider including the following contractual activities and outcomes:

- ◆ Development of an inventory of existing recreational facilities;
- ◆ Development of an inventory of nearby public and non-public sector recreational facilities, such as gyms, tennis centers, or pools and their availability and affordability to the public;
- ◆ Development and use of a statistically reliable public survey;
- ◆ Benchmarking similar jurisdictions;
- ◆ Analysis of recreational trends that may impact park attendance and use; and
- ◆ Recommendations for future recreational facilities.

Information and data gathered from these sources can be absorbed and formatted to provide needed planning direction. The information will also serve as a gauge of the public support that the project can expect to receive during the approval processes.

Public Involvement

Conducting a public interest survey is a viable and useful exercise in developing a park capital improvement program. It is important, as in any type of survey, that the survey be based on good statistical principles. Sampling a sufficient size and cross-section of the community will produce data that can be trusted to represent the community as a whole. These surveys can be conducted in various formats, including the following:

- ◆ Public meetings;
- ◆ Telephone contacts;
- ◆ Email surveys;
- ◆ Personal interviews with community leaders;
- ◆ Focus groups; and
- ◆ Informational booths at community events or venues.

A survey of multiple jurisdictions with similar characteristics allows a means of comparing recreational offerings. The physical elements of other jurisdiction's park facilities are not the only components to be considered in this benchmarking analysis. Operating budgets, capital budgets, size of parks and recreation staff, and demographic data on age ranges, income levels, and educational background are all important for developing a reliable foundation on which to evaluate future needs.

Survey of Existing Parks

Taking stock of the existing park facilities and determining the current and historical usage levels offers a good perspective on what is important to citizens. An inventory of existing parks should also include an assessment of the facilities' physical condition. Finding out what other regional facilities exist, including those controlled by other jurisdictions as well as private recreational facilities, will provide an indication of the types of recreational amenities that the community desires and those that might provide competition. Also, any deficiencies in available facilities, private or public, will become clear and can be considered as the governing body makes long-term recreational plans.

Emerging Recreational Trends

When forecasting a capital program for future parks and recreational facilities, the jurisdiction should be aware of emerging recreational trends. Interest in certain sports and activities fluctuates and what may be important now may not attract future users. Annual public surveys, studies of surrounding jurisdictions, or professional networking may be the best means of monitoring and gauging the validity of trends in the recreational market. Traditional, popular options and the fresh emerging trends need to be considered and evaluated in the planning process.

Land and Property Issues

With respect to the size of park facilities, planners need to determine the required acreage and evaluate options for land that may be available for future parks. The identification of the land area and the location of the land is vital, and the geographic placement of the park within the community is extremely important. Pocket-sized neighborhood parks that meet the needs of individual and adjacent neighborhoods will be generally well received. Large community parks with extensive parking needs, lighted sports fields, and the potential of drawing large crowds may receive overall support but still generate considerable opposition from adjacent property owners. Placement of parks and their associated facilities must be carefully considered.

While an ideal park location is important, land acquisition costs may be a large part of the overall capital budget. Minimizing this expenditure will allow more funding to be concentrated on recreational amenities and associated programming, thus maximizing the benefits of the park itself.

Using Parks as a Buffer

Park sites can also provide necessary buffering zones between incompatible land uses. For example, the space between water or wastewater treatment facilities and a residential neighborhood could include a park. With a park in-between, the residential community is somewhat shielded from less desirable facilities that may generate unpleasant odors or noises. Taking advantage of such opportunities could help control the overall cost of both the treatment facility and the park by having both projects share some of the land acquisition costs and associated improvement costs.

Competition with "For-Profit" Businesses

Park facilities, especially golf courses, tennis centers, fitness centers, and aquatic centers, often face competition from the private market. There are two potential downfalls to blindly entering this type of a market: 1) the public facility may not be able to compete with the privately owned and operated facility, and 2) competition from a jurisdiction that can operate at a lower cost as a result of its tax-free status causes other private businesses to fail. Either way, unhappy constituents who are also voters can have a negative impact on elected officials and governmental staff members.

A great deal of upfront research is necessary to determine the level of demand for a new "competing" recreational

Golf Courses

A local government considering building public golf facilities must develop goals that will be used to measure the project's success. For some jurisdictions, a goal may be to provide an affordable golf experience. In order to be described as affordable, the green fees generally must be established at a lower rate than those of a private course, which may require that the jurisdiction subsidize a portion of the operating and maintenance costs. The following scenarios regarding the ownership, operations, and maintenance of a golf course should be explored during the needs assessment for any potential golf facility:

- Publicly owned and operated golf course with fees offsetting some of the operating costs.
- Publicly owned golf course with controlled rates and operated under contract by a management company. The management company would be paid by the governmental agency for operating the course on behalf of the agency.
- Publicly owned golf course on public property that is operated under contract by a management company. Green fees are not controlled. Under the contract, the governmental agency and the management company would share in the revenues.

During the decision-making process to provide a government-run golf facility, the jurisdiction must also consider that a golf course can serve approximately 240 golfers on the best and longest day of the year. On a similarly sized parcel of land developed with athletic fields or hiking trails, it is possible to serve thousands of people each day.

facility. One needs to accurately measure the level of direct competition that may exist in a particular market and ascertain that it can tolerate additional recreational offerings. The potential fee structure for the new park facility will determine how much competitive pressure the private operators may feel. The jurisdiction needs to make sure that its intent is not to become a competitor in the local recreational market, but rather to provide recreational opportunities not available through the current private sector market, such as low-cost, affordable golf courses.

Park Development Standards

The inventory of existing facilities and the results of any public input process will lead to the development of standards to guide planning efforts. Standards, often expressed on a per capita basis, indicate the number of amenities or size of the facilities to include in parks and can be used to justify projects. Careful adherence to standards minimizes wasted energy and budgets.

The City of Scottsdale, Arizona, developed standards based on national recommendations but tailored each standard to fit the local community. Standards used by the city are displayed in Exhibit 17.1. A good source of guidelines for standards is the National Recreation and Parks Association.[1] Publications such as the *Park, Recreation, Open Space and Greenway Guidelines* published by the National Recreation and Parks Association may also act as a starting point for recommended standards. Standards, although difficult to define, are essential to the successful planning for park facilities. When creating park standards, always consider the public preferences and information discovered as part of the needs assessment process. Each community is different and national standards may not accurately reflect every area.

Exhibit 17.1 Examples of Localized Park Project Minimum Standards

Park Projects	Minimum Standard (per population)
Neighborhood parks	1.0 acre / 1,000
Community parks	2.6 acres / 1,000
Baseball fields	1 / 5,000
Soccer fields	1 / 4,000
Playgrounds	1 / 4,000
Tennis courts	1 / 3,000
Swimming pools	1 / 50,000

Source: Estimates taken from the City of Scottsdale Community Services Facilities master plan, 2004.

Estimating the Costs of Park Facilities

The preparation of a conceptual design and cost estimate is an exercise of choosing a realistic facility plan and a budget. Each scenario should be tested for its feasibility given available resources. This is done by calculating an associated preliminary cost estimate. Too ambitious of a site plan may end up undermining the success of the entire program.

This stage of concept planning determines what recreational amenities are needed, where they will fit on the available land parcel, and how much they will cost. Important components to consider in this preliminary planning process include, but are not limited to:

◆ Layout and density of the park amenities;

◆ Adjacency of proposed activities on the park site;

◆ Topographic features of the selected parcel;

◆ Physical relationship of the park to adjacent properties;

◆ Compatibility to uses of adjoining properties; and

◆ Vehicular and pedestrian accessibility to the selected park site.

In addition to the physical planning of the project, the preparation of the cost estimate is better considered during preliminary processes rather than left to the end. To ensure effort is not wasted on options that are too expensive, estimating costs should be a part of all initial conceptual designs. Specific items to cost include:

◆ Land acquisition, including closing costs and appraisals;

◆ Park equipment;

◆ Building components: restrooms, shade structures (canopies), staff offices, storage buildings, maintenance compounds;

◆ Lighting;

◆ Landscaping;

◆ Hardscapes;

◆ Connection fees for utilities;

◆ Furniture, fixtures, and equipment for buildings and recreation programs;

◆ Public art components that may be desired in the project, including fees paid to artists for development and production of the artwork;

◆ Financing costs, if the project is to be funded by bonds or other borrowing mechanisms;

◆ Inflation costs, if the project is to be completed over several years;

◆ Professional design consultant fees;

◆ Project management and administration;

◆ Cost of construction in general; and

◆ Contingencies.

Example costs for common park features are listed in Exhibit 17.2, but cost may vary from region to region. Local experience, therefore, plays an important role in this budgeting exercise. In addition to capital costs, the associated operating and maintenance costs should also be considered throughout the facility's expected life. Nothing is more disappointing to a capital program than to go through the process of facility construction and then have the facility remain closed because it is too expensive to operate.

Exhibit 17.2 Representative Costs for Park Amenities

Park Amenity	Representative Unit Cost
Lighted ball field	$300,000
Tennis court	$100,000
Lighted volleyball court	$ 50,000
Lighted basketball court	$ 75,000
Playground	$150,000
Large picnic ramada	$ 30,000
Turf (per acre)	$ 15,000
Park building (per square foot)	$ 300

Source: Costs provided by the City of Scottsdale, CIP/Planning Division, 2006.

Park Development by Phases

Often, park projects cannot be completed in one phase. Resource availability or project scale may require that the facility be constructed in phases over several years. Unlike other projects, such as water infrastructure, fire stations, libraries, and other common projects, park projects are very capable of a phased construction schedule where portions of the park are used while others are being developed. Creating a master plan provides a logical approach to complete an entire park project. A master plan that conceptually depicts the fully completed park and identifies distinct phases of the park can be developed. Phasing may also address the potential of growing demand for recreational services. As the population grows and development occurs, more park facilities and amenities may be required.

Common Financing Methods for Parks

Various funding sources are commonly available to jurisdictions for park projects. Park capital improvement plans could utilize any of the following funding sources: general fund contributions, dedicated tax revenue, impact fees, user fees and charges, and grants. Other possibilities may exist depending on an individual jurisdiction's charter and structure.

Local Option Taxes

Some cities and counties have developed policies that levy additional sales or property taxes to support park facilities and recreational programming. In many cases, taxes are approved via referendum to support large capital plans. Often parks and recreation will share the revenue stream with cultural facilities, libraries, zoos, and museums. For example, the City of Miami, Florida, recently began work on a voter-approved bond issue to support over $600 million of capital improvements for parks, recreation and green space, and smaller-scale projects. Communities also may set up specific taxing districts, such as park districts, to collect taxes exclusively for parks and recreation. Dedicating revenue streams allows continual funding for parks and recreation facilities without the competition from other governmental uses.

Impact Fees

Some local governments collect impact fees from new commercial or residential developments in order to develop park projects. Jurisdictions may also require that developers donate land within planned residential developments to the local government for use as a park. In some cases, the developer may be required to construct the park with defined amenities.

Service Fees

Some recreational programs have the potential to be used as a revenue source and jurisdictions may desire to set up the facility as a separate enterprise fund. This approach enables the government to operate like a business and would be structured to recover the cost of operating and maintaining the associated facilities, potentially recouping the capital expenditures over a set time period. Common activities for no-fee and fee-based uses are outlined below:

No-Fee Uses

- ◆ Drop-in use of facilities on a first-come, first-served basis;
- ◆ Local government authorized, sponsored or co-sponsored uses, such as youth sports activities, government budgeted events, or public meetings

with other agencies when provided for in an intergovernmental agreement; and

◆ Joint use of facilities under the terms and conditions of authorized contracts.

Fee-Based Uses

◆ Reservation by citizens when a specific facility or field is for their private use, including athletic league organizations' use of fields;

◆ Use of specialized equipment to control access in order to recover the cost of maintaining and operating those specialized pieces of equipment;

◆ Leisure activities and classes that have direct costs for instructors, staff, supplies, and equipment;

◆ Fundraising events; and

◆ Picnic or similar activity, which may include third-party vendors or event promoters.

Debt Service from User Fees

If revenue bonds are used to finance park facilities, proper analysis should be completed to assure that operating revenues adequately cover any debt service expense. In determining prices for services, the government might want to utilize the services of a professional consultant that will complete a pro-forma and forecast expected usage levels, operating revenues, and costs. Assuming that other revenue sources are not pledged to cover the debt, a consultant's analysis will demonstrate project feasibility and the appropriate level of risk for any investors or lenders. Consultants can also be useful in determining an appropriate fee to gain access or participate in the recreation facility or program.

Grants

The receipt of grants can be another viable funding source for capital projects. Foundations, large corporations, and state and federal government agencies may offer funds for specific projects meeting their funding goals. State programs often provide grant funding for park projects that will protect environmentally sensitive land. Other options could include transportation grants for bike trails or walking paths. The many possibilities for grant funding should be explored. Nonprofit organizations may also provide funding, and community foundations will support projects that work to increase the recreational, educational, or cultural opportunities within the community. Additionally, private or corporate sponsorship of park facilities may be an attractive way of obtaining necessary funding. Similarly, jurisdictions could sell naming rights or enter into contracts to limit only one firm to sell products, such as soft drinks, within the park to raise additional funds.

Operating Impacts

Throughout the capital planning phase for park projects, jurisdictions should recognize the operating costs that are associated with park facilities. Parks that are not properly staffed and maintained will not achieve their full potential. The following should be considered when developing capital projects for parks and recreation purposes:

◆ **Recreational Programming.** Additional park facilities generally create more opportunities for recreational programming. When developing a park, the programming component should not be overlooked.

◆ **Operational and Maintenance Costs.** Proper maintenance of parks is essential to providing recreational assets over an extended time period. Even if the park is new, proper funding should be allocated to regular and preventative maintenance to avoid costly repair or replacement expenses in the future. Personnel considerations would usually include grounds maintenance staff and appropriate benchmarks should exist when determining need for additional staff.

◆ **Supplies and Vehicles.** New facilities may require additional supplies and vehicles to operate and maintain the park. All associated costs should be considered before development of the park facility.

◆ **Equipment Replacement Costs.** Equipment or components within the park may have a useful life that is shorter than the rest of the park. Equipment should be replaced when necessary.

Parks and Grounds Maintenance and Repair

Grounds maintenance is best performed by a staff that is closely associated with the parks and recreation staff. This will permit a hands-on approach to timely inspection and re-

---

Playground Safety

Playground safety is an important aspect of any governmental park facility. Equipment must be updated in order to ensure the safety of the children and adults who will be using it. Rigorous and frequent inspection of all equipment and grounds is absolutely necessary. Preventative maintenance does minimize the occurrence of injuries.

The National Recreation and Parks Association certifies playground safety inspectors through a comprehensive three-day workshop and examination. Information on age-appropriate equipment, Americans with Disabilities Act provisions, safety design, and inspection schedules are available through this certification process.

Note: More information on the Certified Playground Safety Inspector program is found on the National Recreation and Parks Association Web site (http://www.nrpa. org).

pair of park amenities. A grounds maintenance staff should include technicians trained in horticulture (turf and tree management), irrigation, electricians, and construction tradesmen for the repair and installation of equipment and hardscape features such as concrete pads, sidewalks, and walls. Utilization of such staff may be centralized where the same grounds maintenance staff also has responsibilities for the grounds at all government facilities, including schools. The expertise of such staff should also be enlisted in developing site plans, ensuring that the most efficient and safe way to maintain the grounds is achieved without adversely affecting the use of the site.

Exhibit 17.3 shows an example of the range of costs for landscape maintenance for park facilities. Costs may need to be adjusted to more accurately reflect maintenance costs for different areas of the country.

Exhibit 17.3 Representative Costs for Parks and Grounds Maintenance

Grounds Maintenance Item	Representative Unit Cost
Mowing turf (passive or sports)	$56-62/acre/cut
Fertilizers (various types)	$12-20/bag
Pre-emergent	$32/bag
Turf aeration	$290-$350/acre
Hybrid Bermuda sod	$0.50/square feet
Granite (1/2-inch)	$27/ton
Playground sand	$15/ton
Specimen trees (24-inch box)	$112 each
Shrubs (1 gallon/5 gallon)	$2.00 -$6.50 each

Source: Cost estimates provided by the City of Scottsdale, Parks and Grounds Management Division, 2006.

Liability Issues

Local governments need to be mindful of risk insurance and indemnification issues related to park programs. Due to the very nature of activities that take place at park sites and in park facilities, jurisdictions may be exposed to liabilities. Recreational activities inherently have the potential of resulting in personal injuries. Athletes and other park patrons will sustain injuries while participating in any number of sports or other activities on park facilities, and governmental entities can become a target for injury claims.

Individual governments insure themselves in various manners. Traditional coverage through insurance underwriters may be the most straightforward method. Other entities may have the ability and resources to provide self-insurance. Even in these cases, insurance coverage through an outside insurance provider may be prudent for the catastrophic event that would exceed an agency's resources to adequately protect itself.

A jurisdiction's risk management department or outside professional consultants should be consulted to determine the types of coverage appropriate for the specific types of recreational amenities that are provided.

Conclusion

Planning and development of parks and recreational facilities is important to citizens' quality of life and should be given serious consideration by local governments. It is important to involve stakeholders in the entire process to ensure that park facilities meet their needs and expectations. It is also extremely important that the finance office be involved in the planning and evaluation of park projects to properly finance the project and make sure that facility maintenance and programming can be sustained.

The City of Scottsdale, Arizona

The City of Scottsdale offers over 900 acres of parks, including small neighborhood parks, larger community-level parks, four city-owned and managed aquatic centers, and physical fitness centers.

The City of Scottsdale is the home to a unique joint-use multi-purpose park known as the Indian Bend Wash Park System. This seven-mile long, linear park was conceived by citizens and the U. S. Army Corps of Engineers in the 1970s to provide flood protection for the city. Historically, flash floods, common in a desert environment during the summer monsoon season, cut the city in half and significantly hindered transportation and the provision of emergency services. Instead of constructing a concrete channel to control flooding, the city designed and built a greenbelt system of parks. The parks provide flood control along with many recreational opportunities, including baseball and softball fields, golf courses, swimming pools, a series of lakes for boating and fishing, and the spring training facilities for a Major League Baseball team.

Note

1. National Recreation and Parks Association is a membership organization of planners, park professionals, and citizens that works to advocate for making parks, open spaces, and opportunities available to all Americans. Its Web site can be accessed at http://www.nrpa.org/.

│18│

Convention Centers and Meeting Facilities

By Fred Winterkamp

Convention centers are often constructed as part of a larger strategy to promote economic development and tourism. These facilities have the potential to bring in out-of-town visitors who spend money at local hotels, restaurants, shops, museums, and cultural attractions. While large convention centers may get the most publicity, communities of all sizes have constructed and successfully operate convention centers and meeting facilities that host conventions, tradeshows, business meetings, community meetings, banquets, and sporting events. While the industry has seen a dramatic increase in available exhibit space recently, many communities continue to evaluate plans for new or expanded facilities.

A convention facility can be a valuable economic development tool for some communities, but can also be a risky endeavor, and some communities have experienced results that failed to meet expectations. As with many public facilities, unique community characteristics play a large part in determining the best methods for planning and financing a convention center. Development is a multi-step process, taking up to ten years, that will evaluate the risks and financing options, help prevent an unfavorable outcome, and result in a facility that is used to benefit the community for many years.

│ Description of Convention Facilities │

Convention facilities are usually proposed as a method of bringing visitors or businesses to the area and increasing economic activity for the host community. Facilities include small local meeting spaces, regional conference centers, or large international tradeshow and convention facilities.

Jurisdictions have built convention facilities of various sizes, designs, and organizational structures. The three most common include publicly owned stand-alone convention centers, hotels with convention spaces, and public/private partnerships that provide convention center facilities and hotel space. The facility type selected will impact the operating structure and help determine the appropriate finance plan.

Stand-Alone Convention Center

The most widely recognized facility design is a publicly owned stand-alone convention center and meeting facility. These facilities are most common in large cities or areas that attract many tourists or visitors, but are found in communities of all sizes. Stand-alone convention centers come in all sizes to meet various market segment needs. Exposition halls containing less than 100,000 square feet typically seek local or regional business. Some of these smaller facilities serve multiple roles and also host sporting events and other performances. Larger convention facilities with over 150,000 square feet will compete for statewide, national, and international business.

Since publicly owned stand-alone convention centers meet the public purpose requirements as an economic development initiative, tax-exempt funding is often an attractive financing option. Usually, these facilities are managed by the jurisdiction through a convention center authority and/or a visitors' bureau. It is also not uncommon for the government to contract with a private operator to manage the facility.

Convention Hotels

Convention hotels combine exhibition space within a standard hotel and are commonly found in both large and medium-sized cities. Convention hotels typically contain less exhibition space than stand-alone convention centers, but still come in a wide range of sizes. Most events held in convention hotels do not have attendance numbers or enough exhibitioners to fill a large facility and can be accommodated nicely in these smaller facilities. Convention hotels are the most common type of convention center facility and are attractive to many smaller and mid-sized jurisdictions.

Some jurisdictions have built a convention hotel in connection with an existing stand-alone convention center. Hotel projects should be carefully considered because the jurisdiction exposes itself to risks inherent in both the hotel and convention center industries. Many publicly funded convention hotels have struggled to meet overly optimistic projections in feasibility reports due to lower than forecast event attendance and pricing discounts needed to lure business during off-peak times. Since the public purpose of a hotel is more difficult to determine, the impact on tax-exemption and the possible requirement for taxable finance must be carefully examined with any publicly funded hotel project.

Public-Private Partnership

A convention and meeting facility with or without a hotel can also be designed as a public/private partnership. One advantage of this type of facility is that both the private sector firm and the jurisdiction share the burden and risk of funding and operating the facility. Public sector participation in projects to construct hotels and privately owned convention space can provide economic benefits to the community, but involve more risk. Risk can be mitigated somewhat by having the private partner provide a significant portion of the project cost and the use of public funds for transportation improvements, utility infrastructure, drainage systems, and other costs on public spaces that accompany a private facility. Public-private partnership agreements are discussed more thoroughly in chapter 6.

> ### Block Room Agreements
>
> Convention centers often negotiate block room agreements with one or more privately operated hotels near the facility. The block of rooms is effectively controlled by the convention center for use cooperatively with bookings at the convention center. Block room agreements are used to guarantee a competitive price for the room and to ensure that hotel space will be available for conference attendees. Block room agreements will also guarantee that attendees stay at the hotel with the agreement, as many facilities have requirements that attending conferences must guarantee a number of hotel rooms.

Needs Assessment: Planning for Convention Center Facilities

Effective planning for a proposed convention facility should analyze many factors, the most important of which is risk. A jurisdiction needs to understand the benefits and both industry risks and local risks of developing and operating a convention facility. The facility design and operating method should be determined, as this is a major factor in determining the type of convention or businesses the facility services and the appropriate funding approach. A feasibility study that realistically analyzes the industry and the likelihood of developing a successful facility should be developed. Outside consultants familiar with the convention center industry are often engaged in this effort. After a complete feasibility study is preparead, the appropriate funding sources and a finance plan can be developed. Each of these interrelated steps is critical to the design and finance of a successful facility.

Benefits

The convention industry is complex, with significant benefits and risks. The benefits of a successful convention facility are numerous. Communities can take advantage of the increase in economic activity from visitors who spend money at hotels, restaurants, and other local businesses. Local resources such as airports, transit systems, and entertainment complexes benefit from additional customers. Also, conventions, exhibitions, and meetings often create additional business for local construction firms that build exhibits, as well as area florists, caterers, and print shops that provide additional support for participants. Additionally, hosting conventions, exhibitions, and meetings is a potentially profitable business that can leverage existing meeting space and tourism attractions.

Conventions, tradeshows, and meetings also market the community to outsiders. They bring business leaders to the community, increasing the jurisdiction's visibility on a regional, statewide, or national level. Similar to large sporting venues, national and regional conventions raise awareness for the community and activity in the local economy. However, unlike sports venues, conventions usually bring in "new" money and visitors from outside the region. Convention centers have the potential to be self-supporting or even subsidize other programs, but also face the possibility of requiring subsidies to overcome operating shortfalls.

Industry Risk

The convention center industry has seen an increase in the number of facilities over the past ten years, and there is competition to attract both large and smaller-sized conventions. Competition also exists from new technology that allows large groups to meet and communicate via the Internet and through electronic conferencing. More event planners are demanding and receiving pricing discounts and other incentives when selecting facilities to host conventions. As incentives increase, conventions become less profitable to host and in many cases facilities experience operating losses. As more and more facilities are built, the chance increases that a new convention facility will take business away from existing convention centers.

Local Risks

There are several local risks inherent in the business climate and geographic location of a new facility. Typically, a desirable convention facility will only take advantage of its full potential when popular tourism venues and convenient transportation options already exist in the community and can attract travelers to events held in the facility.

As shown in Exhibit 18.1, a recent survey reported that 60 percent to 80 percent of event organizers indicated that hotels and overall affordability were very important to the deciding on a convention location; 40 percent to 50 percent indicated that transportation issues, including access for attendees, transportation cots, and travel distance from home, were also important. The industry's informal "8–8–8" rule says attendees generally work eight hours, sleep eight hours, and play eight hours. The community must provide for all three components. Additionally, other factors, such as concerns with local union requirements, transportation costs, and seasonal weather extremes, will impact the decision by event promoters to choose a location and may contribute to the facility's overall success.

Exhibit 18.1 Site Selection Criteria

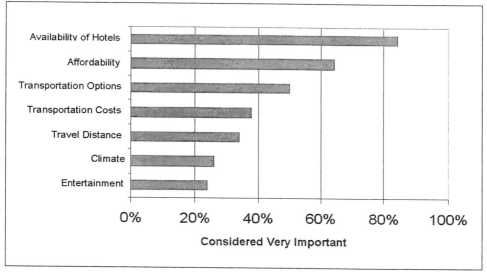

Source: "2006 Meetings Market Report," *Meeting and Convention Magazine* (August 2006).

Defining Success for a Convention Center

One of the first steps in planning for a convention center is to identify goals that the jurisdiction hopes the facility will accomplish. Jurisdictions build convention centers for multiple reasons and can define success in many ways. Goals generally include financial and attendance targets. Additionally, convention centers are often built as part of a larger economic development or tourism strategy and should have goals tied to these efforts as well. The facility's goals will drive the rest of the planning efforts to design, locate, build, and finance a facility that is best positioned to achieve desired outcomes.

Facility Design

Each type of convention center design will attract and limit certain types of business. There is not a "one-size-fits-all" solution that will maximize facility usage. All events will seek a facility that increases attendance through a combination of features to increase logistical efficiency and local amenities. To attract business in this competitive industry, it is important to meet customer needs and include focus groups during planning and design efforts to assure a facility that meets the needs of target customers.

The design of a convention center will impact how the building is marketed to different customers and will impact the facility's ability to accommodate certain events. An open space generally attracts exhibition or tradeshows, but can also contain partitions that allow for more spatial options. Combining open exhibition spaces with smaller meeting rooms can attract events with a professional training or continuing education focus. Typically, these smaller training rooms will be well equipped with technology and audio-visual equipment. Facilities become increasingly attractive when they are equipped to provide food service, package shipping, business centers, and wired to allow links to a broad array of telecommunications and technological tools.

Location

There are common qualities in communities known as successful host locations for local meetings, regional conferences, conventions, and tradeshows. Favorable weather and a long optimal travel season allow for more events. Event planners have more calendar options and indoor/outdoor activity choices in warm weather locations. Event planners will hope to attract more travelers when there are other tourism options in the community that may entice attendees to extend their stay. This can further increase economic benefits for the community because existing tourism attracts events, and event attendees in turn increase attendance at local tourism attractions.

The most successful convention centers have nearby lodging at various price points so event planners can appeal to attendees in many budget categories. Convention planners and promoters will prefer sufficient hotel space in a recognizable flagship hotel very near or adjacent to any convention facility. Once the attendees arrive in the community, successful events will move people to and from the facility in a cost effective manner using local transportation options, like safe and well-marked pedestrian routes, public transit, professionally operated cabs, and well designed road networks with convenient parking options.

Feasibility Report

Feasibility studies should include information obtained throughout the needs assessment analysis along with industry trends to assess the facility's long-term financial sustainability. Past feasibility studies for numerous facilities have repeatedly overstated the profitability of convention facilities, which has caused a number of convention facilities to under perform financial expectations. This should be approached with great care because these reports have been notorious for the dangerous combination of overstated attendance and revenue projections, which result in unfavorable cash flows. As the adage goes, the reports are not called "infeasibility studies" for a reason. The feasibility report should be based on expert analysis of the market for conventions, local conditions, and other similar existing facilities, including facilities that meet or exceed projections, and those falling short of expectations.

History provides lessons when confronting a feasibility study for a convention facility with public participation. The feasibility study should be prepared with conservative estimates. It is not responsible to settle for a "goal line" approach that provides an operating projection that exceeds a break-even cost point. Jurisdictions should request a sensitivity analysis on a range of possible operating projections and a range of possible project costs. The sensitivity analysis should model funding source shortfalls, attendance shortfalls, and changes in the tourism market, such as the one that occurred after the September 11 terrorist attacks. With a sensitivity analysis, the jurisdiction's decision makers can analyze both favorable and unfavorable scenarios and decide if viable strategies and alternatives exist to address potential negative outcomes. This analysis also helps to judge if the risk is worth the benefit.

The facility operators must use realistic expectations as a basis for financial operating projections. Convention facilities reach theoretical capacity when about 70 percent of the total number of available days are rented, because the remaining time and space becomes insufficient to host and load/unload another event. The operator must plan for the less profitable loading and unloading days before and after an event, as well as down time in certain sections for major cleaning and maintenance. In 2004, the average occupancy rate at convention centers with less than 100,000 square feet of exhibit space was 43 percent. Occupancy rates at facilities with 100,000 to 500,000 square feet was 45 percent, and occupancy rates at large facilities with over 500,000 square feet was 52 percent.[1]

When analyzing the cost to participate in the convention, tradeshow, and meeting industry, a community should determine all of the necessary amenities required to attract the desired business. In addition to the construction cost of the facility, the community should evaluate the entire cost of roads, parking, public safety enhancements, and infrastructure for technology and utilities.

Exhibit 18.2 shows part of the long-range strategic plan done prior to expansion of the Orange County, Florida, convention center. The exhibit identifies three possible expansion alternatives and the estimated financial implications of each compared to existing conditions. To generate the cost estimates, consultants performed a complete study of the potential market, existing competition, trends in the industry, and current capacity at the Orange County Convention Center.

Exhibit 18.2 Orange County Convention Center Operating Cash Flow Projection

		1998 Budget	Site A		Clean Site
			1-Story	2-Story	
Operating Revenue ($ million)					
	Event services	15.2	20.7	23.5	22.7
	Rentals	11.5	15.7	17.8	17.8
	Vendor commissions	0.5	0.7	0.8	1
	Forfeited deposits	0.1	0.1	0.1	0.1
	Other	0.7	1	1.1	1.6
	TOTAL	$28.0	$38.2	$43.3	$43.2
Operating Expenses ($ million)					
	Personnel services	15.5	21.1	24	21.7
	Contractual services	1.4	1.9	2.1	2
	Materials and supplies	0.8	1.1	1.2	1.2
	Utilities	5.7	7.8	8.9	8.6
	Repairs and maintenance	2.5	3.4	3.9	3.9
	T-ride assessment	0.5	0.5	0.5	0.5
	Other	4.7	6.4	7.3	6.9
	TOTAL	$31.1	$42.2	$47.9	$43.7
Operating Cash Flows		**($3.1)**	**($4.0)**	**($4.6)**	**($0.5)**

Source: Taken from the long-range strategic plan completed for the Orange County Convention Center in 1999.

Industry Best Practices

While convention center design should be customized to fit the unique segment of the industry it wishes to attract, several industry best practices are common throughout most convention center projects. Generally speaking, all facilities must serve the interests of three groups of people: the visitor or convention attendees, event organizers and exhibitors, and operations management staff.[2] Specific facility features will be dependent on the type convention it hopes to attract. Conventions, tradeshows, seminars, banquets, and community events will have slightly different needs for exhibit space, breakout rooms, meeting rooms, registration areas, parking, food service, and loading/unloading.

Facilities often take advantage of many design features to enhance operating efficiency and lure prospective conventions and meetings. Well-organized loading docks with easy access to event areas help reduce the time and effort of loading and unloading and can reduce the fees charged by many freight companies. A design that avoids chaotic registration processes and long lines for attendees makes the experience more enjoyable. Successful facilities have sizable registration areas and operate technology that allows the event to be run professionally and efficiently. Access to utilities and telecommunication equipment and the infrastructure to support complex audio and video needs will expand the possible conventions or events.

Many facilities are also taking advantage of up-to-date technology features to attract conventions and meetings. Wireless Internet capabilities are now offered facility-wide with advanced infrastructure to ensure reliability in facilities located in Austin, Texas; San Diego, California; Washington, D.C.; and Las Vegas, Nevada. Other trends include offering 24/7 tech support, wired meeting rooms with Internet access, telecommunications, wireless microphones, advanced lighting controls, high-definition televisions, and sophisticated security systems.[3]

Planners for a large international corporate event can work for years and risk millions of dollars on facility rent, marketing, communications, and decorating. Event planners will mitigate that risk by choosing desirable locations with facilities that maximize their chance for success. They will also choose locations many years in advance to allow time to effectively market the event and maximize their return. Having up-to-date facilities and operational procedures that are capable of accommodating the facility's target market will increase the opportunity for success.

Developing a Finance Plan

Convention center projects are extremely complex and require the jurisdiction to take risks unlike most other traditional government projects. The use of professional consultants to provide expertise in cost estimation, market analysis, and construction management support should be considered. Developing an appropriate finance plan is a critical step in the process of planning for a convention center.

The finance plan for a facility can be developed once decisions are made regarding the marketing plan, needs assessment, facility design, and development standards. There are many sources of information to develop a finance plan, and a convention facility or hotel shares many characteristics with the debt needs of any other project. However, a few unique project management issues may require special attention in the finance planning.

The finance plan for a convention facility should address tax issues, reserve levels, construction periods, operational "ramp up," and ongoing costs. The decision to use tax-exempt debt or taxable debt can impact the project cash flows and make the project's timing more complicated.

During the facility's planning and design phases, the jurisdiction should try to maximize cash reserves in potential funding sources. Strong reserve levels will improve credit ratings and provide a hedge against construction cost overruns and other unforeseen project costs. Unlike a newly levied revenue source, an existing funding source with more predictable collections will provide the best opportunity to accumulate reserve funds prior to starting the project. At the end of the project, unused reserve funds can be used to enhance marketing efforts or to retire debt early.

The finance plan should address the construction period and future operating needs. Time will be needed to ramp up facility operations when the facility will drain funding source revenues without producing revenues. While capitalized interest is costly and should not be used carelessly, many projects will require a few years of debt service set aside to cover the construction and initial operating costs. Remember, most events are scheduled and booked years in advance, so a new facility will incur the costs of marketing and sales staff immediately, though the facility may experience limited usage for some period after opening.

Funding Options

While the facility will most likely generate revenue from operations, additional sources are almost always required to cover capital costs or to subsidize any operating loss the facility may incur. Convention center operating revenues generally include fees from conventions, food and beverage sales, parking, and advertising revenue. Average rental rates for convention centers are shown in Exhibit 18.3.

Exhibit 18.3 Average Convention Center Rental Rates

Rate per square foot per day	Trade shows	Consumer shows
Small facilities (under 100,000 sq ft.)	$.097	$.077
Large facilities (over 500,000 sq ft)	$.048	$.047

Source: Heather Kirkwood, "Convention Center Trends," *Expo* (January 2007) (http://www.expoweb.com).

Convention center capital costs are also often financed with debt. The most common funding sources are special tax revenue, grant funding, the use of special taxing districts, and general fund contributions. For some facilities a separate entity or convention center authority will be created to run the facility and manage any debt.

Special Tax Revenue

Public funding for convention facilities is often provided by special tax revenue sources related to tourism, such as hotel occupancy taxes, food and beverage taxes, rental vehicle taxes, or additional sales taxes, and are usually charged in addition to existing general revenue taxes. Often the burden of paying for a portion of special revenue is "exported" and levied on goods and services that are purchased more often by visitors and those living and voting outside of the jurisdiction. Because these special taxes are usually levied with cooperation from the tourism industry to benefit tourism-friendly projects, they may also be used to benefit other tourism-friendly attractions such as professional sports venues, parks, museums, or the arts.

Special tourism-related revenue sources such as hotel occupancy taxes and hospitality surcharges work better when used to fund a publicly owned convention facility. If these sources are used to provide a subsidy for public/private partnerships or private hotels, there may be strong opposition from private groups and existing hotels that do not receive such incentives. When collected in addition to normal general taxes, special revenues derived from tourism activities place the repayment burden on the tourism industry and protect the public from project risks. However, there is a limit to the special revenue that can be collected before pricing levels cause events to move to lower-cost communities that compete for the same business.

It is also important to recognize whether the funding source will be an existing special revenue, or whether a new special revenue source will be enacted for the convention facility project. An existing revenue source will have a recorded collection history and help with credit ratings and provide a financial cushion in excess of projected revenue generated by the facility operation. If a new special revenue source is enacted to fund a convention facility, there will be greater difficulty obtaining credit ratings and greater risks related to using a funding source of unknown potential.

Grants

Convention facilities that bring in visitors from outside the area and aid in economic development efforts within the jurisdiction or region may be eligible for grant funding. Some states may offer economic development grants that can be used to fund infrastructure improvements around the convention facility or the facility itself.

General Fund Contribution

Pledging large amounts of general tax revenue for multi-year obligations to fund a convention facility or hotel is a very risky proposition. There are many examples of convention centers that have not generated the projected revenue, which forced jurisdictions to use general fund revenues unexpectedly. Providing job creation incentives or booking fees are two examples of less risky public funding options. Job creation incentives can be in the form of tax credits, annual tax rebates, or subsidized loans. Discounts involve little risk because the rent discounts are only paid to events once they bring profitable business to the community.

Convention Center Authorities

If debt is required for more complex projects, communities can analyze issuing debt directly versus issuing through a convention authority if that opportunity is available. Financial markets may imply a "moral" obligation if the community issues debt directly under its own name, even if it is limited revenue debt and carries no general obligation pledge. However, projects can sometimes be financed through an "arms length" convention center authority, especially if a primary repayment source of revenue is derived from operations. The investors should be alerted when project revenues and possibly contractual payments made by third parties to the issuing authority would be combined to make debt service payments. The capital markets would evaluate the creditworthiness of all repayment sources. Conduit debt will usually require higher interest costs, and possibly even non-rated or uninsured speculative bonds. Care should be exercised to assure that more risky securities are marketed only to sophisticated investors who will understand the credit and the need for correspondingly high interest rates.

| Operating Impacts |

Participating in the operation of a convention center facility requires entering a traditionally non-governmental function in a competitive and complex industry. Successfully marketing a facility and building client relationships is necessary. Joint marketing efforts with a visitor's bureau will help attract conventions and provide an opportunity to market the convention center along with the community. Using a separate visitor's bureau for marketing may also allow the convention center to avoid any governmental policy on meals, gifts, and entertainment. The convention center industry is competitive and to attract shows the facility must be willing to effectively market itself and provide a well maintained, properly managed facility at reasonable cost.

Ongoing Maintenance

The ongoing maintenance and operating plans of a convention facility are critical to its future financial viability and the level of community benefits it provides. The plans should provide for sufficient maintenance and marketing funds each year. This will keep the facility modern and attractive to clients and allow management to aggressively target businesses to reach the community's economic development goals.

Management Firms

Many jurisdictions do not have expertise in operating large convention facilities and instead contract with a private firm to handle maintenance and operating responsibilities such as bookings, marketing, and food service for the jurisdiction. The contract may specify management fees and possible incentive-based agreements, such as bonuses for achieving a certain attendance threshold. In some cases, different management agreements may exist between the management of the facility and the provision of food and banquet services. In these cases, convention center oversight may be limited to contract management and fiscal management duties. Approximately half of all stand-alone convention centers are operated for the jurisdiction by a private firm.[4]

Using a private firm may have consequences for tax-exempt debt and should be carefully evaluated.

Operating Techniques for Improving Profitability

Many convention centers use creative or unique approaches to improve operations or operating profitability at convention centers. Constructing the facility using energy efficient building materials can reduce utility expenses, and the use of part-time labor for responsibilities such as ushers, greeters, and registration agents can reduce personnel costs. Some facilities also generate additional revenue through exclusive drink-pouring agreements and the sale of advertising space.

Conclusion

In order to successfully develop a convention center as part of a larger economic development strategy, a jurisdiction must undertake the same realistic business planning performed by private sector businesses. The convention industry is complex and competitive, and the best outcome will only result from a coordinated plan to target the right market segment with a properly designed facility funded by appropriate revenue sources. To provide the economic benefits of a successful convention center, the community must have the right mix of infrastructure and amenities cooperating to meet the needs of the client. Convention facilities alone will not bring economic prosperity, but sound planning and management will allow it to be one part of a successful economic development strategy.

Orange County, Florida – Convention Center Expansion

Developing any capital financing plan requires government to predict and overcome unfavorable developments. This kind of contingency planning allowed Orange County, Florida, to successfully complete a convention center expansion despite challenges in the tourism industry. The Orange County Convention Center is a central element of the county's economic development effort. With two million square feet of exhibit space, half of which was added during a 1998 expansion project, the convention center is the second largest in the United States.

In 1998, the county approved a five-year, $748 million convention center expansion to enhance the local economy. The project included a new building and improvements to the surrounding roadways. Using the input of convention industry clients, the county designed the facility expansion to be an efficient venue that would attract even more leading shows. Orange County's 5 percent lodging tax, the tourist development tax (TDT), funded both the original facility and the expansion project.

The finance plan faced an unexpected stress test from the recession in the national economy during 2001 and the September 11 terrorist attacks that led to a downturn in the travel and tourism industries. TDT collections declined significantly in 2002 and 2003. The tourism industry suffered while the country coped with the economy and the aftermath of the terrorist attacks.

On January 15, 2002, the board of county commissioners unanimously approved a revised finance plan that included actions designed to protect existing bondholders and allow time for TDT revenues to recover. To protect the existing investors' coverage levels, the 2002 TDT bonds would be issued as a subordinate lien to the outstanding TDT bonds. Also, the county would issue less 2002 debt than planned, increasing the use of TDT cash reserves to fund the difference. Finally, capitalized interest would be used to lessen the reliance on TDT collections for the first two years. The convention center expansion was completed and opened to host its first show in September 2003.

A large multi-year project is subject to additional elements of risk when the funding comes from revenue bonds backed by a volatile sector tax. That risk increases when growth in the funding source is needed over the life of the project. A sizeable cash reserve provided emergency funds when debt became less favorable. Project plans should always include contingencies for financial challenges.

Source: This case study was based on Sharon Donoghue, Eric Gassman, Stephanie, Taub, and Fred Winterkamp, "Expect the Unexpected: Financing the Orange County Convention Center Expansion in the Wake of Recession and Terrorism," *Government Finance Review* 20 (August 2005): 23-27.

Notes

1. Heather Kirkwood, "Convention Center Trends," *Expo* (January 2007) (http://www.expoweb.com).

2. J. Dana Clark, "Considering a Convention Center: Ten Questions Communities Will Confront" (Haworth Press, Inc., 2004).

3. Patricia Sherman, "Hot Convention Center Technologies," *Expo* (May 2005) (http://www.expoweb.com).

4. Destination Marketing Association International, "CVB Organizational & Financial Profile," 2005.